The
Lost Tomb
of
KING ARTHUR

The Search for Camelot and the Isle of Avalon

Graham Phillips

Photography by Deborah Cartwright

Bear & Company
Rochester, Vermont • Toronto, Canada

Bear & Company
One Park Street
Rochester, Vermont 05767
www.BearandCompanyBooks.com

Bear & Company is a division of Inner Traditions International

Library of Congress Cataloging-in-Publication Data
Names: Phillips, Graham, 1953-
Title: The lost tomb of King Arthur : the search for Camelot and the Isle of
   Avalon / Graham Phillips.
Description: Rochester, Vermont : Bear & Company, 2016. | Includes
   bibliographical references and index.
Identifiers: LCCN 2015037197| ISBN 9781591431817 (paperback) |
   ISBN 9781591437581 (e-book)
Subjects: LCSH: Arthur, King—Tombs. | Camelot (Legendary place) | Avalon
   (Legendary place) | Owain Ddantgwyn. | Britons—Kings and rulers—History.
   | Great Britain—Kings and rulers—History. | Great Britain—Antiquities,
   Celtic. | England—Antiquities. | Great Britain—History—To 1066. |
   BISAC: BODY, MIND & SPIRIT / Mythical Civilizations. | BODY, MIND &
SPIRIT
   / Spirituality / Celtic. | SOCIAL SCIENCE / Folklore & Mythology.
Classification: LCC DA152.5.A7 P47 2016 | DDC 942.01/4—dc23
LC record available at http://lccn.loc.gov/2015037197

Printed and bound in the United States by Versa Press, Inc.

10   9   8   7   6   5   4   3   2   1

Text design by Debbie Glogover and layout by Virginia Scott Bowman
This book was typeset in Garamond Premier Pro with Baskerville Cyrillic used as the
   display typeface.
Photography by Deborah Cartwright
Drawings by Graham Phillips

To send correspondence to the author of this book, mail a first-class letter to the author c/o Inner Traditions • Bear & Company, One Park Street, Rochester, VT 05767, and we will forward the communication, or contact the author directly at **www.grahamphillips.net**.

The

Lost Tomb

of

KING ARTHUR

Discarded

"Another must-read for anyone interested in the often inconvenient truth of history from the audacious and persuasive Graham Phillips. This book will challenge much of what you think you know about Arthur—but in a good way!"

LYNN PICKNETT, COAUTHOR OF *THE TEMPLAR REVELATION* AND
*TURIN SHROUD: IN WHOSE IMAGE? THE TRUTH BEHIND
THE CENTURIES-LONG CONSPIRACY OF SILENCE*

"The history of King Arthur, and whether he truly existed, has been studied by many scholarly disciplines—it is an immense jigsaw puzzle. In this book, Graham Phillips brings these pieces together to form a coherent picture of who the historical Arthur actually was. Always engaging and informative, this book penetrates the mystery of one of England's iconic heritage figures."

STORM CONSTANTINE, AUTHOR OF
THE MAGRAVANDIAS CHRONICLES

"Just when you thought the legend of King Arthur was a fairytale, Graham Phillips shatters the illusion with historical facts, discoveries, and theories that challenge everything you thought you knew about the once and future king. Compelling read for all questers of the truth."

ANDREW GOUGH, WRITER, PRESENTER, AND EDITOR OF
THE HERETIC MAGAZINE

PRAISE FOR OTHER BOOKS
BY GRAHAM PHILLIPS

In loving memory of my sister Margaret

Contents

Acknowledgments

The author would like to thank the following people for their invaluable help: Deborah Cartwright for the wonderful photography; Yvan Cartwright for compiling the index and for fantastic IT support; my researcher Maia Wille; Jodi Russell for extra research material; Sally Evans, Dave Moore, and Claire Silverman in helping with translations; and Jon Graham, Kelly Bowen, Mindy Branstetter, Jeanie Levitan, Manzanita Carpenter, and all the team at Inner Traditions.

INTRODUCTION

A Flesh-and-Blood Historical Figure

What follows is the full, untold story of my quest to do what no one had done before: to identify a real, living figure behind the legend of King Arthur and, ultimately, to discover his grave. When the book *King Arthur: The True Story* was published in 1992, which I coauthored with Martin Keatman, our claim to have discovered a historical King Arthur created something of a sensation. However, that book was originally intended as a comprehensive guide to the Arthurian legend in general, and only the final section included the last-minute identification of the man behind the King Arthur story, made shortly before the book went to press. As a second book was anticipated but never materialized, the true-life historical detective story leading to that discovery was never told. Since that time an astonishing body of evidence has accumulated to support this theory as to who King Arthur really was. I have brought to light formerly obscure manuscripts, initiated archaeological investigations, and have followed a trail of compelling historical clues. Although my continuing research into the King Arthur mystery has been featured in a variety of newspapers, magazines, and television documentaries over the years, none of it has previously been published or broadcast in anything but its barest outline. Now that I have finally located what I believe to be the historical King Arthur's grave, it is time for this book to be written.

Before I start I should probably explain why—even before I began my search for King Arthur and his final resting place—I consider him to be worth serious consideration as a historical figure. The Arthurian story we know today is filled with themes and events that seem pure fantasy: magicians, witches, the supernatural, mythical beings, damsels in distress, and all the rest. These tales developed over many years, from the mid-twelfth century to the modern day, each retelling becoming more elaborate and fanciful. This King Arthur of the imagination—the "floaty man," as I once heard him jokingly described—is not the character I sought. Rather, I was looking for a flesh-and-blood, historical figure upon whom the legends might have been based. Before the romantic Arthurian stories of the Middle Ages were composed, there were earlier accounts portraying the now fabled king in a purely historical context, unfettered by such flights of fancy. One of the oldest such texts is found in a manuscript cataloged as Harleian MS 3859 in the British Library, London, which contains a work attributed to a ninth-century British monk called Nennius. Nennius's *The History of the Britons*—which dates from three centuries before the first of the unlikely Arthurian tales were composed—propounds that Arthur had been a powerful British leader who successfully fended off foreign invasions around the year AD 500. It records a number of episodes associated with Arthur, known from both earlier contemporary sources and through modern archaeology to have been genuine historical events. I will be examining Nennius and other such documentation at length, but for now it is important to stress that these sources, together with recent archaeological discoveries, make a compelling case for Arthur's existence.

Why then, you may be asking, do many historians and other scholars continue to doubt King Arthur was a real, historical figure? Well this is partly because when most people think of the Arthurian story, they recall the medieval and modern fanciful tales. Clearly King Arthur as he is depicted in these elaborate fictions did not exist. More significantly, however, from the academic perspective, no contemporary inscription or historical documentation, or any archaeological find from the period in question, has yet been uncovered bearing Arthur's name. But this, as I shall argue, is actually irrelevant. There are many historical figures—whose existence academics seldom question—who also lack any surviving contemporary mention: Jesus Christ, to name just one. On the contrary, the latest literary and archaeological discoveries do far more to *prove* King Arthur's existence than they do to *refute* it. In this book I not only hope to persuade you that King Arthur was a historical figure, and that many themes in the Arthurian story were based on real events, but that I have discovered both his true Camelot and his long-forgotten tomb.

As I am writing this book for a general readership, I should also clarify a few points. First, concerning dating terminology: it is said that science books written for a popular readership should always avoid confusing mathematical equations (except Einstein's $E = mc^2$). In the same spirit I will be keeping certain terms regarding historical periods simple to avoid confusion. Strictly speaking, the term *medieval,* from the Latin meaning "Middle Ages," refers to the European period from the final collapse of the Roman Empire in Western Europe in 476 until the fall of Constantinople in 1453. No need to worry about these events or why they are significant at the moment. The important point is that today most people, when pondering British history, tend to think of the terms *medieval* and *Middle Ages* as referring to the era of Gothic castles and knights in armor, between 1066, when Saxon England was invaded by the Norman French, and 1485, when Henry VII beat Richard III at the Battle of Bosworth Field, establishing the Tudor period of Henry VIII, Elizabeth I, and William Shakespeare. For this reason, and for convenience, I shall be following this popular conception. In this book medieval and Middle Ages refer to the period of British history from 1066 through 1485.

Concerning earlier British events historians call the period between the Roman withdrawal from Britain in AD 410 and the Norman invasion of England in 1066 the Early Middle Ages, but most laypeople know it as the Dark Ages, so named because it was a time when civilization struggled to exist. There are many reasons why academics dislike this description, and they are valid, but to keep things simple I will be using the term *Dark Ages* for the period of British history between the end of the Roman era in 410 and the Norman conquest of 1066. An even earlier period was the Roman occupation itself. Between the years AD 43 and 410, the Romans ruled Britain, and the two centuries after they left is referred to by historians as the post-Roman era, although archaeologists prefer the term *sub-Roman*. I shall be using the term *post-Roman* to refer to the period between the Roman withdrawal in AD 410 and the time the invading Anglo-Saxons, from northern Germany, had seized much of what is now England by the mid-600s. I appreciate that this overlaps with the early Dark Ages, but don't worry, I shall ensure that all dating is perfectly clear.

So here are my terms for the periods of British history we shall be examining:

> AD 43–410: Roman
>
> AD 410–660: Post-Roman
>
> AD 410–1066: Dark Ages
>
> AD 1066–1485: Medieval or Middle Ages
>
> AD 1485–1603: Tudor Period
>
> (See Chronology on pp. 245–47.)

Also concerning dating, you will notice that I have been using the abbreviation AD. For those who may not know, it is short for the Latin *Anno Domini,* meaning "In the year of the Lord," referring to the time since Jesus is thought to have been born—namely AD 1. The millennium year AD 2000, for example, is said to have been two thousand years since the birth of Christ. The years before Jesus's birth are referred to as BC, meaning "Before Christ." The year Julius Caesar died, for instance, was forty-four years before the assumed date of Christ's birth, and so is referred to as 44 BC. Today academics tend to use the abbreviations CE, meaning "Common Era," instead of AD, and BCE, meaning "Before the Common Era," instead of BC. However, as most people are more familiar with the former, and to keep things simple, I shall be using the AD and BC abbreviations for dating.

Finally on the point of dating: something that can often be a source of confusion to the layperson is century numbering. We are living in the 2000s, but we call it the twenty-first century rather than twentieth; the reason being that the years from AD 1 to AD 99 are the first century (following the assumed date of Christ's birth), and 100 to 199 are the second, and so on. This means that the years 1100 to 1199 are the twelfth century, the years 1200 to 1299 are the thirteenth, and so forth. So when I talk about the fifth century, I am referring to the 400s, and when I talk about the sixth century, I am referring to the 500s. I realize that historians may be wondering why I am bothering to explain all this, but as I said, this book is intended for a general readership, and some people may never have considered it.

I must also make something clear regarding translations. The translating of original medieval and earlier texts relevant to the Arthurian enigma—from such languages as Latin, Old Welsh, Old French, and Anglo-Saxon—often leads to conflicting versions of such works, which can be somewhat confusing for the general reader. (Online, for instance, you will probably find a variety of differing translations of the works we shall be examining.) As I intend to express the content of such manuscripts as accurately as possible, all translations throughout this book are my own, or made on my behalf, taken from the primary source material, unless otherwise stated.

One final point, regarding references: often I have cited the original references used at the time of investigation, although many are more up-to-date publications, concerning the latest archaeological or historical research, or works now in print and still readily available. Anyway, enough of all this: let's get on with the book.

1

Here Lies King Arthur

It is England in the year 1191. With King Richard I away in the Holy Land fighting the Third Crusade, at court in London there is political turmoil as the king's brother Prince John schemes to seize the throne. In England at large there is grinding poverty. The ruling nobles, of French blood following the defeat of the Saxon English by the invading Normans over a hundred years earlier, have reduced the native peoples to the virtual slavery of serfdom. Yet, according to some, there is hope. A Saxon hero is said to have arisen from among the peasants and has taken refuge in Sherwood Forest, from where he challenges Prince John, robbing the rich to feed the poor. In the popular imagination, this is the age of Robin Hood. Curiously, 1191 also marks the birth of another British saga, one that will come to rival even the legend of Robin himself—the story of King Arthur.

The English town of Glastonbury, nestled amid isolated marshland some hundred and twenty miles west of London, is home to the Benedictine monastery of Glastonbury Abbey, many of its buildings destroyed by fire seven years before. The monks are working hard to restore the place to its former glory, and while digging new foundations beneath the Lady Chapel (a side chapel in the main abbey building), they uncover a long-forgotten tomb. At a depth of around sixteen feet, a hollowed-out oak trunk containing two skeletons is unearthed. To have been interred in such a prestigious location, these individuals must surely have been highly revered. Perhaps they are the bones of saints! Excitedly, the monks continue to excavate and soon find something to reveal the identity of the remains. A lead cross around a foot long is found, bearing the Latin inscription:

HIC IACET SEPULTUS INCLYTUS REX ARTHURIUS IN INSULA AVALLONIA CUM UXORE SUA SECUNDA WENNEVERIA[1]

[Here lies buried the renowned King Arthur in the Isle of Avalon with his second wife Guinevere]

They have, it seems, discovered the tomb of Britain's most iconic hero: Arthur, king of the ancient Britons, whose final resting place has remained a secret for seven hundred years.

If this discovery is authentic, then the book you are about to read is little more than a wild goose chase. But—I assure—it is not. In the following pages I will be telling the story of my search for the final resting place of King Arthur. In so doing, I will be revealing the remarkable truth behind the mythology and folklore, and ultimately I will unmask the mysterious historical figure upon whom the legend was based. Coincidentally, my research actually began in 1991—exactly eight hundred years after the alleged discovery of Arthur's grave—during a visit to the splendid ruins of Glastonbury Abbey (see plate 1). I never imagined it would be the start of a real-life historical detective story that was to last for twenty-five years. In the following pages I will be taking you step-by-step through this fascinating search for King Arthur's tomb, beginning where I myself began: by examining the monks' purported discovery of 1191.

Before getting started I should probably present a brief outline of the popular Arthurian story that has evolved over many centuries. Some readers may remember it vaguely from their school days or only know some aspects from various TV shows or movies, while others may be unfamiliar with it altogether. In various renditions it usually goes something like this:

Long ago, when Britain was divided and without a king, barbarian hordes laid waste the once fertile countryside. The throne lay vacant for a just and righteous man who could free the people from their servile yoke and drive the invaders from the land. But only he who could draw from a stone the magical sword Excalibur could prove himself the rightful heir. Years passed and many tried, but the magnificent sword stood firm and unyielding in the ancient, weathered rock. Then, one day, a youth emerged from the forest and, to the amazement of all, succeeded where even the strongest had failed. The people rejoiced: the king had come— and his name was Arthur.

On accession to the highest office in the land, King Arthur set about restoring the shattered country. After building the impregnable fortress of Camelot and founding an order of valiant warriors, the Knights of the Round Table, the king rode forth to sweep aside the evil that had beset the kingdom. The liberated peasants took him to their hearts, and Arthur reigned justly over his newly prosperous realm, taking for his queen the beautiful Lady Guinevere. Even a terrible plague, which ravaged the country, was overcome by the newfound resolve of Arthur's subjects, for they mounted a quest to discover the Holy Grail, a fabulous chalice that held the miraculous cure for all ills. But as happens so often during an age of plenty, there are those whom power corrupts. Eventually, a rebellion tore the kingdom apart: an armed uprising led by Modred, Arthur's treacherous nephew. Yet there was a dark witch that lay at the heart of the strife: the scheming enchantress, Morgan. During a final battle Modred was at last defeated, and Morgan destroyed by Merlin, Arthur's trusted advisor and court magician. But all did not end well, for Arthur himself was mortally wounded.

As he lay dying on the field of battle, the last request by the once mighty Arthur was that Excalibur, the source of all his power, be cast into a sacred lake and lost forever to mortal man. When the magical sword fell to the water, an arm rose from the surface, catching the weapon by the hilt and taking it down into the crystal depths. When the great king was close to death, he was taken away on a boat bound for the mystical Isle of Avalon, accompanied by a group of mysterious maidens. Many say that he died and was buried upon the island, yet there are those who believe that Arthur's soul is not to be found among the dead. It is said that he only sleeps and will one day return.

This, in essence, is the fabulous tale of King Arthur and the Knights of the Round Table as most people now know it. In one form or another, it has been told the world over. Across the globe the story of King Arthur has long been a bestseller.

It is also important, before continuing, that I explain something concerning the academic consensus regarding Arthur as a historical figure. Some respected scholars genuinely contend that this seemingly improbable story was based to some extent on a man who really existed. The story of King Arthur, familiar today, derives mainly from tales committed to writing in the Middle Ages, from the early 1100s to the late 1400s, which portray the fabled king as living around the year 500. As far as I can tell, historians seem to be divided fairly equally between those who consider this Arthur to have been based on a genuine historical figure, although they maintain that many mythological and fictitious elements were interpolated into the story over the centuries, and those who regard him simply as legend with no basis in reality. Archaeologists, on the other hand, tend to be more hostile to the idea of a historical King Arthur. Historians study historical documents, and early documentation from the Dark Ages, from as early as the 800s, suggests that a figure called Arthur did lead the Britons at the time the legendary monarch is said to have lived. However, these works were written over three centuries after the period in which Arthur is purported to have existed. Hence the roughly fifty-fifty split in opinion among historians. Archaeologists, on the other hand, excavate historical sites and form their opinions from what they dig up. As nothing from the period around AD 500 has ever been discovered bearing Arthur's name, they generally contend that he was a product of pure fiction. Or, at best, they make no comment at all. Despite various claims, no firm evidence has ever been uncovered to resolve the issue one way or the other. Certainly, no one has found his grave.

That is—I hope to convince you—until now. In this book I present my arguments for Arthur as a historical figure; among other things I have, I believe, located his seat of power and his final resting place. I will propose, too, that even many of the seemingly fanciful elaborations in the Arthurian saga developed from genuine post-Roman customs, beliefs, and traditions of the Britons prevalent at the time he lived. (*Britons,* by the way, is the term applied to the native British before the Anglo-Saxon conquest of most of England by around AD 700.) Before I began my investigation, I had already consulted the original source material concerning King Arthur and had come down on the side of those historians who considered him to have been based on a real British leader who lived around the year 500. (Obviously, or I wouldn't have bothered searching for him.) But throughout I have tried to keep an open mind: if what I discovered showed him to be nothing but an unsubstantiated legend, I was willing to give up the search. I could have started this book by discussing in detail my reasons for siding with the "yes camp" for Arthur's historical existence, but as I want to take the reader through my investigation in the order it occurred, and so as not to confuse the issue, I have left this evidence—both historical and archaeological—for later chapters. So I ask, while you read, that you keep an open mind, suspend disbelief if necessary, and trust me that my reasons are sound for accepting that Arthur—at least, as a down-to-earth British warlord of the late fifth and early sixth centuries—might indeed have existed.

Finally, you may well be asking: How come Phillips found King Arthur when no one else did? Serious scholars who have previously researched the Arthurian enigma have tended to be historians, literary scholars, folklorists, or archaeologists, who examined the problem primarily from the perspective of their particular discipline. It reminds me of the old East Indian allegory of four blind men (or men who are in the dark) who try to identify an elephant. One man touches the thick, rough leg and thinks the elephant is a pillar; another feels the long, thin tail and concludes it is a rope; a third touches the smooth, tapered tusk and believes it to be a horn; and the fourth, who touches the wrinkled trunk, deduces it to be a tree branch. Though they all accurately describe what they are feeling, none has sufficient overall information to know what the object really is.

Because of the scarcity of written information concerning the period in Britain during which Arthur is said to have lived, the metaphorical nature of medieval literature, the obscurity of mythology, and the incomplete picture reconstructed from archaeology, academics have also been working in the dark. No single branch of learning has enough information to solve the enigma of King Arthur. If these academics had shared their knowledge, they might have been able to get a clearer picture of who King Arthur was. Sadly, historians, literary scholars, folklorists, and archaeologists seldom consult one another, let alone work together.

What I have tried to do is to take an overall approach and, where necessary, incorporate each of these subject areas. The answer, I decided, is to combine them all. To me the Arthurian mystery is like a giant jigsaw puzzle: many of the pieces are there, but they are spread among these various subject areas. I have taken an overall approach, piecing together the historical, literary, mythological, and archaeological evidence and finding vital clues that had previously been ignored or overlooked. Furthermore, until I conducted my research, some pieces had been missing entirely. Earlier researchers lacked methods and knowledge that are now available: geophysics has grown; scientific instruments have been developed to reveal what's buried under the ground without digging; new technological dating methods are available; hitherto unknown medieval manuscripts have been discovered; and new archaeological sites have been excavated, all revealing fresh evidence unavailable to earlier investigators. This, I believe, is why I have succeeded where others failed. This might all sound a bit arrogant, but all will be explained. Besides, someone has to blow my trumpet, and I doubt many other Arthurian investigators will.

Whether or not the monks of Glastonbury Abbey really did find the remains of King Arthur and Queen Guinevere in 1191, the event certainly marked the birth of the Arthurian saga as we know it today. At the time the legend of King Arthur was well known even beyond England: in France, Germany, and as far south as Italy and Spain. It was said that Arthur had been a Christian monarch who, around the year 500, ruled the isle of Britain. Today Britain includes the countries of England, Scotland, and Wales, which, together with Northern Ireland, make up the United Kingdom or UK. Arthur's Britain, however, included only what is now England and Wales. According to medieval belief Arthur had fought numerous campaigns overseas, where he was hailed a hero for defending the last enclaves of the fallen Roman Empire from the hostile pagan tribes of the East. (The Roman Empire in the West had finally collapsed in 476.) Arthur was, it was told, the last of the Romans to protect the West from the barbarian onslaught, long enough, in fact, for the Christian kingdoms of the post-Roman era to become established. (During the late Roman Empire, the term *Roman* was applied to anyone with Roman citizenship, regardless of his or her country of origin.) Arthur was more than just a military hero; he was believed to have founded the dynastic powers of medieval Europe and to have been the savior of the Roman Catholic Church.

Although Arthur's reign was recorded in various ancient works, and extensive mythology, fables, and other early tales had sprung from his supposed exploits before the late twelfth century (that we shall be examining later), the story so familiar to us today—of Camelot and the Knights of the Round Table—only developed after the monks' purported discovery in 1191. Indeed, it came about as a direct result of that event. Because of King Arthur's fame and perceived status, news of the Glastonbury find spread quickly, prompting writers and poets across Europe to cash in on the invigorated popularity of the legend. Within a year or so, the famous Arthurian romances began to appear: tales of King Arthur in poetry and prose that became some of the most prolific works of the entire medieval era. ("Romance" was a style of heroic literature that became popular throughout Europe in the Middle Ages.) There can be no argument that the alleged discovery of the Glastonbury tomb was a momentous event in the development of the King Arthur story; however, it is somewhat questionable in a modern-day historical context regarding a search for any truth behind the Arthurian legend. Does it really prove, as it appears at face value, that King Arthur existed as a historical figure? Or was it, as many historians now agree, nothing more than an elaborate medieval hoax?

The event itself probably did occur—or at least something like it—in Glastonbury in 1191, as it was recorded just two years later by the contemporary cleric Gerald of Wales, an eminent scholar and respected chronicler of his times.[2] There is, however, some confusion concerning what precisely was written on the lead cross. Gerald, who wrote that its inscription read "Here lies buried the renowned King Arthur in the Isle of Avalon with his second wife Guinevere," was archdeacon of Brecon, over a hundred miles away, and does not appear to have seen the item for himself. In the late 1200s another historian of the time, a Glastonbury monk called Adam of Domerham, records that, without mentioning Guinevere, the inscription had simply read:

HIC IACET SEPULTUS INCLITUS REX ARTURIUS IN INSULA AVALONIA[3]

[Here lies interred the renowned King Arthur in the Isle of Avalon]

This does not necessarily mean the discovery was a fraud. Gerald of Wales might simply have misinterpreted what he was told, while Adam of Domerham—having been a monk at the abbey and so having presumably seen the item himself—may have made an accurate recording of the inscription. Today, however, archaeologists would need more persuasive evidence that the monks of Glastonbury really had found King Arthur's grave. The bones themselves would require dating with modern scientific techniques, while the cross would need to be examined by experts on artifacts from the period Arthur is said to have lived. Sadly, neither the bones nor the cross exists today. Or if they do, we have no idea where they are. In the 1190s, the skeletons and the artifact were put on display in the abbey and later reinterred beneath a new marble tombstone beside the high altar. Today, the spot is marked by a sign standing on an open-air lawn at the heart of the abbey ruins. In 1539 Glastonbury Abbey was closed by King Henry VIII during the English Reformation when the last abbot was hanged, drawn, and quartered, and the buildings were left to decay. Hope that the bones might still lie buried where the high altar once stood was dashed in 1962 when the English archaeologist Dr. Ralegh Radford excavated the site and found no human remains.[4] There were, though, distur-bances in the soil to indicate that there had once been a grave at the site, as there also were at the site where the bones seem to have origi-nally been found. All, however, that can really be determined from this is that the monks *may* have found some bones as described. The lead cross is another story.

Unlike the bones, the cross is known to have survived the Reformation. Back in 1278 it was recorded as being seen by the English king Edward I when he visited the abbey; it is said to have been laid on top of the marble tomb for all to see. Evidently, the cross remained here on public display right up until the abbey was dissolved by Henry VIII, after which it came into the possession of the king's antiquarian John Leland who recorded having examined it in 1540. (An antiquarian was an enthusiast of antiquities, anything to do with the past, rather than a historian who reconstructed the past by study-ing old documents.) As late as 1607 one of the late Elizabeth I's royal historians, William Camden, handled the artifact and had it drawn as an illustration for his work *Britannia,* a groundbreaking histori-cal survey of Britain and Ireland.[5] From this illustration we at least know what the cross looked like and what the inscription actually said. We can also surmise, as Leland and Camden both worked for the monarch, that once it had been removed from the abbey, the cross remained in possession of the Crown. The English monarchy was overthrown for a period during the mid-seventeenth century when Parliament, and then the puritan general Oliver Cromwell, ruled the country, and the cross was probably pilfered from the royal household at this time. It was in fact last reported to have been in the possession of one William Hughes, a Protestant cleric attached to Wells Cathedral only six miles from Glastonbury, in the early 1700s. What happened to it next remains a mystery.

Although we can no longer examine the cross, we do have William Camden's illustration to study. It shows the Latin inscription, which translates most directly as: "Here lies interred the renowned King Arthur in the Isle of Avalon." So it seems Adam of Domerham's thirteenth-century interpretation was approximately right. However, the pictured inscription reveals that Adam did not provide the Latin wording verbatim. It is significantly cruder than he relates. Today most historians doubt the cross's authenticity, at least as a genuine sixth-century artifact. It is pointed out that the Latin appears too rough and ready to date from around the year 500, Arthur's supposed time. In fact, the wording on the cross differs as markedly from a sixth-century inscription as modern English prose differs from a Shakespearean text. British clerics of the twelfth century still wrote in Latin, but it was no longer their native tongue, and the language had undergone considerable transformation from the everyday spoken form used by the Britons of the immediate post-Roman era when Arthur is said to have lived. This does not inevitably imply that the monks of 1191 staged a hoax, but it does suggest that *someone*, way after Arthur's time, fashioned the cross for reasons of his or her own. Indeed, the wording itself implies that the cross was fashioned *many* years after Arthur's time.

The inscription not only informs us that the cross accompanies Arthur's bones but that the place where he rests is none other than the mystical Isle of Avalon. The oldest surviving reference to Avalon appears in the writings of the Welsh scholar Geoffrey of Monmouth in the year 1136, in his *History of the Kings of Britain;* although he fails to say where it is, Geoffrey tells us that Arthur was taken there after his final battle.[6] Accordingly, it is generally assumed by literary scholars that Geoffrey, or possibly one of his close contemporaries, invented the name. Thanks to the Arthurian romances that were written after the monks' supposed discovery, the Isle of Avalon is today firmly associated with the burial place of King Arthur. Nevertheless, there is no known literary evidence that anyone prior to 1136 ever used the word *Avalon*. There are indeed associations between Arthur and an enchanted island in more ancient works than Geoffrey of Monmouth's, but in these it is not called Avalon but Annwn (pronounced "Ann-wun"). So it seems the name Avalon was not the original name of the island upon which Arthur was thought to have been buried, further undermining the authenticity of the cross inscription. Yet even if Avalon had been the name of the island in Arthur's time, the cross inscription would still be somewhat spurious. Presumably, the people who laid him to rest, and those who lived thereabouts, would need no reminding of where they were. It would be like someone today inscribing my gravestone with the words: "Here lies Graham Phillips in the town of London." The most likely scenario, therefore, appears to be that a person or persons unknown *after* 1136 were responsible for inscribing the cross.

It might perhaps be that someone between the years 1136 and 1191, *before* the monks' excavation, found the bones, decided for reasons best known to himself or herself that they were Arthur's remains, and innocently fashioned the cross to celebrate the event. This, however, seems most unlikely. The abbey had been founded in the seventh century, although an earlier ecclesiastical building may have stood on the spot even as early as Arthur's apparent era. Major rebuilding and enlargement of the monastery occurred in the 900s, and the building that was eventually destroyed by fire in 1184 had undergone no significant renovations since this time. It is, therefore, highly unlikely that anyone would have had reason to dig up the floor of the Lady Chapel and excavate down to a depth of sixteen feet before the fire reduced it to rubble. The reasonable conclusion is that whoever made the cross made it *after* the fire, at the time the monks were excavating. But if it was a hoax, why bother? What could be the motive?

Today Glastonbury might be little more than a relatively unknown, low-income town were it not for its Arthurian associations. True,

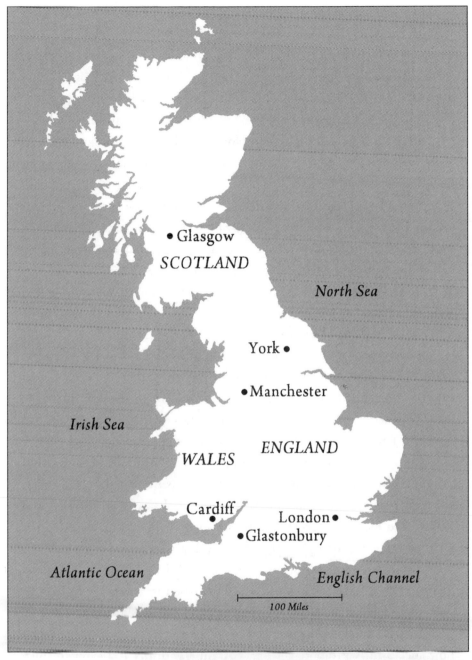

Fig. 1.1. Britain today,
as England, Scotland, and Wales.

Glastonbury has some lovely scenery, but so do many similar-sized towns in western England whose inhabitants struggle to make a living. Tourism was once a big earner for England's West Country—I know, I once lived there. But today, with the ease and popularity of holidays abroad, many of these towns, including the town where I used to live, are a shadow of their former selves, with boarded-up buildings, collapsing infrastructure, and high unemployment. Their populations are way above the average age, the young having left to find jobs in the cities. Farming communities have been decimated, while fishing villages have been turned over largely to the elderly and retired. But standing defiant among them is Glastonbury. Not only is its tourist industry thriving, its high street is lined with stores selling every kind of astrological, mystical, and occult paraphernalia. During the season its restaurants and bars are filled to capacity, and the town square throngs with Wiccans, pagan sightseers, and New Age travelers. The reason for this demographic anomaly is nothing less than the legend of King Arthur.

In the flower power era of the 1960s, the legend of King Arthur—at least the romantic, magical version of the tale—became vogue. Hippies descended on the town of Glastonbury in droves, following what the media dubbed the Grail Trail. I have to admit that I was one of them. I remember hitchhiking there one day when I was at college and was amazed to see so many hippies milling around like some kind of a mini San Francisco of the time. But I was more astonished to see the handwritten signs adorning the windows of nearly all the bars and stores: "No Dogs. No Long Hair. No Hippies." The locals detested the weirdos infesting their peaceful town. Today all that has changed. The once Bohemian nonconformists the locals did their best to vanquish ultimately got jobs, made money, and returned to the town to live. In fact, today, many of the older residents are ex-hippies, and the town's population is made up largely of their children and grandchildren, who now successfully promote the area's Arthurian links and cater to tourists from around the world. It is true to say that if it wasn't for the monks' purported discovery in 1191, Glastonbury's tourists and many of its residents would simply not be there. The King Arthur industry actually saved the town. But this was not the only time the Arthurian legend came to Glastonbury's aid. After the fire in 1184, Glastonbury Abbey desperately needed funds for rebuilding, and the only way to raise such money, as today, was to attract visitors. Now it's tourism, but back in the twelfth century, it was pilgrimage. And the sure way to lure pilgrims was with sacred relics.

Strictly speaking, relics (derived from the Latin word *reliquus,* meaning "left behind") were the bones of holy men and women whom the church had proclaimed saints. To be considered for sainthood (or canonization), it was not enough for the individual to have simply performed good deeds; he or she needed to have performed miracles, such as levitation, stigmata, and visions but above all miraculous cures and healings. In medieval England the average life expectancy was around thirty years (in fact, it didn't rise much above this until the late nineteenth century), and sickness and deformity were commonplace. Without the benefits of modern medicine, people relied on prayer and religious devotion to make them better. According to beliefs at the time, the bones of a saint were endowed with the sacred healing powers the individual enjoyed in life. To pray over or, better still, to touch the bones of a saint could not only cure you but might endow you with spirituality and increase your chances of going to heaven. Today, we are familiar with how Catholic places of worship are designated to saints: Saint John's Church, Saint Catherine's Abbey, Saint Patrick's Cathedral, and so forth. The reason for this is that early ecclesiastical buildings were consecrated to (named after) the saint whose bones were said to be interred there. Saint Peter's Basilica in the Vatican, for instance, is so called because it is said to be built over the tomb of Jesus's disciple Peter. In medieval times the churches, abbeys, or cathedrals that held the remains of the most illustrious saints would attract the most visitors who would make a special journey, or pilgrimage, to visit the site. These medieval religious tourists were the pilgrims (not to be confused with the Pilgrims who settled the New World in the seventeenth century). On Holy Days (from where our term *holidays* derives), hundreds, sometimes thousands, would descend upon a church housing the remains of a famous saint, where the bones were often on display in a casket known as a reliquary, which the pilgrim could touch while praying for healing or salvation. Relics were big business. Ecclesiastical communities would not specifically charge for pilgrims to encounter their relics, but donations were gratefully accepted. It would be a brave pilgrim who would expect the saint to answer his or her pleas without offering what he or she could afford (or often ill afford). Some abbeys grew extraordinarily rich from the proceeds of their relics, and there was intense competition between them. Those with the relics of the most celebrated saints got the most tourists. If one doubts the remarkable allure of what many today would regard as mere superstition, just visit Lourdes in southern France, a place where, it is said, the Virgin Mary manifested to a young girl in the 1850s. For over a century and a half, Catholics from around the world have flocked to the shrine marking the spot where the Virgin is believed to have appeared. Even non-Catholics, and many who are not even religious, visit the place by the thousands in the hope of miraculous cures. The small town's population is only around fifteen thousand, but it has around three hundred hotels and a staggering five million visitors every year.

In medieval times much of England's population believed in miraculous healing, and it was to sacred relics that they turned. By the twelfth century, the business of relics had expanded to include not only bones but the appendages of saints—severed hands, fingers, heads, even genitalia—which were placed in glass-fronted caskets of elaborate design for all to see. Additionally, objects that had once belonged to saints were also regarded as relics: cups, combs, sandals, anything the saint had used. Ultimately, the earthly remains and belongings of eminent kings and queens were also regarded as relics, and this is where King Arthur comes in. Examples of early English monarchs considered divine and whose relics various abbeys claimed to possess, are Alfred the Great, who defeated the pagan Vikings in the late ninth century; the pious and aptly named eleventh-century King Edward the Confessor; and Edmund the Martyr, who died for his faith in 869. Arthur was considered a far more illustrious ruler than any of these. It was he who is said to have saved Christianity in its darkest hour. The Glastonbury monks of 1191, therefore, had a powerful motive for hoaxing the discovery of King Arthur's tomb. One thing we know for certain is that Arthur's supposed remains, which were put on display, attracted so many pilgrims that enough money was raised to save the abbey and rebuild it as one of the most magnificent in all England. (Only Canterbury, the seat of the country's archbishop, was finer.)

In 1991, when I first began my investigation into the Arthurian legend, beside the main roads entering the town of Glastonbury, signboards saying "The Isle of Avalon" welcomed tourists. This seemed strange to me at the time, as the area is not an island. Today, Glastonbury sits amid a small cluster of hills, its highest being Glastonbury Tor with a solitary stone tower at its summit that can be seen for miles around on the fertile Somerset plain. Though much of the surrounding lowland has been drained for farmland over the past few hundred years, eight centuries ago it was heavily flooded, and Glastonbury was surrounded by reed marshes and connected to the mainland by a narrow strip of land. It was indeed an island of sorts when the monks were digging in 1191. But was it the Isle of Avalon?

We will be returning to examine the legend of Avalon itself in chapter 4, but for now our concern is whether Glastonbury has a legitimate claim to be the mystic isle. Did its association with Avalon only arise with the alleged finding of the bones and the lead cross? Is there any evidence that anyone prior to 1191 regarded Glastonbury as Avalon? The answer seems to be no. Early historians appear completely unaware of any such notion. One of the foremost historians of the medieval period is William of Malmesbury, a monk from Malmesbury Abbey in the county of Wiltshire in southern England. In 1130 he spent time at Glastonbury and compiled a detailed history of the abbey.[7] William, who has been described as the most learned man in twelfth-century Europe, was well versed in the Arthurian legend and had written about King Arthur in 1125.[8] However, in his history of the abbey, although he refers to many folktales and legends concerning Glastonbury, not once does he mention Avalon. In fact, he makes no reference of King Arthur's connection with the town whatsoever. If we rely on William's treatise on Glastonbury Abbey, it not only provides evidence that Glastonbury had no early associations with the Isle of Avalon but it also demonstrates how the monks' Arthurian claims deserve to be treated with skepticism.

The Holy Grail is another theme of the King Arthur story that today is associated with Glastonbury. In the late 1190s one of the authors of the many new stories written about King Arthur was the French poet Robert de Boron. Robert was the writer chiefly responsible for the Grail legend we know today, for he was the first to describe it as the cup used by Christ at the Last Supper. The Bible relates how one of Jesus's followers, a rich man named Joseph of Arimathea, laid the body of Christ in a tomb after the Crucifixion. According to Robert, Joseph used the sacred cup to collect blood from the crucified Christ, thus endowing it with miraculous healing powers. Joseph, Robert de Boron tells us, led a group of Christian followers who, forced to flee Roman persecutions in Palestine, traveled to England where they founded a church and hid the Grail for which King Arthur's knights ultimately searched.[9] In Robert's narrative the place where Joseph hides the Grail is Avalon. However, he fails to tell us where Avalon is and makes no reference at all to Glastonbury. William of Malmesbury's treatise of 1130 makes no mention of Joseph of Arimathea or the Holy Grail, but in 1247 a new handwritten copy made by the Glastonbury monks adds that the church founded by Joseph's followers, where they are said to have hidden the Grail, was none other than Glastonbury Abbey. This is compelling evidence of fraud by the Glastonbury monks, presumably in an effort to cash in on Robert de Boron's popular tale.

There is additional evidence to indicate the monks were up to no good. It turns out that Arthur's was not the first sacred grave the Glastonbury brothers allegedly found. Writing in his history of the abbey completed in 1291, the Glastonbury cleric Adam of

Domerham records that back in 1184, immediately after the fire, the monks claimed to have unearthed the remains of Saint Patrick. This discovery did not go down well with the church in Ireland, whose members were furious to hear that the bones of their patron saint were on display in England. Their own claim that Saint Patrick had lain peacefully at rest in Down Cathedral in Ireland for six centuries was upheld by the Archbishop of Canterbury, and the bones at Glastonbury promptly disappeared. But it didn't end there. Within a few months, the monks were at it again, this time claiming to have found the bones of England's most popular saint, the tenth-century Saint Dunstan. This went down even less well with the archbishop, for Dunstan's tomb was already to be found in Canterbury itself.[10] Yes, the Glastonbury monks had quite a track record for finding spurious holy relics.

It is, I think, fairly safe to conclude that the purported discovery of King Arthur's grave in 1191 was indeed a hoax. The monks may well have found the bones buried as they described (as construed from Radford's excavation), but *whose* bones was probably a mystery. Someone then had the bright idea to make out that they were King Arthur's remains, and the lead cross was fashioned as "proof." Perhaps most of the monks were unaware of the fraud. It would only take one person to toss the item into the pit. Whoever was responsible, however, this time it worked: no one else made claim to already posses King Arthur's relics, and they were widely accepted as genuine.

This was the conclusion I reached in 1991, and the following year the findings were published in my first book on the Arthurian legend.[11] This seemed to have had some influence in the town of Glastonbury because before too long the signboards welcoming tourists to the Isle of Avalon disappeared. Evidently, the town council decided the claim was now too shaky to endorse. Thankfully, the Arthurian tourist industry remained unaffected or I might have found myself lynched.

I may have cast doubt on King Arthur's grave being in Glastonbury, but I had become hooked on the Arthurian legend. From what I'd researched, I was sure that Arthur had been based on a real-life historical figure, the reasons for which I will shortly reveal. So if Arthur was not buried at Glastonbury, where was he laid to rest? The whereabouts of King Arthur's grave has remained a mystery for fifteen hundred years. What with the global fame of the Arthurian legend, surely its discovery would rank among the most celebrated historical finds of modern times. I decided to make it my personal quest to finally uncover his tomb.

2

Camelot

When I first began my search for King Arthur's tomb and the origins of the Arthurian legend, I decided the best way to start was by trying to locate the fabled Camelot. After all, this was said to have been Arthur's capital and seat of power. Before continuing I should explain that the place I was looking for was not a castle; at least it would not have been originally. If Arthur lived around AD 500, as the legend holds, then he would never have occupied a huge stone keep, surrounded by battlements, towers, and decorative turrets, with a portcullis, drawbridge, and moat. British fortifications of the late fifth and early sixth centuries were not massive Gothic castles but wooden stockades built atop earthen banks. Camelot would have been a fort, or fortified town, rather than a castle. Furthermore, Arthur and his warriors would have appeared very different from the shining knights so familiar today; armor was generally leather and chain mail, in the fashion of the late Roman army. The reason Arthur is now perceived as a medieval-style king of many centuries after his alleged lifetime is that writers of the Middle Ages tended to set ancient stories, such as the legends of Greece and Rome, in their own historical era and in a context of knighthood and chivalry. They couldn't do much else. It took modern archaeology to reveal how people of that bygone time really lived.

Searching for the supposed site of the magnificent Camelot was easier said than done; no place with that name exists today, nor is its location revealed by any historical documentation or map. Although the Arthurian romances from the late twelfth to the fourteenth centuries portray Camelot as a fabulous city, the grandest in all Britain, remarkably none of the authors tell us where it actually is. The earliest surviving reference to provide any specific location for the legendary Camelot was by the English author Sir Thomas Malory in the late 1400s. Thomas Malory wrote the most famous of all the medieval Arthurian romances between 1450 and 1470. Published under the French title *Le Morte d'Arthur* (The Death of Arthur), it was an amalgamation of many of the previous King Arthur tales that had appeared since the purported discovery by the Glastonbury monks in 1191. These earlier works were widely read, but Malory's rendition was to take the Arthurian legend to an altogether different level of popularity. Before this time, all books and documents were handwritten and so took a multitude of scribes countless hours of painstaking work to laboriously copy. Obviously, this severely limited the number of people who actually got to read the early Arthurian tales. Malory's *The Death of Arthur* was to change everything.[1]

Although it had been invented by the Chinese as early as the 1040s, the printing press did not reach Europe until four centuries later, and the first operational device in England was introduced by William Caxton of London in 1475. Caxton was delighted to print Malory's work, and it was he who chose to publish under the French title. Although the book was written in English, Caxton evidently considered French to be more sophisticated. Malory actually titled his work *The Whole Book of King Arthur and His Noble Knights of the Round Table*. *The Death of Arthur* was originally only the name for the last section. The catchier title clearly shows the wily Caxton had his eyes firmly set on sales, and sales he achieved. When it was published in 1485, it became an unprecedented success. As one of the first extensively available books to be printed in England, it became the country's first bestseller. (Even the bestselling book of all time, the Bible, was not printed in English for another century.) *The Death of Arthur* is pretty much the Arthurian tale we know today, in essence the theme for many of the modern Hollywood epics, including the famous John Boorman movie *Excalibur*.

In his work Malory breaks with something of a literary tradition dating back three hundred years by being the first Arthurian author to provide a precise location for Camelot. He reveals that it was Winchester Castle in the county of Hampshire in central southern England. In Malory's time Winchester Castle was indeed an impressive structure, and it had served as a royal residence until the fourteenth century. However, it was not so much the building itself that persuaded Malory that it was the site of Camelot but something it contained. In the castle's Great Hall was none other than King Arthur's round table. We know it was there in Malory's time as it is referenced by the English chronicler John Harding in 1463.[2] From what he tells us, it seems that Winchester Castle was widely regarded as Camelot during his day. Although much of Winchester Castle has long since been demolished, the Great Hall still survives. More remarkably, so does the round table. Eighteen feet in diameter, made of solid oak, and weighing approximately one and a quarter tons, it is now a table top without legs hanging on the wall. It resembles an enormous dartboard, painted in green and white segments said to indicate where the king and his knights once sat, and in the segment indicating King Arthur's place is the painting of an enthroned and bearded king. Around the rim are written the names of Camelot's knights, and in the middle there is a huge red and white rose encircled by the words: "This is the Round Table of King Arthur with 24 of his named knights."

So was Malory right: Is Winchester Castle really the fabled Camelot? Well, the building that survives today, and the larger castle that was there in the 1400s, was certainly not Camelot. It was only built in the thirteenth century, but fortifications of various types had existed on the site from as early as Roman times (AD 43–410), when Winchester was one of the largest cities in Britain. During the Saxon period (AD 550–1066), it even became the principal city of all England for a while, and a statue of the most celebrated English king to rule from here, Alfred the Great, stands proudly at the heart of the town.

In theory, therefore, the site of Winchester Castle could have been the seat of a King Arthur who is said to have lived around the year 500. Nevertheless, the castle's case for being Camelot relies principally on its round table. Is it really a genuine Arthurian relic as Malory and his contemporaries clearly believed? Or is it, like the Glastonbury lead cross, just another medieval fake?

Well, to start with, we have the same old problem. Like the association between Glastonbury and Arthur's burial site, there is no surviving reference to King Arthur having a round table before the twelfth century, over six hundred years after the alleged Arthurian era. Nonetheless, the oldest known historical reference to Arthur having a round table does date from almost forty years before the purported discovery of Arthur's grave. It is found in the work of a Norman poet named Wace from the Isle of Jersey off the coast of France. (At the time few people had surnames. They were either called "someone of somewhere," such as Geoffrey of Monmouth ["de" in French, as in Robert de Boron], or they were simply known by their Christian names, such as Wace.) Completed in 1155, Wace's *Romance of Brutus*—or *Roman de Brut* in its original French—is a history of Britain in poetic verse.[3] According to Wace the round table was a royal conference table that seated fifty of Arthur's knights. The reason for it being round, rather than rectangular, was to promote a sense of equality among Arthur's noblemen. No one could sit at its head. Wace claims he was not the source of the round-table story, saying that he learned of it in Brittany, a part of northern France where many Britons had fled after England was progressively invaded by the Germanic Anglo-Saxons in the late fifth and sixth centuries. Unfortunately, much of Wace's *Romance of Brutus* is as much fiction, or at least mythology, as it is historical reality. For example, the title is derived from the name of one Brutus of Troy, a purely mythological figure who is said to have been Britain's first king. Wace includes this medieval fallacy as a historical event in his narrative. So how seriously should we take his Arthurian theme of the round table?

In support of Wace some literary scholars have indicated the similarities between his account of the round table's purpose and historical references to ancient Celtic courts, where chieftains and their leading warriors would sit in a circle so that feuding over precedence could be avoided. The Celts were the native peoples of Britain before, during, and immediately after the period of Roman occupation, usually referred to as the Britons (as other parts of Western Europe such as Ireland were also Celtic). It is possible, therefore, that this evidently common tradition may have led to a British king conceiving the idea of a round table during the sub-Roman period (the term archaeologists use for fifth- and sixth-century Britain). Alternatively, the round-table motif may have originated in France where Arthur could have been confused with another ancient hero, Charlemagne the king of the Franks (the early French). Charlemagne, who reached the height of his power around the year 800, when his empire united much of Western Europe, did possess a celebrated round table. According to his biographer and courtier Einhard, Charlemagne's round table was decorated with a map of Rome.[4]

The round-table concept may have been associated with the early Arthurian legend as Wace claims, or it may have been a later interpolation. When I first visited Winchester in the early 1990s, there seemed no way of knowing one way or the other. However, my suspicions concerning the Great Hall's "round table" were aroused when I learned that it was the fashion in Thomas Malory's day for castles to house such round tables to emulate the Arthurian court. Just a few years before Malory was writing in the 1450s, the powerful René, Duke of Anjou in France, not only had a magnificent round table assembled but also had an entire castle constructed in the style of Camelot to house it.[5]

Soon after Arthur's grave was said to have been found in Glastonbury and the Arthurian romances began to appear, it became the trend across Europe for festive events known as "Round Tables" to be staged. These involved feasting and jousting and nobles dressed in costume as King Arthur's knights. The first of such Camelot scenarios is recorded in 1223, and by the late thirteenth century, the events were commonplace to celebrate victories, weddings, births, and sometimes—in the case of unpopular individuals—even deaths. In England, for instance, King

Edward I held one at his wedding in 1254, another in 1284 to celebrate his conquest of Wales, and yet another in 1290 for the betrothal of his daughter, and he supported still more held by his barons.[6] His grandson Edward III took the tradition a step further and decided to create an order of knighthood based on the Knights of the Round Table. This he inaugurated as a round-table tournament held in 1344 and erected a huge circular building for the purpose.[7] (Incidentally, the institution he founded still survives today and is called the Order of the Garter; it is one of the highest awards to be bestowed by the monarch. Its knights include former prime minister John Major, the queen's husband, Prince Philip, and, believe it or not, the emperor of Japan.) Such pageants continued during the Middle Ages, right through the fifteenth century, when Malory was writing, and as late as 1566 Mary Queen of Scots had a round table made for an Arthurian masquerade held in Scotland to celebrate the baptism of her son.[8] Many such events are recorded as having a round table made specifically for the purpose. It seemed, therefore, that in Malory's day there may have been dozens of fake "round tables" kicking about. Was the Winchester item merely one of them?

At the time I was pondering Winchester's Camelot connection in the early 1990s, the tourist literature I obtained at the Great Hall appeared noncommittal concerning its round table's authenticity. It did, however, reveal that the surface painting was a later addition. The inscription around the center of the design is in Middle English, a language that did not exist until the late twelfth century, but the central rose motif can be dated more precisely. It is a red and white Tudor Rose, the emblem of the Tudor dynasty, which only came to power in 1485. As Middle English had pretty much died out to be replaced by what we would recognize as "Shakespearean English" (technically, Early Modern English) by the early sixteenth century, the painting can therefore be dated as somewhere between 1485 and 1525. However, the pamphlet assured the visitor that the table itself was very much older. In essence, it implied the jury was still out on the matter of its true age. On the contrary, after a bit of digging through Winchester's city library (there was no Internet back then, remember), I found that the jury had in fact returned its verdict as long ago as 1976. In that year the eminent British archaeologist Martin Biddle, later professor of medieval archaeology at Oxford University, had the table scientifically examined. Two types of dating were employed: dendrochronology, which could determine the age of wood by studying tree rings, and radiocarbon dating, which could establish the age of organic remains by chemical analysis. The first estimated a date of around 1270, and the second around 1290. These should not, though, be considered precise results. The margin of error for the radiocarbon dating was some fifty years, and the dendrochronology some thirty years either way. Additionally, the tree-ring analysis only determined when the tree was felled (when it died), not when the wood was actually used for the table. Even taking all this into account, the earliest possible date for the Winchester Round Table is around 1240—seven centuries after King Arthur's perceived era. Unfortunately for the Great Hall, its relic was almost certainly one of the feasting "round tables" made in the thirteenth century for Edward I, most likely the one constructed for the betrothal of his daughter in 1290, particularly as the event is recorded on April 20 of that year as having occurred in Winchester itself.[9]

The Winchester Round Table may explain the belief that the town was Camelot in Thomas Malory's time in the mid-1450s, but today we know it cannot be considered as evidence that Winchester was the celebrated capital of King Arthur. But there is a more damning indication that the town was never originally regarded as Camelot. Although it is claimed that Arthur did rule from a splendid, impregnable castle in earlier accounts, the oldest surviving reference to the name Camelot is found in the work *Lancelot* by the French poet Chrétien de Troyes (pronounced "Cret-ee-an de Twor," Troyes is a town in north-central France), written around 1180.[10] In this poem Chrétien also refers to the town of Winchester; significantly, however, he treats it as a completely separate place. Sadly, Winchester's claim to being Camelot had pretty much dissolved.

Soon after I published these findings, Winchester's Great Hall tourist literature was updated to include Radford's results, just as

Glastonbury's "Avalon" signboards had been removed. Luckily, I avoided a potential lynching as visitor levels remained unchanged, while many of Winchester's Camelot advocates continued undeterred. Whereas some of Glastonbury's unflinching Avalon proponents had used the argument that monks would never lie, Winchester's devotees began muttering about the unreliability of scientific tests. All the same, Winchester was yet another British town I should probably best avoid.

But if Winchester was not King Arthur's capital, where was I to concentrate my search? Well, to start with, wherever the legendary city might have been, it is unlikely to have borne the name Camelot. As I mentioned, the oldest extant reference to the word is found in the poem by Chrétien de Troyes around 1180. Although earlier writers, such as Geoffrey of Monmouth, talk at length about Arthur's magnificent city, not once do they record its name. The inference, therefore, is that the true name of the legendary city had been long forgotten by the twelfth century. This obviously made my search for a historical King Arthur considerably difficult. Like the subsequent Arthurian romancers, Chrétien fails completely to provide any indication as to where Camelot might be found. But are his predecessors of more help?

Geoffrey of Monmouth, writing around 1136, does say that Arthur held court for a while in the town of Caerleon in south Wales, over one hundred miles west of Winchester, and some modern historians have suggested that it may have inspired the concept of Camelot. In Roman times it was a military outpost with a large civilian population, and Geoffrey says the ancient Roman ruins were still visible during his time. Modern excavations have again uncovered these remains, including an amphitheater (arena) that some local enthusiasts have suggested might have been the origin of the round-table legend. Personally, I failed to see how a stepped, stone structure built to accommodate over six thousand spectators to such venues as gladiatorial contests could be regarded as a round table. Nevertheless, many of the guides I encountered on my visit to the Roman arena in 1991 were convinced by the idea. Questioning them concerning Caerleon's claim to be Camelot, I pointed out that, like Winchester, the first author to name Camelot, Chrétien de Troyes, also refers to Caerleon as a completely separate place[11] and that Geoffrey of Monmouth only included it as a location where Arthur held court for a short period during campaigns. They were, however, undeterred. Indeed, some were positively hostile. Caerleon, it seemed, was yet another place I should probably steer clear of.

Another tourist site that makes claim to being Camelot is Tintagel (see plate 2) on the north coast of the county of Cornwall in the far southwest of England. I arrived at the height of the holiday season to find it teeming with sightseers of all nationalities. Like Glastonbury, Tintagel's tourism has been bolstered by its Arthurian links. The streets were filled with stores bearing names like The Camelot Gift Shop and restaurants such as Merlin's Café. There were hotels decked out in Arthurian style and a museum dedicated to the King Arthur legend. Known as King Arthur's Hall, it even had its own round table made from solid granite. Along with the impressive building, it had been created in the 1930s by a somewhat eccentric millionaire who made his money from custard. Tintagel has a real castle, though. It stands just outside the town on what is virtually an island surrounded by foaming sea, linked to the mainland by a narrow ridge of rock. The ridge crumbled long ago, so to reach it I had to cross a dizzying footbridge and ascend a tiring flight of steps. The castle appeared much older than Winchester's Great Hall. Its ruined stone walls, resplendent with archways, battlements, buttresses, and arrow slits, stood ancient, weathered, and spectacular above the Atlantic breakers crashing against the cliffs below. This, according to the tourist literature, was the true site of Camelot.

Tintagel is yet another location first associated with the Arthurian legend by Geoffrey of Monmouth, asserting that it was here that Arthur was born. Although Geoffrey presented his *History of the Kings of Britain* as a historical text, his portrayal of Arthur's birth is, to say the least, somewhat fanciful. He tells us how Arthur's father, Uther Pendragon, had designs on Igraine, the wife of Gorlois the Duke of Cornwall. Aided by a magic potion prepared by Merlin the magician,

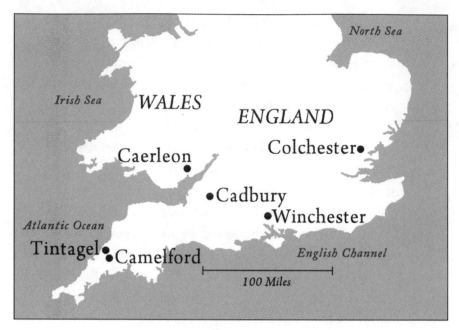

Fig. 2.1. Proposed Camelot sites in England and Wales.

Uther was transformed for a time into the form of Gorlois, and as such he visited the duke's castle at Tintagel and made love to Igraine. Thus Arthur is conceived. On the death of Gorlois, Uther makes Igraine his queen, and Arthur is born at Tintagel Castle.[12] Whether or not I was to believe any of this, or even if it had been based on some earlier tradition, it all seemed completely irrelevant to my search. Not once does Geoffrey say that Tintagel was the site of King Arthur's magnificent capital. Indeed, as far as I know, none of the original Arthurian romances ever suggested it was. It was simply said to be Arthur's birthplace. Even so, although the castle is very old and it did indeed once belong to an Earl of Cornwall, it cannot have been the birthplace of someone who lived around the year 500. It was only built in the early 1100s. In fact it was built for a Lord Reginald, the Earl of Cornwall, who, perhaps more than coincidentally, was the brother of Geoffrey of Monmouth's patron—the man who commissioned him to write his book. Most historians I spoke to believed that Geoffrey had concocted the story in order to please his sponsor. As with Glastonbury and Winchester, the publication of my research made little difference to Tintagel's tourist industry; today there's even a stunning cliff-top lodge called Camelot Castle Hotel, done out in the most elaborate style, complete with four-poster beds and even a mock round table in the lobby. Despite my reservations concerning its Arthurian authenticity, I happen to like Tintagel. Not only was I shown absolutely no hostility by the locals, but its shops and museum still sell my books even today. It was, at least, a place to which I could fearlessly return.

In stark contrast with the thronging Tintagel, the next stop in my search for Camelot was a lonely and isolated spot in the county of Somerset, around ten miles southeast of Glastonbury. This huge grass-covered earthwork called Cadbury Castle has been claimed by local people to have been the site of Camelot for a good few hundred years. No castle stands there today; in fact none ever did. Surrounded by a band of woodland, the hilltop site consists of a series of roughly circular ditches and high, steep-sided banks approximately fifteen hundred feet in diameter, enclosing a flat expanse large enough to encompass a modern English village. Cadbury Castle is what is known as a hill fort, a defensive earthwork built in pre-Roman times, perhaps as early as twenty-five hundred years ago. Originally the ring of embankments would have supported wooden stockades, and the central area would have contained a fortified settlement of thatched dwellings of heavy timber and rough stone. Although it predates the supposed Arthurian period by as much as a thousand years, such sites were refortified in the fifth and sixth centuries. Indeed, archaeological excavations conducted here in the late 1960s showed that it was reoccupied around the year 500, precisely the time Arthur is said to have lived. Leslie Alcock, the director of the dig, actually titled his book on the excavation *Cadbury/Camelot*.[13] So unusual was it for an esteemed archaeologist to link his name with the Arthurian legend that many Arthurian enthusiasts even today accept that Camelot has been unearthed at Cadbury.

You may guess what's coming next. Yes, I had my doubts. Although it was extensively refortified during the period Arthur is said to have lived, so were many other similar pre-Roman hill forts throughout

Britain. These include the hill forts of Dinas Powys and Lodge Hill in Wales; Old Oswestry and The Wrekin in central England; Chûn Castle and Castle Dore in Cornwall; and Barbury Castle, Hod Hill, and Maiden Castle in southern England. In fact, there are literally dozens all across the country where archaeology has shown intensive reoccupation during the supposed Arthurian time. After the Romans left Britain in AD 410, law and order quickly broke down in many parts of the country, and by the year 500 there were invasions from Germany, Denmark, Scotland, and Ireland. The old hill forts proved to be the most readily defensible locations. Nothing discovered during Leslie Alcock's excavations even remotely suggested that the fabled King Arthur had any more links with Cadbury Castle hill fort than any of the others. In fact, contrary to popular belief, Alcock himself never said Cadbury was Camelot. He merely named his book in reference to local folklore that held the location was Arthur's capital (and perhaps with his eye on sales). The oldest known reference to Cadbury Castle being Camelot is found in the work of Henry VIII's antiquarian, John Leland (the man who examined Glastonbury's lead cross), who visited the district in 1542, reporting that local people believed it was the site of Camelot, probably as the word *Camel* was found in the name of the nearby village of Queen Camel.[14] Queen was added in the thirteenth century, coming from Queen Eleanor, the wife of Henry III, who owned the land at the time. Previously, it was just called Camel, which many Arthurian enthusiasts have seen as evidence that this was the location of Camelot. However, this was not its original name; in the tenth century it is recorded as Cantmael, derived from the Celtic meaning "District of the Bare Hill." Considering the fact that the local folklore appears based on a name the location did not have until many centuries after the Arthurian era, Cadbury Castle's specific case for being Camelot pretty much evaporates.

Just how much of the country was I to wander before finding anywhere with a substantial or at least a truly ancient claim to being Arthur's legendary capital? There were two other places that had been suggested by various authors as possible candidates for Camelot, but these I soon rejected. The Roman name for Colchester in the county of Essex to the northeast of London was Camulodunum, which might, with some imagination, be regarded as being the origin of the name Camelot. It was certainly the principal city in early Roman Britain, but by the time Arthur is said to have lived around the year 500, it was firmly within the territory conquered by the Anglo-Saxons and had been for around fifty years. Then there was the town of Camelford in Cornwall. It does not even seem to have existed before being recorded in the thirteenth century, as it is not so much as mentioned in the Domesday Book, an exhaustive survey of England commissioned by King William I and completed in 1086. In any event, it seems that both of these locations could be dismissed, as the word *Camelot* most likely originated in the fertile imagination of the poet Chrétien de Troyes or one of his close contemporaries, as no one before the 1190s gave a name to the fabled city.

I had, it seemed, run out of places to go: my hunt for Camelot—for the time being at least—had led to a complete dead end. In my search for the historical King Arthur, I decided to turn to another Arthurian theme. What about the legend of Excalibur, the sword in the stone, and the Lady of the Lake? Could they help in my quest to discover the true origins of the Arthurian saga? As unlikely as it might seem, the story of King Arthur's fabled weapon may well have emerged from genuinely ancient traditions.

3

Swords of Power

According to the familiar story, Arthur became king at the age of fifteen by drawing the sword Excalibur from a block of stone. It was said that the man who could accomplish this task was destined to rule the Britons, and all before Arthur had failed. Could this seemingly fanciful yarn be based on some kind of historical event? Surprisingly, historians have suggested a potentially authentic origin for the sword-and-stone story. It concerns the way swords were made. Swords were cast in a stone mold; when the molten metal cooled and set, the finished sword blade was literally removed from a stone. Some scholars have suggested that this is the origin of the Arthurian story of a sword coming from stone. Nice idea, but personally I don't buy it. Nearly all swords were made this way. If this was the origin of the legend, wouldn't it make King Arthur's purportedly unique sword as common as any other? There is, though, another theory regarding the birth of the legend that involves a real sword stuck in an actual stone.

Remember I said that by the time of the Glastonbury grave discovery, the notoriety of the Arthurian legend had spread as far south as Italy. Well, in the Italian province of Tuscany, local people are still proud to assert that the sword-and-stone story began there. In a chapel near Saint Galgano Abbey in the district of Chiusdino, there is a rock from which a sword hilt protrudes. The weapon is said to have been plunged into the rock in 1180 by an Italian knight called Galgano after he renounced warfare to become a monk. When he died the pope made him a saint, and a chapel was built around the sword in the stone, which had become regarded as a holy relic. Quite how the knight managed to secure a sword in solid rock is something of a mystery, but however he did it, it stuck fast. As it was said to possess miraculous healing powers, during the Middle Ages various pilgrims—including a couple of rival abbots—tried to steal the relic, but none could remove it from the stone. To deter such attempts the abbey monks put mummified hands on display, declaring them to have belonged to would-be thieves whom God had punished by having them devoured by wolves, evidently leaving behind the offending appendages.[1] Nowadays, the relic is protected by a thick Perspex acrylic screen, so there's no point going there to try your hand. (No pun intended.)

The sword visible today would seem to be the original item, as metal testing has dated the weapon to around AD 1200. This dating has led some researchers to agree with local opinion that Galgano's sword inspired the Arthurian sword-and-stone idea, as the theme first appeared in the Arthurian romances at this time. Medieval authors, they suggest, interpolated the episode into the continually evolving King Arthur story. The oldest known inclusion of the sword-and-stone motif in the King Arthur saga is by the poet Robert de Boron (the same man who introduced the Holy Grail into the Arthurian romance) in a poem titled *Merlin*.[2] Robert's *Merlin* can be dated to around the year 1200, so the anecdote of the Galgano sword could well have been known to him. However, there is one vital difference between Robert's tale and the story of Galgano. It may come as something of a surprise to those familiar with the modern version of the story: in Robert's original tale, the sword is not embedded in a stone but in an anvil, which stands on a stone. Later writers tended to leave out the anvil in favor of the sword-in-the-stone theme we know today, and this might well have been influenced by the account of the Galgano sword. The sword-in-an-anvil motif, however, would suggest that the Arthurian episode was inspired by a separate source and merely modified after the fame of the Italian event. In fact, some scholars have advocated that the Galgano story was inspired by a preexisting Arthurian tale. Either way, it was the *location* of the incident in Robert's poem that was of interest to me. Arthur does not gain his sword in some remote village in Italy but in the capital city of England.

Although other medieval authors had concentrated on the sword in the stone, rather than the anvil theme, Sir Thomas Malory in the fifteenth century returned to Robert de Boron's original rendition. Indeed, he retells Robert's account almost verbatim. As Robert's poem only survives today in fragmented form, I decided to concentrate on Malory's *The Death of Arthur* as my starting point, as he appears to have had a full copy of the *Merlin* poem in his possession. As I said, most people are familiar with the story of how Arthur, as a young man, proves himself rightful king by drawing the magical sword from a stone when no one else could. In the acclaimed movie *Excalibur* of 1981, and in many other Hollywood, TV, and literary portrayals of the event, Arthur pulls Excalibur from a large boulder or stone block that had stood defiantly in woodland or open countryside for many years. Besides originally being in an anvil, it may come as a further surprise to know that this modern rendering of the tale differs considerably from the original on three other accounts. First, the weapon is not Excalibur but a completely different sword. Second, the sword had not been there for years but suddenly appeared. And third, the event does not take place in some isolated setting but right in the heart of London.

Malory actually provides a specific location in London for the event. According to him, after a service on Christmas Day in what he describes as "the greatest church in London," when the congregation are leaving, they are shocked to see something in the churchyard that had not been there before: a large square, stone block upon which stands an anvil, and embedded in the anvil is a sword, the hilt and part of the blade protruding. Around the sword—whether on the anvil or the stone is not clear—are words written in gold: "Whosoever pulls this sword from this stone and anvil is born the rightful king of England." (At the time Malory was writing, the word *England* was often used to refer to Britain as a whole [see chapter 7].) The greatest nobles try and fail to remove the sword, until New Year's Day when Arthur finally succeeds.[3]

Leaving aside the likely reality of the stone-pulling incident itself for a moment, does the original setting of the event where Arthur is proclaimed king imply that the origins of a historical King Arthur might be found in London?

Malory follows Geoffrey of Monmouth's version of Arthur's birth at Tintagel Castle, after his father King Uther sleeps with Igraine. As trouble is brewing in the nation and the baby's life is in danger, Merlin persuades the king to allow him to bring up the child in secret. This he does by giving the infant to one Sir Ector and his wife who raise him as their own in an undisclosed location. In fact, it is they who call the child Arthur, so even Uther and Igraine are unaware of their son's true name. When Uther Pendragon dies without an heir, the country slides into civil war, and for many years, without a king, the barons struggle for supremacy while foreigners plunder the country. Only a new, undisputed king can possibly hope to return peace and prosperity to the land. All this time Arthur remains ignorant of his lineage, believing Ector to be his father.[4] One day, when Arthur is fifteen, he is out riding with his adopted father and elder brother Sir Kay, on their way to tournaments to be held beside the churchyard where the sword in the anvil stood. En route, Kay discovers that he has forgotten to bring his sword and asks Arthur to return home to fetch it. Failing to find his brother's sword at home, on his return journey Arthur gets lost and ends up in the churchyard where he sees the sword in the anvil. Unaware of its significance, he decides to take it for his brother to use. With no one around he effortlessly pulls the sword from the anvil where all others have failed. Inadvertently, Arthur has proved himself rightful king. When news spreads and the barons gather to dispute that such a lowborn individual could possibly be their ruler, Merlin—once the revered advisor to Uther Pendragon—appears on the scene to reveal Arthur's true identity as the dead king's son and true heir to the throne.[5]

Once more the historicity of these events should not concern us at present. What's important is that they provide a specific location for Arthur's beginnings. Malory suggests that the place where Arthur had been living was fairly close to the London churchyard where the sword in the anvil stood. He and his adopted family had been on their way to take part in the very tournaments that were to be held on New Year's Day beside the London churchyard, and they arrive there well within a day. In fact, we are told that Sir Ector even conducts his daily business within the town of London. Today London is a huge city covering an area of seven hundred square miles, but in the Middle Ages it measured little more than a single square mile. Accordingly, Arthur's childhood home was evidently thought to have been in the countryside not far from the city. Although an unladed horseman might cover thirty-five miles on a good day, in midwinter on mud tracks, fifteen miles would be about the limit. As we are told that Arthur first returned home and, when he failed to find his brother's sword, rode to the tournament site to arrive well before the event began, we can deduce that Arthur was imagined to have lived fairly close to where the sword in the anvil stood. Yes, I realize that there are some rather glaring inconsistencies in the account. How come Sir Kay forgot to take his sword to a tournament in which he was to take part? And how come Arthur managed to get there before his family, after a detour back home? However, as I have said, it was the locations Malory had in mind that specifically interested me, rather than the action. If he took the story from Robert de Boron's twelfth-century original, which Robert in turn claimed to have taken from an earlier account, then it is possible that this medieval tale concerning Arthur becoming king originated with a much older, though now elaborated legend regarding Arthur spending his youth near London (in fact, in what is now within the boundary of London itself) and being proclaimed monarch in the city. So could such a legend genuinely relate to the time Arthur is said to have lived, around AD 500?

Malory says that the churchyard in question surrounded the "greatest church in London." Today that would be Saint Paul's Cathedral, as it was in Malory's time, and indeed right through the Middle Ages. Malory even names Saint Paul's as being the possible location for the episode, saying, "Whether this [church] was Saint Paul's or not, the French book does not say."[6] (The French book to which he refers appears to be Robert de Boron's *Merlin*.) Nonetheless, Saint Paul's had been London's most important church for centuries, so it's hard to imagine what other church it could be. (Westminster Abbey—where England's kings and queens are crowned and royal marriages are held—was indeed a great church, but until the sixteenth century, well after Malory's time, Westminster was a different city from London, geographically separated by open countryside.) Although Saint Paul's went through many periods of reconstruction, culminating with the building we see today erected in the late 1600s, the location is recorded as having been the seat of the bishops of London since 604. This is significant, as the seats of bishops were cathedrals, and there had been bishops of London since the Romans ruled Britain in the fourth century.[7] It is possible, then, that there had been a Saint Paul's Cathedral during the time Arthur is reckoned to have lived, around AD 500. But what could possibly be behind a story as fanciful as the sword and anvil or stone?

Even though the sword was originally depicted as being in an anvil, it is the stone upon which it rested that ultimately assumed the greater importance. Strangely, although in Robert de Boron's account the sword is in an anvil, he makes no reference to its significance. Neither indeed does Malory. Moreover, the fact that most of the dozens of Arthurian authors between Robert and Malory omitted the anvil altogether further suggests it was the stone rather than the anvil that was considered the essential element of the anecdote. When I read Robert's account specifically saying that the stone represented "the power of Christ," the episode took on a completely new perspective.[8] Although it is said that the sword and anvil mysteriously appeared during mass, it is not made clear by either author, Robert or Malory, whether or not the stone was already there. If it was, then, going by Robert de Boron's words, the stone actually fitted into a historical context.

From the time the newly converted Roman Christians brought their faith to Britain, in the mid-fourth century, they adopted a policy that may seem unusual to us today. They did not immediately try to eradicate paganism, rather they replaced it gradually. Paganism was not outlawed by the Romans; it was merely discouraged. In fact, the

Romans adopted this policy throughout their empire as part of a clever strategy to convert pagan peoples called *Interpretatio Christiana,* meaning "Christian Reinterpretation." Rather than expect folk to immediately convert and abandon generations of deeply held beliefs, the canny Roman Church allowed the process to occur slowly. Saints progressively supplanted the old gods, pagan festivals little by little replaced days of pagan observance, and temples were gradually substituted for churches. For example, the traditional date for the birth of the sun god Sol Invictus became Christmas, the birth of Christ; temples to the moon goddess Diana became shrines to the Virgin Mary; and the regular bull-blood-drinking feasts to honor the god Mithras were replaced by the weekly Mass of the Eucharist, where consecrated wine was drunk; and most importantly for our current investigation, there are numerous examples throughout the British Isles of churches built on formally sacred pagan sites. In several such examples there still survive ancient stones, once venerated by the pagan Britons as representing their gods, which had been reconsecrated as Christian monuments. For instance, in Llanwrthwl churchyard in Wales in western Britain, there is a six-foot such stone; in Saint Clement churchyard in Cornwall in southwest England, there stands a ten-foot stone; and in the churchyard of Rudston in Yorkshire in northern England, there is a massive twenty-five-foot pagan megalith. Many churches have smaller such stones, such as Lanivet and Cuby churches, both in Cornwall. As part of their policy of *Interpretatio Christiana,* the Roman Christians deliberately built churches right next to these stone monoliths and blocks, which no longer represented the ancient deities, but *the power of Christ.* As this is exactly how Robert de Boron describes the stone in the Arthurian event, and as it is actually said to have stood in the churchyard, could it have been such a reconsecrated monument? Was there any historical evidence that such a stone had once been in the churchyard of Saint Paul's Cathedral in London?

Near Saint Paul's there is indeed a block of limestone that still survives that local tradition holds to be the very stone from which Arthur drew the sword. Approximately seventeen inches high, twenty-one inches wide, and twelve inches thick, it is known as the London Stone (see plate 3). (Evidently it was once larger, closer to the size of the Arthurian stone described by Robert de Boron.) This ancient stone is recorded as marking the place of legal declarations; moreover, it was specifically associated with a sword of power. Surviving records dating from as early as eleven hundred years ago refer to the stone as having great ceremonial significance: it marked the traditional place where laws were passed and proclamations issued; and after 1189, when Henry Fitz-Ailwin became London's first mayor, the inauguration ceremony expressly required the new incumbent to strike the stone with his sword to validate his entitlement to govern the city. Just how far back the tradition between the London Stone and a sword of authority actually goes is unknown, as earlier records are scanty, but it is quite possible that it had existed in some form or other for centuries. Today the stone is set into a niche in the wall of a building opposite London's Cannon Street Station, protected by a glass case and an iron grill, some ten minutes' walk from Saint Paul's. It has only been there since 1962 and had previously been moved on several occasions as new buildings were erected, and there are no records earlier than the 900s to tell us where it originally stood. Nevertheless, it has always been close to Saint Paul's, and so it might well have originally stood in the cathedral churchyard as local legend asserts. I therefore concluded that the London Stone could indeed have inspired the setting for the sword-and-stone episode as related by both Thomas Malory and originally by Robert de Boron (although they both have an anvil on the stone), particularly since Robert penned his story just a decade after Henry Fitz-Ailwin's inauguration as mayor. A genuine stone in Saint Paul's churchyard that was associated with civic authority and with a sword of power: an ideal theme—and one familiar to readers at the time—for Robert de Boron (or his source) to have incorporated into the ever-evolving legend of King Arthur.

All the same, although I might have found the origin of this particular Arthurian theme, it might simply have been a medieval interpolation. The stone may well have been here during the period Arthur is said to have lived—in the 1960s, Museum of London archaeologist Peter

Marsden suggested the stone was of pre-Christian Roman origin—but there are no records concerning its ceremonial function or indeed anything about it earlier than around AD 900.[9] So I was left with no more evidence to associate a historical King Arthur specifically with the city of London than to link him with any of the proposed Camelot sites. Nevertheless, I did formulate an idea as to how the notion of a sword imbedded in an anvil upon a stone *might* have originated with a historical Arthur. It was the odd combination of the two items that got me thinking.

As we have seen, like Malory, Robert fails to explain the anvil's significance, while most medieval authors chose to leave it out altogether: so why the two items? There was, I discovered, an intriguing phonetic peculiarity concerning the words *stone* and *anvil*. Before continuing I need to explain whom King Arthur and the Britons were seeking to repel. I have mentioned that he was fighting the Anglo-Saxons, but this is a simplification. The Angles and the Saxons were originally different peoples from adjacent regions in the far north of modern Germany. The Angles invaded the northeast and east of England, while the Saxons invaded the south and southeast. So if he did unite the Britons around AD 500, Arthur would either have been fighting the Angles or the Saxons but presumably not both at the same time. Ultimately, the invaders formed an alliance, and by the 700s they where collectively referred to as the Anglo-Saxons, and ultimately just the Saxons, but during the historical Arthurian period—the post-Roman era—they were separate invaders. With this in mind, I found it fascinating that in Latin (the Roman language spoken widely throughout Britain in the early Dark Ages), the word for a large stone, such as that on which the anvil stands in the Arthurian episode, is *saxum,* a word that sounds very similar to Saxon. So similar, in fact, that at some point the two words could easily have been confused. Add to this that the English word *anvil* is similar to the name Angle, and it is possible that an original version of the story portrayed Arthur taking the sword from the Angles and Saxons—that is, the fight out of them (he seized the initiative from his enemies)— and the words ultimately became mistranslated as "anvil" and "stone."

Might this eventually have evolved into the legend of Arthur drawing a sword from an anvil and stone?

So was this the evolution of the Excalibur story? A theme incorporated through mistranslation into the Arthurian legend during the Dark Ages and popularized in the Middle Ages by the story of Galgano's sword, while a setting for the event was based on the traditions associated with the London Stone around the year 1200? Well—yes and no. It could be the origin of the sword-and-stone motif but not of Arthur's enchanted sword. As I mentioned earlier, in the medieval Arthurian romances, the sword in the stone (or anvil) was a completely different weapon from the famous Excalibur. So could the tale of Excalibur itself help me in my quest?

Most people's familiarity with the King Arthur story comes from its various renditions on TV and in the movies, where the two swords are usually one and the same. But in the medieval tales, right up to Malory's time, Excalibur was not the sword in the anvil or stone. Arthur obtains Excalibur well after he has drawn the unnamed sword that proves him king. Excalibur, as the name of Arthur's second sword, appears to originate with the work of Geoffrey of Monmouth in the 1130s where he calls it Caliburnus, or Caliburn for short, leading to later authors using the more lyrical name Excalibur.[10] Initially, it was not endowed with magical properties; rather, as the French poet Chrétien de Troyes in his *Perceval* composed in the 1190s explains, it was "the finest sword ever made, which sliced through iron as if through wood."[11] In other words, it was an exceptionally well-made weapon but not enchanted. It was not until the early 1200s that it took on a mystical aspect. From then on different authors attributed various supernatural qualities to Excalibur: when drawn its blade shone so brightly that it blinded the enemy; its wielder could not be defeated if he kept faith; it could only be lifted by the true king; and it had the power to dispel witchcraft. Even its scabbard was said to possess magical properties, as anyone wearing it would not bleed from wounds.

But these were all medieval tales, written down well over half a

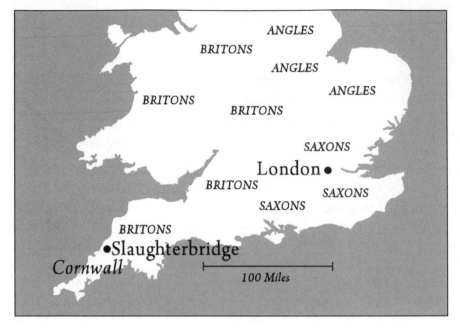

Fig. 3.1. Areas in southern Britain occupied by the Britons, Angles, and Saxons around AD 500.

millennium after Arthur is said to have lived. Are there any stories concerning a special sword associated with the fabled king before the Middle Ages? There are, and they survived in an area of Britain not occupied by the Anglo-Saxons: Wales in the west of Britain. Wales had and still has a separate language from the rest of Britain. In the Welsh language—derived from the tongue of the native Britons, as opposed to English, which originated with the Anglo-Saxons—there are a number of old stories featuring King Arthur that seem to date from before the medieval Arthurian romances. In some of these Welsh narratives, such as the tale of *Culhwch and Olwen* (Culhwch, pronounced "Cul-hoo-k" or "Ilhuk," is a legendary hero and Olwen is his lover), which dates from the eleventh century,[12] and *The Spoils of Annwn*,[13] dated on linguistic grounds to around AD 900—over two centuries before the work of Geoffrey of Monmouth—Arthur's sword is called Caledfwlch (pronounced "Caled-voolch"), meaning "unbreakable sword." (Specifically, the name appears to be a combination of the Welsh words *caled,* meaning "hard," and *bwlch,* meaning "breach," that is, it could cut through anything.) It seems likely that this is where Geoffrey derived his name for Arthur's sword, latinizing it as Caliburnus, or Caliburn, as it is usually abbreviated in English translations. So it seems that the tradition regarding Arthur having a unique sword, whether magical or not, did exist before Geoffrey of Monmouth and the subsequent Arthurian romances of the Middle Ages. But could the Excalibur legend help me narrow my hunt for a specific location concerning Arthur's origins? One feature of the story, I decided, might indeed prove helpful, particularly in my search for Arthur's grave, and that was the tale of the Lady of the Lake.

The Lady of the Lake first appears in a series of Arthurian tales known as the Vulgate Cycle. (The term *cycle,* in this context, is used for stories or poems dealing with the same themes.) Coming from the Old French *vulgāre,* meaning "to popularize," they were composed by a series of anonymous authors from around 1220 to 1240. (Strictly speaking, those that were composed after 1230 are usually referred to as Post-Vulgate by literary scholars, but for convenience I shall use the term *Vulgate* to cover them all.) In the Vulgate stories the Lady of the Lake is a mysterious water nymph from whom Arthur originally receives Excalibur. Eventually, it is returned to her in the now famous scene. After his final battle, when Arthur lies mortally wounded, he orders his knight Girflet to cast Excalibur into a nearby lake. After twice disobeying the king's wishes, the knight reluctantly consents. When the sword is thrown, the arm of the Lady of the Lake rises from the surface, catches the weapon by the hilt, and takes it down into the watery depths.[14] This is the incarnation of the tale later elaborated by Thomas Malory, although in his version it is Sir Bedivere and not Sir Girflet who assumes the role. While other medieval authors cast Galahad, Lancelot, or even Perceval in this part, the event itself had become firmly entrenched in the saga by the end of the Middle Ages. Although the episode would seem to be one of the more fanciful aspects of the Arthurian story, it was worth considering the possibility that the legend could lead me to a real location where Arthur was originally thought to have died. Obviously, if he historically existed, finding where he died might lead me to the general vicinity of his grave. So where, exactly, was the lake in question believed to have been?

So often in the Arthurian saga, locations are hard to identify. As I had found with Camelot, none of the medieval authors tells us where the Excalibur lake actually is. Even Malory, who did identify Camelot as being Winchester Castle, is silent on the matter. And as you might expect, there are a number of lakes in the British Isles that local folklore asserts to be the resting place of Excalibur. In Wales, for instance, there is Lily Ponds near the town of Bosherston in South Wales, and Llyn Llydaw and Llyn Ogwen in Snowdonia, North Wales (*llyn* is Welsh for "lake"); Cornwall has Loe Pool near Porthleven and Dozmary Pool on Bodmin Moor; England boasts a stretch of the River Brue at Pomparles Bridge near Glastonbury; even Scotland has an Excalibur lake, Loch Arthur near the town of Beeswing. However, all but one of these can pretty much be discounted. Three are undoubtedly relatively recent inventions. Lily Ponds did not even exist until the 1700s, when it was created as a garden feature by the landowner; Loe Pool was only brought into the story by the poet Tennyson in the late 1800s; and there are no known Arthurian tales or poems whatsoever before modern times that mention Scotland's Loch Arthur. Two are fairly spurious. Pomparles Bridge is not named in any early Arthurian story. It is only referenced in passing in association with Excalibur by the antiquarian John Leland in the 1500s, who says that local people believed it to be the place where Arthur's knight threw the sword to the Lady of the Lake. I dismissed this site quite quickly. After all, if this was the location the romancers had in mind, then the mysterious water nymph would have to be the Lady of the River. Llyn Llydaw's claim does come from a medieval tale, titled *Vera Historia Morte de Arthuri* (The True History of Arthur's Death); dating from around 1300, it locates Arthur's last battle nearby. As much concerning Arthur in the work is at odds with earlier authors, it is generally considered as an unreliable source by literary scholars. And one is based on an irrelevancy. Llyn Ogwen's case comes from an indirect association referenced in a series of short medieval Welsh poems known as *Trioedd Ynys Prydain* (The Triads of Britain).[15] In one of the triads (which we shall be discussing later), it is said that Arthur's knight Sir Bedivere is buried on Mount Tryfan, which overlooks the lake. According to Thomas Malory in the mid-1400s, it was Sir Bedivere who cast Excalibur to the Lady of the Lake, and consequently local folklore assumed the lake beside his purported burial site to be the lake in question. However, Bedivere was not the knight originally associated with the Lady of the Lake episode. The oldest known rendition of the story is found in one of the Vulgate stories, known as the Vulgate *Mort Artu* (Death of Arthur), composed around 1230, over two centuries before Malory's time, and here the knight who throws Excalibur into the enchanted lake is not Bedivere but Sir Griflet.[16] Accordingly, whether or not Bedivere was buried near Llyn Ogwen is completely immaterial to its case for it being the Excalibur lake, and since Bedivere is irrelevant, the case collapses. This left me with Dozmary Pool, a small, remote lake with a surface area of around thirty-seven acres in the bleak, windswept uplands of Bodmin Moor in the county of Cornwall. As it was the most famous of the lakes linked to the Arthurian story, and with a stronger case than most, I felt it warranted further investigation.

Dozmary Pool's claim to being the lake where Arthur's sword was cast lies exclusively with its proximity to a place where Arthur is said to have fought his last battle: a field in an area called Slaughterbridge, only ten miles away. The bridge itself crosses the River Camel, which various Arthurian scholars have asserted to be the location of Arthur's final conflict. Many of the medieval Arthurian narratives affirm that King Arthur's last battle was fought at a place called Camlann; it is even mentioned in an older chronology known as the *Welsh Annals,* compiled as early as 955.[17] As no place still bears that name, the location of the Battle of Camlann is open to speculation, and one of the favorite contenders has been Slaughterbridge, some Arthurian researchers suggesting that the name of the river at the site, the Camel, derived from the word *Camlann.* We will be returning to the Battle of Camlann itself and its various possible locations in chapter 12, but for now we need to establish the authenticity or otherwise of this particular site in order to consider the likelihood of the nearby Dozmary Pool as the Excalibur lake. Today, there is an Arthurian visitor center at Slaughterbridge, which includes an exhibition room, nature trail, scenic garden, children's play area, and a gift shop. The area, some twenty acres in size, also includes the purported battle site where lies an inscribed horizontal stone around nine feet long and three feet wide, known locally as King Arthur's Stone, which is said to mark the very spot where Arthur fell. The stone has been reliably dated to the early sixth century and so could well date from the period Arthur is said to have lived.

On the face of it, Slaughterbridge is a good contender for the site of Arthur's last battle. Geoffrey of Monmouth, writing in the 1130s, says Arthur's final battle was beside a river somewhere in Cornwall, implying that it was fought for control of a strategic river crossing or bridge, whereas the Jersey poet Wace, writing in the 1150s, specifically refers to Cornwall's River Camel as the location of the battle. So, at the site in question, we have a bridge called *Slaughter*bridge—seemingly suggesting a bloody skirmish was fought here—which crosses the River Camel, specifically named by Wace. However, as I researched the local history, there emerged a number of problems. The "slaughter" element in the name of the location comes from the Old English word *slohtre,* meaning "marsh," so is not in itself evidence that any battle was fought here. Most of the medieval romancers place Arthur's last battle in southern or central England, rather than Cornwall, and the earliest reference to the conflict in the *Welsh Annals* suggests it was fought in Wales. Although Wace specifically places it on the River Camel in Cornwall, he uses Geoffrey of Monmouth's account of the battle as his source, which he paraphrases almost exactly, implying that this Cornish location was solely down to Geoffrey. We have already questioned Geoffrey of Monmouth's reliability when it comes to his Cornish Arthurian connections, such as placing Arthur's birth at Tintagel Castle in order to please his patron's brother, the Earl of Cornwall, who owned the place. Slaughterbridge is only twelve miles from Tintagel, and it too was

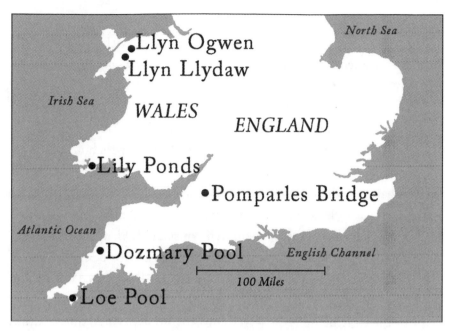

Fig. 3.2. Traditional locations for the lake into which Excalibur was cast.

owned by this same Earl of Cornwall. In fact, he owned much of the county, which explains why he was earl of it. So, according to Geoffrey, Arthur was born and ultimately fell on the estate of his patron's wealthy brother. As such, I didn't have much confidence in Geoffrey of Monmouth's account per se when it came to locating the site of Arthur's last battle. But there was still the inscribed stone.

When I first saw the inscription on King Arthur's Stone—upon which its dating is primarily based—I was mystified as to why anyone had ever associated it with King Arthur. In Latin the weathered inscription reads: LATINI IC IACIT FILIUS MA [. . .] RI, meaing "Here lies Latinus, son of [probably] Macarus." As it is clearly the grave of someone called Latinus, where does the Arthur link come in? The oldest known reference to the stone appears in *The Survey of Cornwall* by the antiquarian Richard Carew published in 1602.[18] Here, he tells us that "the folk thereabouts will show you a stone bearing Arthur's name." Presumably, he never saw it himself. Interestingly, another Cornish antiquarian, William Borlase, in his *The Antiquities of Cornwall* (abridged title) published in 1769,[19] suggests that the locals mistakenly concluded that the last letters read MAG URI, which could, with some imagination, be considered a rendering of the Latin words *Magni Arthur,* meaning "Great Arthur." A lot of imagination, I would think.

As far as I was concerned, all that was really left to suggest any association between Slaughterbridge and the early King Arthur legend was the *cam* element in the name of the River Camel, which also appears in Camlann, the apparent name for the location of Arthur's last battle. As we shall see when examining the battle of Camlann itself, there are many such places in Britain bearing the affix *cam.* At this point it could just as well have been any of them. All considered, Slaughterbridge did not impress me as having a particularly strong case for being the site of the Battle of Camlann, and as such the nearby Dozmary Pool's claim for being the Excalibur lake seemed equally unconvincing.

For the time being my research into the mystery of Arthur's sword, or swords, had taken me no further in my quest to identify a historical King Arthur than my search for Camelot. So where was I to turn next? I decided to concentrate specifically on where Arthur was supposedly buried. No, not Glastonbury, but the Isle of Avalon. In the Geoffrey of Monmouth account, and in many of the later Arthurian romances, after his last battle the mortally wounded Arthur sailed off to the mystical Avalon. So where exactly was the enchanted Isle of Avalon originally thought to have been?

4

Avalon

After Excalibur is thrown to the Lady of the Lake, the mortally wounded King Arthur sails away to Avalon, an enchanted island of healing and eternal youth, accompanied by three mysterious maidens. This is the story familiar throughout the world today. When I first began researching the Avalon legend, I regarded it as the least likely of the Arthurian themes to be rooted in any kind of real Dark Age history: magical swords, water nymphs, enchanted islands, mystic cures, and immortality. No way! Astonishingly, I was very much mistaken.

Initially, when I examined the medieval accounts of the episode, it all seemed little more than a fairy tale. Nevertheless, I examined them thoroughly as I wanted to find out how, when, and particularly where the legend started. It might, I hoped, provide clues to a historical Arthur's origins and where he might in reality have been laid to rest. The oldest use of the name Avalon is found in Geoffrey of Monmouth's *History of the Kings of Britain.* Written in Latin around 1136, he calls it *Insula Avallonis*—the Isle of Avalon. Geoffrey was from Britain, and the Roman Empire had long since collapsed, so why Latin? During the early medieval period, following the conquest of England by the Normans from northern France in 1066, Britain had three separate languages: English, French, and Welsh. To complicate matters English was a collection of distinct regional dialects, meaning that someone from one part of the country could barely understand someone from somewhere else. So for convenience many authors of the time wrote in

Latin—the language used by the church and understood by the educated classes—and Geoffrey of Monmouth was no exception. He mentions Avalon twice. First, telling us simply, without elaboration, that the king's famous sword was forged there and again later when referring to Arthur's demise.[1] Translated into English, he writes: "And the famous King Arthur was himself mortally wounded, and carried to the Isle of Avalon to be healed of his wounds." And that's it. He tells us nothing whatsoever about the place: not where it was, who lived there, and what relevance it had in the overall narrative. However, in a further Latin work on the Arthurian legend, titled the *Life of Merlin,* written around 1150, he does say more.[2] In this, he refers to the island as *Insula Pomorum* (Isle of Apples) and reveals who dwelt there:

> There, nine sisters rule. . . . She who is chief among
> them is the most skilled of healers, excelling her sisters
> in beauty. Her name is Morgan, and she knows the
> properties of herbs to cure the sick.[3]

Arthur is taken to Avalon to be healed by Morgan:

> [On the island] Morgan received [Arthur] with honor,
> and placed him [Arthur] on a golden bed in her
> chamber. . . . After some time, she told him that his
> health could be restored only if he stayed with her.[4]

So, according to Geoffrey, Avalon is an island ruled by a sisterhood of nine female mystics, the leader of whom is a healer called Morgan who attempts to cure Arthur with her abilities. He fails to say whether Arthur lived or died, but the Jersey poet Wace, in his French poem the *Romance of Brutus* of 1155, implies the island gave Arthur immortality.[5] He tells us that:

> Arthur himself was mortally wounded. . . . [He was]
> taken to Avalon in the hope that he might be healed.

[And] he is still there, awaited by the Britons, for
they say that he will return to live again.[6]

(You may be wondering why, if this was a poem, it fails to rhyme. It
does—sort of—in the original French.) Strictly speaking, Wace suggests that Arthur is not exactly immortal but rather that he is dead
and awaiting rebirth at a time of his country's greatest need. According
to Wace, therefore, it would appear that Arthur's preserved body was
entombed somewhere on the Isle of Avalon.

Wace came from the island of Jersey off the northern coast of
France. At the time the north of France was ruled by the English
kings following the Norman conquest of England; consequently the
Arthurian story became as popular in France as it was in Britain. Many
early Arthurian romances were composed by other French authors;
a number of these were by the poet Chrétien de Troyes, and one
includes the next surviving reference to Avalon. In his long poem *Erec
and Enide,* composed around 1170, Chrétien speaks of a banquet held
by King Arthur where one of the guests is described as coming from
the Isle of Avalon.[7] Like Geoffrey, he also refers to Morgan in association with Avalon, calling her Morgan le Fey,[8] a name used by many
of the subsequent romancers, although one of them, the English poet
Layamon, calls her Argante, which appears to derive from Old Gaelic
meaning simply "the Queen." Around the year 1200 Layamon composed a reworking of Wace's poem, a Middle English work called simply *Brut* ("Brutus," a mythical founder of Britain), in which Arthur is
sailed to the enchanted Isle of Avalon by two mysterious women, where
the isle's queen, called Argante, tends to Arthur's wounds.[9] (Middle
English was one of three developing forms of the English language,
coming after Old English, or Anglo-Saxon, and before Early Modern
English as spoken by William Shakespeare. To be accurate Layamon
wrote in the Midland [central] dialect of Middle English.) About
the same time Robert de Boron wrote his Latin *Joseph of Arimathea.*
Robert's tale does not include an account of Arthur's demise, but it
does incorporate the Holy Grail into the Arthurian saga, which he

tells us was ultimately hidden in the "Vales of Avalon."[10] The *Vulgate Mort Artu* (see chapter 3), written in French prose around 1230, is the oldest known inclusion of the Lady of the Lake and the episode where the knight Girflet throws her Excalibur.[11] In this rendition, after he has cast the sword into the lake, Girflet sees a barge approach a nearby shore in which there are a number of women, one identified as Morgan le Fey, who takes the dying Arthur aboard and sails him off to Avalon. Ultimately, Thomas Malory in the late 1400s, writing in Late Middle English, describes how the knight Bedivere carries Arthur to a barge, after he has returned the sword to the Lady of the Lake.[12] In the barge are Morgan le Fey and three other women described as "three queens," one of whom is the Lady of the Lake herself, and they sail Arthur away to the "Vale of Avalon."

So where exactly was Avalon supposed to be? The mysterious island where Arthur is either entombed, buried, or in a state of suspended animation. The place where, if the legend was based on some semblance of truth, I might find the famous king's grave. Sadly, as was becoming all too familiar, none of these authors reveal where it actually is. The only one to give even an approximate location is Robert de Boron, who says that it is somewhere in the west of Britain. Britain has hundreds of offshore islands, which is why it's called the British Isles, and nearly all of them are off the west coast, so this was of little help. Geoffrey of Monmouth does suggest that it may be off the coast of Cornwall, as this is where he locates Arthur's final battle, but I had already come to view Geoffrey's Cornish Arthurian connections with some suspicion (see chapter 2). One possibility that seemed more reasonable was that the island might be off the coast of Wales. In chapter 1 I mentioned how works predating Geoffrey of Monmouth referred to an enchanted island in association with King Arthur, which was called Annwn. These works were all early Welsh stories.

Annwn, as a mysterious, magical land, is mentioned in a number of anonymous old Welsh tales, such as *Cad Goddeu* (The Battle of the Trees) and *Pwyll* (named after a Welsh prince), and specifically in association with King Arthur in *Culhwch and Olwen,* written in the eleventh century.[13] There are remarkable similarities between the legends of Annwn and Avalon. In an even earlier tale, *Preiddeu Annwfn* (Spoils of Annwn), Arthur actually sails to the island of Annwn in search of a magic cauldron, said to have supernatural powers.[14] (The oldest surviving copy of *The Spoils of Annwn* is found in a fourteenth-century manuscript known as The Book of Taliesin, in the National Library of Wales, but it is believed by literary scholars to be a copy of a much earlier poem, as its language and syntax date from around the year 900, predating the earliest Arthurian romance by well over two centuries.) In this tale Annwn is specifically depicted as an island, said to be the home of nine saintly maidens who guard a magic cauldron, a metal cooking vessel.[15] The medieval Robert de Boron tells us that the Holy Grail (which in many Arthurian tales Arthur's knights go in search of and ultimately return to their king) is a sacred drinking vessel, hidden on Avalon, and subsequent Arthurian romancers include a community of so-called Grail Maidens as its guardians. Geoffrey of Monmouth even has Avalon ruled by the same number of *nine* sisters. The Welsh tales also include a mythological figure called Bran: he was said to have been a onetime ruler of Annwn and the first guardian of the magic cauldron.[16] In Robert de Boron's story, the man who took the Grail to Avalon was a follower of Joseph of Arimathea, called the very similar Bron. In the Welsh version Bran is a demigod who lives the duration of many lifetimes and ultimately suffers with a wounded foot, while in Robert's account Bron survives for centuries as the first guardian of the Grail, permanently troubled by a wounded leg.[17] Bran's potential links with the Holy Grail go even deeper.

The Welsh tales say that after Bran died his severed head was preserved as a kind of oracle—it speaks and gives valuable advice to those who possess it. This "talking head" idea is thought to have derived from the pre-Christian Celtic practice of preserving the head of a high-status individual, such as a priest or king, in the belief that it could communicate with the living.[18] (In reality, a seer, or trance medium, would most likely get high on some plant extract or other in the presence of the skull and commune with whatever came into his or her *own* head.) Bran's head is said to have been the greatest of such relics, and in an early Welsh poem called the *Three Unfortunate Disclosures,* King Arthur himself is said to have acquired it.[19] In an early Welsh tale called *Peredur* (author unknown), the hero Peredur, one of Arthur's courtiers, bears a striking resemblance to King Arthur's knight Sir Perceval as he appears in the medieval romances.[20] The oldest known inclusion of Perceval in the Arthurian saga is found in a work by Chrétien de Troyes known as *Le Conte du Graal* (The Story of the Grail) completed around 1190.[21] In this, Perceval is the knight who searches for and eventually finds the Grail, first seeing it during a strange banquet held in the great hall of a mysterious castle:

> A squire entered [the hall] from a chamber, holding a white lance . . . and from its point there dripped red blood . . . Perceval watched but he refrained from asking its meaning. . . . A damsel [then] came in with three more squires, holding in her hands a graal [Chrétien's spelling of "grail"].[22]

Now compare this to the *Peredur* narrative, where the hero attends a banquet in a Welsh castle in an almost identical setting:

> And he [Peredur] saw two young men enter the hall . . . bearing a long spear with blood flowing from the point. . . . And as he [Peredur's host] did not explain the meaning of what he saw, Peredur refrained from asking. . . . [And] then two maidens entered, holding a large salver between them, upon which was the head of a man.[23]

It is patently clear that with a few minor variations, these are both the same story, one taken from the other, or both taken from some earlier source. Although *Peredur* now survives only in a mid-fourteenth-century manuscript, like the other Welsh Arthurian tales, it probably originated with a much older rendition. In fact, the character of Peredur appears in a Welsh genealogy (family tree) dating from 988, preserved in the British Library, and going by this he was considered to have lived around the same time as King Arthur.[24] So the most likely scenario would place the Welsh tale well before the time of Chrétien de Troyes. Either way there is an intriguing disparity between the two accounts: whereas Chrétien has his damsel holding the Grail, the *Peredur* author's two maidens are bearing a severed head. Although, as we have seen, Robert de Boron, around the year 1200, is the oldest known author to depict the Grail as the cup used by Christ at the Last Supper, he is not the earliest writer to name the relic and to include it in the King Arthur story; Chrétien de Troyes did so some ten years earlier. The origin of the word *grail,* or *graal* in Chrétien's original, is hotly disputed. Interestingly, Chrétien describes it not as a chalice, as Robert does, but as a golden platter or large serving dish. We shall be examining the Grail legend later, but for now the important point to bear in mind is that the sacred item was originally a large plate and not a drinking vessel. (As we shall see, subsequent authors portrayed the Grail in many different guises: it was depicted as a holy relic, such as a mystical chalice, sacred jar, or a magic stone; or as an allegorical concept, such as immortality, mother nature, or a royal bloodline; and even as a representation of the Virgin Mary, the Holy Spirit, or Jesus himself.) In Chrétien's version, on this plate is the sacramental bread of the Catholic Mass, representing the body of Christ, whereas in the *Peredur* narrative, on the salver—a large serving platter—there is a severed head. The *Peredur* author does not explain its meaning, suggesting it would have been familiar to his readership, but it was almost certainly one of the "talking heads" of early Celtic religion (see page 59). In the Welsh tales Bran's head is the most sought after of these talking heads, leading most literary scholars to conclude that it was meant to be his. The demigod Bran was the original guardian of the magic cauldron, and in the Arthurian romances the original guardian of the Grail is the semi-immortal Bron. The head of Bran and the Holy Grail are therefore undoubtedly connected, and as the Welsh King Arthur tales appear to predate the medieval Arthurian romances, then it is reasonable to conclude that the Grail, bearing the symbolic "body of Christ," is a Christianization of the original magic cauldron combined with the sacred head of Bran theme. (It's not important whether or not the magic cauldron or Bran's head was based on real or imaginary relics—something we'll return to later—the point is that the literary evidence indicates that they were associated with the story of King Arthur well before the Middle Ages.)

So the Isle of Avalon and its Holy Grail portrayed in the medieval Arthurian romances appear to be themes both taken from earlier, Welsh King Arthur tales. Geoffrey of Monmouth was the first author to include Avalon in the Arthurian saga, and he claims he took his account of Arthur's life from "a certain very ancient book written in the British language," which presumably meant Welsh.[25] (Geoffrey was from Monmouth in Wales, so he was presumably fluent in the language and could translate such works.) What the book was called he fails to say, but it could have been a work containing Welsh tales concerning the Isle of Annwn. (It is thought that there were probably many such Welsh Arthurian stories in existence during Geoffrey's time, which no longer survive; indeed, it is astonishing that without modern methods of document preservation, any have survived at all.) Many subsequent Arthurian romancers, such as Wace, also claimed to have had access to earlier "British" tales and chronicles, and so they too might have taken their various themes from similar narratives.[26] As these early references to Annwn were all in Welsh tales, I decided that Wales might be the best place to search for where the enchanted island was originally thought to be. I noted that certain modern authors contended that Annwn was simply a name for the Celtic otherworld, the spirit realm of mythical beings, but in the Welsh tales I examined, it was certainly regarded as a physical place, and in *The Spoils of Annwn,* it was clearly an island (see p. 59). The problem was—as ever—none of them say exactly where it is. There was, though, an intriguing account written during Geoffrey's lifetime that could point to one particular island. I found it in the medieval work of William of Malmesbury.

William of Malmesbury is considered by modern scholars to have been a particularly reliable chronicler for his time and has been described as the foremost English historian of the twelfth century. Some have even gone so far as to suggest that he was the most learned man in Europe. While a monk at Malmesbury Abbey in the county of Wiltshire in southern England, William wrote his Latin *Deeds of the English Kings,* completed in 1125 (a few years before Geoffrey of Monmouth's works), in which he talks about King Arthur in some detail.[27] William explains that many fanciful legends had built up around Arthur, although he is certain that the fabled king had been a genuine historical figure who fought the Anglo-Saxons around the year 500. In fact, he tells us quite a lot about the Arthurian legend as it existed at the time (which we will return to in chapter 13, see p. 241), but unfortunately he does not refer directly to Avalon. However, in another of his works, the *Ecclesiastical History of Glastonbury,* completed in 1130, he does mention an island that appears to be it.[28] (Not Glastonbury. As we have seen, that was added into copies of the monograph by later monks.) In the work William makes reference to the travels of Augustine, the first archbishop of Canterbury in the late sixth century, and includes a copy of a letter Augustine wrote to the Pope. It reads:

> In the western part of Britain there is a large royal island . . . abounding in the beauties of nature and providing all the necessities of life. Upon it, the first neophytes of Catholic law founded a church.[29]

This appears to be the same place that Robert de Boron later mentions when he says that Joseph of Arimathea's followers brought the Grail to Britain and took it to the Vales of Avalon, where, he tells us, these early Christians, the first to land in Britain, founded a church. They were indeed some of the "first neophytes of Catholic law." In the sixth century the term *Catholic* was synonymous with Christianity, as there were to be no Protestant sects for another nine centuries. *Neophyte* means a new religious convert, and *first neophytes* was Church terminology for the original followers of Christ, such as Joseph of Arimathea, whom the Bible says had known Jesus personally, and his companions. It might seem unlikely that Christians would have come to Britain as early as the mid-first century AD, but there were regular shipping routes to Britain, where merchants came to trade for tin and copper, and as the country had not yet been invaded by the Romans, it was a safe haven for a persecuted faction such as the Christians to settle.[30] In fact, the Roman author Quintus Tertullianus (also known as Tertullian), writing in the second century, expressly makes reference to such early Christians settling in Britain,[31] while Hilary, Bishop of Poitiers in France in the mid-fourth century, specifically states that disciples of Jesus had built a church here.[32] There was only one island immediately off the Welsh coast that fitted Augustine's description: the Isle of Anglesey in northwest Wales. It was a large island, some 276 square miles, the largest in England and Wales, and it was a royal island. In Augustine's time it was the seat of the kings of the Welsh kingdom of Gwynedd in northwest Wales. It was not only an extremely fertile region, the grain basket of Wales, but was famous for growing apples. Remember, Geoffrey of Monmouth refers to Avalon as the "Isle of Apples." Moreover, in the first century it had the largest copper mines in Europe, was visited regularly by Roman merchants, and so was a relatively easy destination for early Christians to secure passage.

Anglesey is the English name for the island, coming from Ongullsey, meaning "Hook Island," which it was called by the Vikings when they invaded parts of Britain in the ninth century. The Romans called the island Mona, from where the modern Welsh derived their name for it: Môn. What the original Britons called the island is unknown. It might even have been Annwn, who knows? It was something of a long shot, but I decided to visit Anglesey as a possible site for Avalon. It was easy enough to get to, as it is only about a quarter of a mile from the mainland, separated by the Menai Strait, which is spanned by a road bridge. Although, on my first visit to Anglesey, I failed to uncover any further evidence for it being the location the earliest Arthurian authors had in mind when writing of Annwn or Avalon, an archaeological site on the island did provide me with a completely new perspective on the story of the Lady of the Lake.

When I arrived on Anglesey, I made for the island museum in the town of Llangefni. Called Oriel Ynys Môn (Isle of Môn Gallery), it was a new building only recently opened by the queen. It housed displays of many historical artifacts found on the island, and one particular exhibit had me transfixed. It was an archaic iron sword blade, unearthed from the bed of one of Anglesey's dried-up lakes, which the museum guidebook said was believed to have been cast into the water centuries ago as an offering to an ancient water goddess. Excalibur had been thrown into a lake, to a mystical water nymph! Could there be a connection? Hurriedly, I asked a staff member about the find and was told that it was just one of hundreds of ancient Celtic treasures uncovered from the bed of the now dry lake of Llyn Cerrig Bach (Lake of Small Stones) in the northwest of the island in the 1940s. Archaeologists believed that these artifacts had been deliberately thrown into the lake as tributes to a water deity around two thousand years ago. The museum attendant told me how archaeologists across Europe had found many such artifacts that had been cast into pools, rivers, and lakes by the Celtic peoples of northwest Europe—before, throughout, and even after the Roman era. Known as votive offerings, the consensus was that they were precious gifts to various water goddesses, as the Romans actually made reference to the practice.[33] The Romans even adopted the custom themselves, by throwing their own valuables, often coins, into sacred pools in the hope that the resident goddess would heal their afflictions or grant their wishes. It is generally thought that such traditions gave rise to the custom of wishing wells, into which we throw money even today. The Celtic peoples, of which the Britons were one, together with the Romans, regarded these water deities as goddesses of healing.[34] All this put what had seemed nothing more than a medieval fairy tale into a realistic historical context, consistent with post-Roman Britain, the period in which Arthur is said to have lived. Could the story of the wounded Arthur's sword being thrown to the Lady of Lake, I wondered, have emerged from this custom of votive offerings? Was It originally perceived to be a tribute to a water goddess in the hope of healing the king? Indeed, such votive offerings often included swords—I'd actually seen one of them in the museum.

Today the site of Llyn Cerrig Bach is at the end of Anglesey Airport runway, but when I was there in 1991, it was a largely disused Royal Air Force base. However, much of the old dried-up lake was outside the base perimeter on common land, so I could freely wander around. The first pieces from the Celtic hoard were unearthed here in 1942, when ground was being cleared for a runway extension. After World War II archaeologists found more than 150 artifacts, including seven swords, six spearheads, cauldrons, a shield, a bronze trumpet, horse gear, and iron bars that were used as currency by the ancient Britons. (These days most of the finds are housed in the British Museum in London, including the sword that was once on display in Anglesey.) Dating the artifacts, archaeologists determined that they had not been cast into the lake all at one time but over a period of some four hundred years between around 300 BC and the late first century AD.[35] In fact, the final dating corresponds with a known historical event. The Roman historian Tacitus, writing in the early second century, says that Anglesey had been an important center of learning for the druids, the Celtic priesthood, and when the island was conquered by the Romans around AD 60, they slaughtered or enslaved the population, destroying their places of worship.[36] This was probably when the lake ceased to be used as a place of votive offering.

After visiting the museum I drove to Llyn Cerrig Bach, near the village of Llanfair-yn-Neubwll. Here a local farmer showed me where many of the items had been discovered, in what is now a peat bog. It was, he told me, because they had been preserved in peat that the finds had not rusted away. He also explained that the original lake had once been much larger than the peat bog that now survives and included three smaller lakes to the immediate southeast. Evidently the area had been drained for farmland years ago, but it was still low-lying land, except for a small hillock in the middle, on which now stood a radar mast for the airfield. It was when he told me that this hillock had once been an island in the center of the lake that I was struck by another epiphany. Everyone always seemed to assume that the island in the King Arthur story lay across the sea. But what if it was a lake island? Although, in the Arthurian romances, the vessel that transports Arthur to Avalon is not described in any detail, it is usually said to be a "barge." (Malory, in his original Late Middle English, for example, describes it as "a lytyl barge," a little barge.) A barge is not a seafaring boat but one used for inland travel on rivers or across lakes. In fact, the more I thought about it, the more likely it seemed that Avalon was originally considered a lake island. Just before Arthur is carried off to Avalon, he gets his knight to cast Excalibur into a lake where the Lady of the Lake retrieves the weapon; then, immediately afterward, Arthur is put into the barge. Reading between the lines, it would seem that Arthur is taken across the very same lake, particularly as the Lady of the Lake is one of the three women awaiting him on the boat. Were lake islands considered sacred in Celtic times?

Before continuing I should perhaps explain a little about the Celts. The Celts came originally from Austria around 800 BC and were able to settle much of what are now France, Britain, and Ireland by about 500 BC. They did this virtually unopposed because of their superior weaponry. Their weapons were made from iron, while the native inhabitants had only softer bronze. Celtic swords could easily bend or even slice through those of their enemies. The Celts were, therefore, the chief Iron Age inhabitants of northwestern Europe, supplanting the earlier Bronze Age peoples. (The Bronze Age refers to the period in which implements were made from bronze, and in Britain it dates from around 2000 BC, although it was not extensively used until about 1200 BC, while the British Iron Age dates from the seventh century BC until the coming of the Romans in the late first century AD.) The Celts shared a common culture, artwork, and religion and a collective group of regional dialects of the language we now call Gaelic. The problem facing modern historians is that until the Romans conquered the Celts, they had no form of written language, leaving us with Greek and Roman writers to tell us much of what we know of them. One aspect of the culture the Romans considered particularly odd was that in Celtic society men and women enjoyed equal status. In fact, women accompanied men into battle, and there were even warrior queens, such as the famous Queen Boudicca

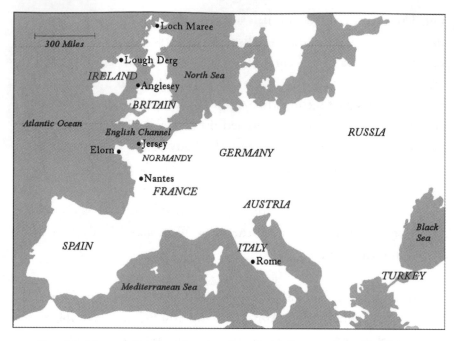

Fig. 4.1. Map of Europe, showing locations discussed in this chapter.

who fought the Romans in Britain. The Romans also regarded as peculiar that the Celts, in the countries they inhabited, lacked an overall state. Instead, they were organized around smaller tribal kingdoms.[37] However, they did have a kind of ruling elite, a priesthood known as druids, probably derived from the Celtic word *dryw,* meaning "seer," who lived above and beyond tribal society. The druids traveled where they liked and were welcomed and revered in each kingdom they visited. The Greek historians Diodorus Siculus, writing around 36 BC, and the Roman historian Strabo, writing about the time of Christ, say that the druids acted not only as priests but also, because they were held in such high regard, intervened to stop tribal wars. (In effect, they were somewhat similar to Buddhist lamas of old Tibet.) They lived outside the tribal villages, in the countryside, in simple settlements of round, wood and thatch huts that we might today call monasteries. However, unlike later Christian monks and nuns, the druids were not usually bound by an oath of celibacy; both male and female druids often lived together in a sort of commune. Exceptionally esteemed druids, though, *did* seem to have refrained from sexual relationships and lived either alone or in small communities in remote or relatively inaccessible locations.[38]

Much of Celtic Europe was eventually occupied by the Romans. France was successfully conquered by Julius Caesar in 51 BC, and Britain was invaded by the Emperor Claudius in AD 43. France became part of the Roman province of Gaul, and what is now England and Wales became the Roman province of Britannia. The Romans, however, failed to conquer Scotland and Ireland, where a Celtic way of life continued until well after the collapse of the Roman Empire. Although the Romans allowed the conquered Celts to continue some of their religious practices, and to venerate their own gods, they ruthlessly suppressed the druids, whom they regarded as a threat to their authority. As part of this policy, they destroyed the druid sanctuaries. However, in the mountainous regions of Scotland and across the sea in Ireland, they survived for many more centuries, and it is here that archaeology has revealed much about druid settlements. When Scotland and Ireland were gradually Christianized, during the late fifth and early sixth centuries, these sanctuaries were not obliterated; rather, they were replaced with churches, shrines, and monasteries. In fact, in these countries there developed a strange hybrid of paganism and Christianity known as the Celtic Church, an institution that the Catholic Church later did its best to eradicate.[39]

Returning to my question: Were lake islands considered sacred in Celtic times? The answer is yes. Remember how the Romans recorded that certain esteemed druids would live in small, remote communities. Well, these were very often said to have been on islands in lakes or rivers. There are many examples throughout the Celtic world, recorded by early Christian missionaries and investigated by archaeologists. For instance, in Ireland there was one on Lough Derg (Island of the Red Eye) in Country Donegal. On an island now called Station Island, there is a monastery known as Saint Patrick's Purgatory, dating from the fifth century, which stands on the site of an ancient druid settlement. Early monks from the monastery record that it had been the last druid sanctuary in Ireland. In Scotland there is Loch Maree, in which there stands the Isle of Maree where, in the year 672, the Christian missionary Saint Maelrubba converted a community of druids who lived there in seclusion. There still survives a ring of standing stones on the Isle of Maree, some thirty feet in diameter, which has long been known as the Druid Circle. Archaeologists have excavated the site and dated it to around 100 BC, indicating that it had been erected, presumably for ceremonial purposes, by the ancient Celts.[40] I already knew of these islands from research into druidism I had carried out for a previous book, but it had never occurred to me that the Arthurian Avalon might have been based on such a place. But now, standing in the dried-up lake of Llyn Cerrig Bach, staring over to the hillock at its heart, I felt sure I should be looking for an island in a lake. The original Avalon could perhaps have been this very site, but I hoped not. It had never been excavated, and there was no way it would be in the foreseeable future; I could not even visit the hillock, as it was now home to a military radar mast. I decided, however, that I didn't need to worry too much. There would probably have been many, perhaps hundreds, of sacred druid lake islands in Britain, any of which may have inspired the legend of Annwn or Avalon. The statistical chances of Llyn Cerrig Bach being the location of the mystic isle were remote. Nevertheless, I still had to decide on the best candidate among what I assumed would be dozens of potential contenders, which would no doubt take some considerable doing. As I was already in Wales, I decided my next stop should be the National Library of Wales in Aberystwyth, on the coast some eighty miles to the south. It has one of the best collections of ancient Welsh and early British manuscripts in the world.

A somewhat austere, white-stone building, overlooking the sea beside the campus of Aberystwyth University, the National Library of Wales houses over four million printed volumes. Hidden among them, there might lie vital clues to solving the Avalon mystery. Arthur is professed to have lived around AD 500, and so if the story of Avalon was based on a real location, it would presumably have been an island with sacred associations during this time. Arthur's Britain had consisted of what is now England and Wales, or at least parts of them, so I was presumably looking for a lake island in either of these two countries. For the Avalon theme to relate to an actual site, it would have to have been somewhere still considered hallowed by the Britons of the late fifth or early sixth centuries. I already knew that there had been sacred lake islands in pre-Roman Britain and probably during the Roman era; my first task at the library, however, was to decide if such ancient pagan sites would still have been venerated by the Britons around AD 500.

Many pagan Celtic practices, I discovered, had endured the Roman occupation of Britain and had enjoyed something of a revival when the Romans departed. Soon after the Roman legions left in AD 410, law and order rapidly collapsed, and Britain fragmented into its pre-Roman tribal kingdoms, of which there were dozens. Although many of the town-dwelling Britons had adopted Christianity by this time, paganism still thrived in the countryside. The word *pagan* actually comes from the Latin word *paganus,* meaning "country dweller," and referred to those living outside the towns that refused to convert to Christianity and continued to worship their old gods. (The word *heathen,* incidentally, has a similar origin; it means "heath dweller," a heath being an area of wild countryside.) Without the presence of the imperial army, many Roman towns were sacked and plundered by the "country dwellers," whose leaders had assumed control of the various new kingdoms, and paganism reasserted itself—something that greatly concerned the Catholic Church. Even after the Roman withdrawal from Britain, the empire struggled on for a few more decades until Italy was invaded by the Germans and the last western emperor was deposed in AD 476. (It was not actually the end of the entire Roman Empire; it continued in the East, in places like Turkey, as we shall see later.) Remarkably, the German conquerors of Italy converted to Christianity, allowing the Church in Rome to survive. Learning of Britain's slide into idolatry, the pope (or Bishop of Rome, as he was known at the time) sent various missionaries to reconvert the Britons. One of these was Germanus, the Bishop of Auxerre in France, who had remarkable success around the year 429.[41] However, the efforts of Germanus soon resulted in unwelcome consequences for the Roman Church. What ensued was a hybrid style of British Christianity, heavily influenced by paganism, which flourished over the rest of that century and was prevalent in Britain at the very time Arthur is said to have lived. It was not until the pope's envoy Augustine came to Britain in 597 that the Roman Catholic Church reasserted itself.[42] Although few written records survive from Britain during this period, archaeology has shown that many pagan conventions continued alongside, and also as a part of, British Christianity as practiced at the time. For example, archaeologists have found depictions of Celtic goddesses alongside contemporary images of the Virgin Mary, inscriptions to honor pagan deities appear beside the name of Christ, and stone circles, used by the pagans as places of worship, were simultaneously being utilized for Christian services, as demonstrated by Mass chalices being discovered, deposited alongside Celtic pots decorated with images of ancient gods.[43] It was, I concluded, very possible that the old druid lake islands were indeed being used again as sacred sites around AD 500. What I needed next was to find firm historical or archaeological evidence to establish the precise locations of such sites.

I discovered that the National Library of Wales had a dedicated archaeology section, so that's where I concentrated my research. Did anyone working there have knowledge of lake islands being occupied for religious or ceremonial purposes in post-Roman Britain? A member of the department was particularly helpful, explaining how a team from the University of Wales was excavating a potential site at that very time. The dig was taking place at Ynys Bwlc (Stockade Island), which stands in Llangorse Lake in the Brecon Beacons (hills), about sixty miles to the southeast of Aberystwyth. The excavation had been inspired by a reference in the Anglo-Saxon Chronicle, written in the late 800s, which records that the island was still being used as a royal residence by a Welsh chieftain in the ninth century. Artifacts unearthed at the site, such as jewelry and pottery fragments, revealed that the site had been occupied as early as the sixth century, well before it had been used as a palace.

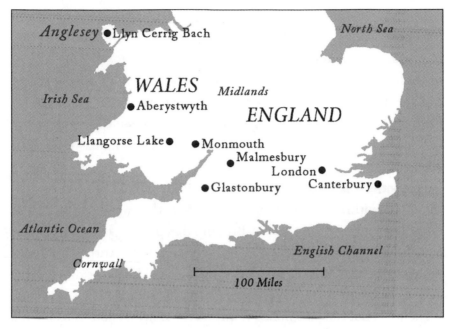

Fig. 4.2. Map of southern Britain, showing locations
discussed in this chapter.

The problem was that no clues survived indicating the island's function at that time; a platform of rocks and earth had been erected across the small island as foundations for the palace in the 800s, destroying vital evidence concerning its earlier occupation.[44] When I asked about archaeological excavations on other British lake islands occupied in the post-Roman era, I received a disappointing reply. Evidently, there had been none (at least, that they knew of). Unlike the later Dark Age era, virtually no written manuscripts from the post-Roman period survive to lead archaeologists to promising locations to excavate. With the limited resources available to British archaeology, potential dig sites from the period around AD 500 were just too uncertain a venture. In fact, I was told, specifically excavating lake islands was prohibitively expensive. Just getting the equipment and personnel to and from Ynys Bwlc, for example, was proving so costly that the dig was threatened with closure.

Archaeology has always been grossly underfunded, and there are thousands of British sites, from every period of time, crying out to be excavated. Only the most promising locations warrant the attention of archaeologists: sites for which there is ample historical documentation to support the notion that there is something worth uncovering. Almost no historical records whatsoever survive from Britain dating from the period after the Romans left in the year 410 until the Anglo-Saxon era from around AD 700. During this post-Roman era, life was just too turbulent: buildings and places of learning, such as monasteries, were continually being looted, pillaged, and burnt. Moreover, with the break from continental Europe, Britain found itself starved of parchment— there was nothing to write on. Even records that were kept had little chance of long-term survival in Britain's damp, rainy climate.[45] By the eighth century some semblance of civilization had returned, and new monasteries were built in which documents could be kept dry, but the period of interest to me was a very different matter. Bad news all round. I had just about resigned myself to the fact that my Avalon search would be just another dead end when the librarian told me something that put an exciting new complexion on my entire lake island theory. He cited examples of sacred islands recorded by ancient Greek and Roman authors in Celtic Gaul. The Greek historian Strabo, in his *Geographica* (Geography) written around AD 7, describes an island on the River Loire, near the town of Nantes in northwestern France, that was occupied exclusively by a community of Celtic priestesses.[46] Such priestesses are again mentioned by the Roman geographer Pomponius Mela, some four decades later, in his *De Situ Orbis* (A Description of the World), where he describes a similar island, this one at the mouth of the River Elorn, some 180 miles farther northwest. Once again it was inhabited only by priestesses, one of them an oracle (a medium) for a Celtic deity.[47] When the librarian read from a copy of Pomponius Mela's work, I was pretty much bowled over: "Its priestesses, holy in perpetual virginity, are said to be nine in number." Additionally, Mela says that they had the power to "cure wounds and diseases incurable by others."[48] Nine island-dwelling holy women led by a female oracle who heal the sick! He might as well have been describing Avalon with its nine venerated women led by the healer Morgan le Fey. Such island communities, I was told, seem to have been common throughout the Celtic world, and they almost certainly existed in Britain. I was convinced that sacred lake islands, such as Avalon is portrayed in the Arthurian saga, had existed during Celtic times, although I still lacked firm evidence for that particular convention enduring in Britain itself into the period Arthur apparently lived. However, I did have a new line of inquiry that might lead me in that direction: the nine priestesses. In the Arthurian tale Avalon and its nine mystic women are associated with healing, and the enchantress Morgan is their leader. It was time to turn my attentions to Morgan le Fey and Avalon's mysterious maidens.

5

Morgan and Her Sisters

Those familiar with the modern Arthurian story will recognize Morgan—or Morgana, as she is sometimes called—as being Arthur's half-sister and chief rival, the evil sorceress who plots his demise. The original Morgan was quite different. Geoffrey of Monmouth fails to provide her with any background, and it is Chrétien de Troyes who first portrays her as Arthur's sister. It was only in later romances that she became the "wicked witch," a concept ultimately adapted by Thomas Malory. In the original stories she is a benign healer and prophetess and the ruler of Avalon, and many scholars propose that she was based on an ancient Celtic deity called Mórrígan (pronounced "Mor-rig-ahn"), meaning "great queen." Nothing now survives in early Welsh texts concerning Mórrígan, but a great deal does exist in the mythology and old literature of Ireland. Wales, as we have seen, was occupied by the Romans, suffering turmoil for centuries after the end of their rule. Celtic Ireland, however, remained free from foreign occupation until 1171, when the Norman English started to invade. Consequently, far more unfettered Celtic mythology, once shared by the Irish and mainland Britons, remained in Ireland than in either England or Wales. In Irish mythology Mórrígan was a war goddess who guided the spirits of valiant warriors to the afterlife on a magical boat, similar to the Greek ferryman Charon transporting souls

across the River Styx; she was also paradoxically associated with healing. Likewise, in the Arthurian stories, Morgan sails the mortally
wounded Arthur to Avalon—in some tales to be healed, in others to
be laid to rest.

Although Morgan, in the King Arthur saga, is not specifically
a goddess, she *is* portrayed with supernatural powers. Rather than
being a goddess, she seems to *personify* a deity. This is suggested by
her name. Chrétien de Troyes, in 1170, is the first to refer to her as
Morgan le Fey, meaning "Morgan the Fairy." Today, the word *fairy*
is associated with tiny, mythical creatures with gossamer wings, a
theme popularized by the Victorians, but in its original medieval
context, the word *fairie* referred to an enchanted person. Generally,
in British and Irish mythology, fairies were completely human in
size and appearance and were gods and goddesses in mortal guise.[1]
Sometimes they were men and women possessed by the spirits of
deities. In ancient times, in cultures throughout the world, it was
believed that divinities could temporarily occupy the bodies of gifted
mortals, much like modern mediums are said to channel spirits. In
Greece and Rome such people were known as oracles,[2] while in Celtic
society the role would be assumed by the head druids. As we saw in
the last chapter, the Roman writer Pomponius Mela refers to the chief
among his nine, island-dwelling Celtic priestesses as an oracle. We
can assume, therefore, that this woman was one such druid. Putting
all this together, it is reasonable to infer that Morgan in the original
Arthurian legend, who heads Avalon's sisterhood of nine, was considered an oracle of the goddess Mórrígan. Could it be, I wondered,
that a historical King Arthur was laid to rest on an island sacred to
Mórrígan or the dwelling place of her oracle? I needed to discover
more about this ancient goddess.

I soon discovered that literature pertaining to Mórrígan was best
preserved in the National Library of Ireland in Dublin. In its huge
circular reading room, I was free to examine English translations of
the definitive collection of early Irish manuscripts, books, and articles
by various literary scholars and other related archaeological material

in the library's vast archives. Here my reading revealed that many of the mythological characters with whom I had become familiar in my Welsh studies also appeared in Irish mythology but with slightly different names. For example, the Arthurian hero Culhwch is attributed with similar deeds to the Irish hero Cuchulain, and the god-king Nudd Llaw Eraint, meaning "Nudd of the Silver Hand," closely parallels his Irish equivalent Nuada Airgetlám, meaning "Nuada Silver Hand." Such mythical figures were clearly one and the same. As the original Celtic language once shared by both Wales and Ireland had diverged into Welsh and Irish Gaelic, it was very possible that something similar had occurred with Mórrígan: a deity once known by a single name had come to be called Mórrígan in Ireland and Morgan in Wales. If so, Morgan le Fey was presumably named after the goddess she was thought to channel. But there was much more to link Mórrígan with Morgan le Fey than just their names.

I soon discovered that a number of Irish tales included the figure of Mórrígan, both as a goddess and in mortal guise. Although preserved in copies dating from medieval times, many are thought on linguistic grounds to be very much older, perhaps having been composed as early as the 700s. In some—such as *Togail Bruidne Dá Derga* (The Destruction of Da Derga's Hostel),[3] *Lebor Gabála Érenn* (The Book of the Taking of Ireland),[4] and *Cath Maige Tuired* (The Battle of Magh Tuireadh)[5]—Mórrígan is accompanied by three sister goddesses called Badb (pronounced "Bave"), Macha (pronounced "Maxa"), and Anann (pronounced "Anarn"). Together with Mórrígan, they are said to be the children of Ernmas, the Irish mother goddess (referenced in *Lebor Gabála Érenn* and *Cath Maige Tuired*). In the medieval Arthurian romances, an unspecified number of women accompany Morgan in the barge from Avalon, but Thomas Malory expressly says that Arthur is taken to Avalon by "three queens."[6] Could these three queens have been based on Mórrígan's three sisters? All three were Celtic water goddesses, and one of them—Macha—was specifically associated with a sacred lake island.

Remember how Geoffrey of Monmouth also calls Avalon the Isle of Apples? Well, in Middle Welsh, the language of Wales as it was spoken during Geoffrey's time, the word for "apple" was *abal,* as it still is in Irish Gaelic. In Irish legend there is even a magical island called Emain Ablach (The Place of Apples) from which some scholars believe the name Avalon derived. It is the subject of a very early Irish story still preserved in Dublin's Trinity College, just a block away from the National Library. In the *Immram Brain* (The Voyage of Bran), dating from around AD 700, the hero Bran (the same Bran we met in the last chapter) sails to Emain Ablach, said to be an island of immortality and healing where no one ever gets sick.[7] It is also referred to as the Land of Women, as its guardians are a sisterhood of kindly sorceresses. Its name and description are so similar to Geoffrey's Avalon that he probably, it has been argued, used it as the template for his Isle of Avalon. What I found particularly interesting is that in Irish mythology there are a number of *real* islands referred to as Emain Ablach. One of them, like the hillock at Llyn Cerrig Bach, remains as a hill at the heart of a dried-up lake. Today it is also called Emain Macha (The Place of Macha), named after one of Mórrígan's three sisters who is said to have once dwelt there.

Nowadays, the site of Emain Macha is a low hill, some two miles west of the city of Armagh in Northern Ireland, surrounded by a bank and ditch around eight hundred feet in diameter. There is now a visitor center beside the hill called the Navan Centre (UK spelling), which includes a re-created Iron Age village, complete with reenactors, along with a café and museum. On the hill itself there are two mounds surrounded by circular ditches, one twenty feet and the other one hundred feet in diameter, that are the sites of what archaeologists believe were two Celtic temples built from wood. The entire complex has been dated to around 95 BC and seems to have been in use for over five hundred years until the spread of Christianity in the fifth and sixth centuries AD. Although the site is often referred to as Navan Fort, as it was later used as a fortified residence of local chieftains, archaeologists are certain that it was not originally built for defensive purposes. Rather it was some kind of religious or ceremonial compound.[8] The bank surrounding the entire site was constructed on the outside of the ditch, the opposite of what would be expected if it was intended for fortification. As the Irish Celts had no form of writing until Christian times, there are no records of how the place was used or who lived there. However, as it is associated with the goddess Macha in mythology, it could well have been a sacred island run by a community of priestesses or female druids, like the contemporary Celtic islands mentioned by Strabo and Pomponius Mela (see chapter 4).

Other examples of sacred Celtic lake islands with two druid temples, such as those on Emain Macha, have been found in both Ireland and Scotland, and they too were associated with important water goddesses; for example, the islands in Lough Derg and Loch Maree discussed in the last chapter. Early monks from the monastery of Saint Patrick's Purgatory on Station Island in Ireland's Lough Derg record that there had been two pagan shrines on the island that they reconsecrated as places of Christian worship in the sixth century and over which they built churches. One of these had been a cave believed to have been the dwelling place of a lake goddess called Cliodna, and the other had been a stone and thatch building where the sick were tended.[9] On Scotland's Isle of Maree, archaeologists have excavated two similar sites.[10] One was a circle of standing stones dated to around 100 BC (see chapter 4), and the other was a pool shrine, recorded by monks in AD 672 as being sacred to a water goddess called Slioch. At this pool, fed by a natural spring, archaeologists have uncovered votive offerings, such as jewelry and coins, dating from as late as the sixth century AD. At both sites monks erected churches, and they reconsecrated the pool as a holy well. Holy wells survive in great number throughout Western Europe, where pagan shrines, once dedicated to female water deities, were sanctified as sacred to Christian saints, such as Saint Mary, Saint Catherine, and Saint Brigit.[11] (Another example of the Roman Catholic policy of "Christian Reinterpretation" we saw in the chapter 3.) Local tradition still calls the island on Loch Maree the Isle of Chapels, in reference to

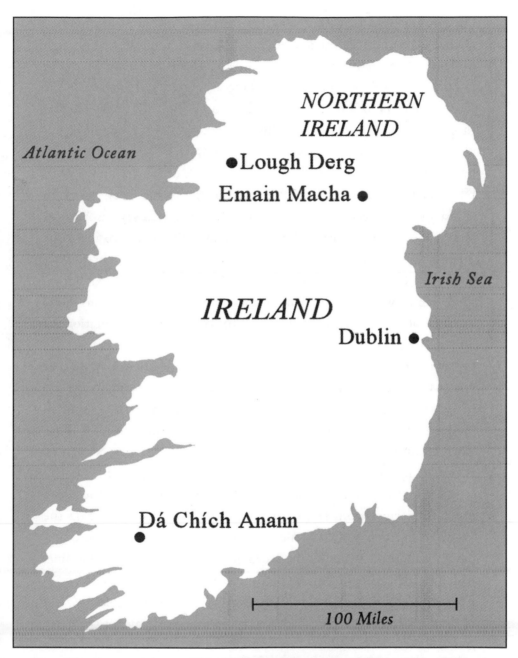

Fig. 5.1. Map of Ireland, showing locations
discussed in this chapter.

the two churches that once stood there. Today the ruins of only one of them, the one with the holy well, still survives to be seen. Although evidence of the early occupation of the lake island at Emain Macha in Ireland is less well preserved, as it was reconstructed and fortified in the seventh century, comparisons with these other sites led archaeologists to speculate that the original earthwork was a similar twin-temple complex sacred to a water goddess, in this case Macha. (Interestingly, Irish mythology also refers to the site as "The Twins of Macha," possibly in reference to these two temples.) So, just as the Celtic deity Mórrígan appears to have been incorporated into the Arthurian saga as Morgan le Fey, the oracle, healer, and ruler of Avalon, it seemed to me to be a reasonable assumption that Macha, one of Mórrígan's three sister goddesses, could have inspired the character of one of the Arthurian three queens who also dwelt on the enchanted isle. But there was more. Another of Mórrígan's sisters appeared to have been the inspiration for none other than the Lady of the Lake.

We have already seen how Thomas Malory specifically states that one of the three queens was the Lady of the Lake.[12] Writing in the late fifteenth century, he calls her Nynyue, usually rendered as Nimue in modern English translations. The authors of the much earlier Vulgate stories, composed over two centuries before, called her Ninianne, although in the first of them to include her (the *Vulgate Merlin,* ca. 1230), she is called Vivianne.[13] The "Viv" element in the name probably derives from the Latin *viva,* meaning "living," while the "anne" element is of Old French origin, a language spoken throughout England and Wales by the Norman rulers of Britain at the time, which in turn comes from the Breton Gaelic Ana, a Celtic water goddess recorded in Roman Gaul. (Breton Gaelic was the Celtic dialect of Brittany in northern France.) In the Irish legends one of the three goddess sisters is called the very similar Anann, so the original name of the Lady of the Lake could well mean "The Living Anann." In other words, she is the goddess Anann incarnate. Indeed, the Anann of Irish mythology is associated both with lakes and miraculous cures; she is said to appear on sacred ponds to heal wounded warriors in the guise of a swan. In County Kerry in southwest Ireland, there are two adjoining hills called Dá Chích Anann, "The Breasts of Anann," once considered sacred to the goddess. Below the hills, beside an ancient stone-walled enclosure called Cahercrovdarrig, "Fort of the Red Claw," there is a pool fed by a natural spring, once sanctified to Anann but now a Catholic holy well.[14] Here archaeological excavations have uncovered votive offerings, such as weapons, domestic items, and various other trinkets, dating from before the pool was consecrated as a Christian shrine. Remarkably, until as late as the 1940s, local people would still gather at the site to perform a May Day festival, including a ceremonial procession involving the throwing of coins and other personal belongings into the well, which was considered to promote good health.[15] All said, Anann bore a striking resemblance to the Lady of the Lake, the water nymph to whom Arthur's sword was thrown when he was mortally wounded. She was a goddess associated with sacred lakes and pools and with the practice of votive offerings, particularly with regard to the healing of warriors. Furthermore, she was one of Mórrígan's three sisters, and the Lady of the Lake was one of the three queens who took Arthur to Avalon.

There could be little doubt that Morgan and the three queens in the Arthurian tale of Avalon were original Celtic concepts. This meant, at the very least, that the story elaborated by the medieval Arthurian romancers had to have been based on much earlier Dark Age legends. Moreover, in pre-Christian times there had been lake islands occupied exclusively by pagan priestesses and healing oracles, but those we know of were all in Celtic Ireland and France. What about Celtic Britain? Might a historical King Arthur—a British warrior—have been taken to a priestess, regarded as a healing oracle, living on a sacred lake island inhabited by nine holy women? Or, at least, was such a tradition included in the Arthurian legend in its original form? We have seen how there probably were such sacred lake islands in England and Wales, such as those at Lynn Cerrig Bach and Llangorse Lake, but because there are far fewer records concerning pre-Roman Britain as there are of France, and Christianity came to Britain well before Ireland, there is much less information from which to base an opinion. Nevertheless, we do have indirect evidence to suggest that such island healing sanctuaries run by women not only existed in Britain but still survived at the time Arthur is said to have lived.

As we have seen, in Britain the Romans adopted Celtic pagan customs, although they usually changed the names of the native deities to match their own. So, Celtic tradition did survive the Roman occupation in a Romanized form, specifically as Romano-British religion. When the Roman Empire adopted Christianity as the state creed in the fourth century, a hybrid faith emerged in Britain, where Celtic pagan practices, sacred sites, and deities were incorporated into Christian worship (see chapter 4). Even though the Romans had tried their best to eradicate them, we know from early Welsh writings that even the druids managed to survive in isolated locations. This pagan-influenced Christianity endured throughout Britain until well into the sixth century. Moreover, so did the druids. Astonishingly, they reemerged after the Roman withdrawal in AD 410 but known under a new name—the bards. To research the bards I needed to return to the National Library of Wales. (I wish we'd had the Internet back then.)

Although the origin of the word *bard* is obscure, bards are best known as Dark Age Celtic poets; many of their poems still survive, relating the exploits of Welsh warriors of the time. The works and deeds of historical bards of the sixth and seventh centuries, such as Aneirin and Taliesin, are preserved in medieval copies of early Welsh literature, such as *Llyfr Coch Hergest* (The Red Book of Hergest), preserved in the Bodleian Library, Oxford, and *Llyfr Gwyn Rhydderch* (The White Book of Rhydderch), *Llyfr Aneirin* (The Book of Aneirin), and *Llyfr Taliesin* (The Book of Taliesin), preserved in the National Library of Wales. (Incidentally, Shakespeare is known as The Bard as he is regarded as the greatest of poets.) But the original bards were not only poets, they were also considered to possess prophetic powers and were renowned as healers, even wizards. We will be examining bards in more detail later, but for now all we need to bear in mind is that what's recorded concerning them is almost identical to what's known of the druids. Bards featured prominently in the post-Roman Celtic Church in Britain, and some of them were even made saints, such as Saint Herve, a Welsh bard born in 521 who founded an abbey and was venerated as a healer and miracle worker. There were female bards, too, such as Heledd, a seventh-century princess from what is now central England. We have already seen how certain lake islands were still being occupied, or reoccupied, as sacred sites during the period Arthur is said to have lived around AD 500, and these places were most likely occupied by bards. Historical records are scarce from this era, and so it is hard to determine what such sites were used for, but healing sanctuaries seems a good bet. Some records do survive from more accessible locations, such as those that later became the sites of ecclesiastical buildings: for instance, Saint Melangell's Church near the Welsh village of Llangynog in the county of Powys. The sixth-century Saint Melangell was a female Christian bard who founded a healing sanctuary run exclusively by women, which stood where the church now stands.[16] (Intriguingly, Melangell is the patron saint of hares, and the hare is her symbol found carved on the church. The hare was also the symbol of the Celtic moon goddess, further implying that this Christian saint was also regarded as a pagan priestess.)

Returning to my question: Could the wounded Arthur have been taken to a healing sanctuary run by such women on a holy island? Was this the origin of the Arthurian Avalon theme? In pre-Roman Britain there had indeed been lake-island sanctuaries run by Celtic priestesses, and in some areas—the pagan, country-dwellers' districts—they endured the Roman occupation. After the Romans left they again assumed importance as neo-Christian bardic shrines. So a wounded Celtic warrior of Arthur's time could well have been taken to such a site. Equally, the sword of a historical Arthur might have been cast into the lake surrounding such an island as a tribute to a water goddess in the guise of a Christian saint. There is no doubt that the custom of votive offerings did continue with the early Christians. Many examples exist of post-Roman treasures dating from the fifth and sixth centuries being unearthed from now dry springs, such as near the towns of Caerwent and Flint in Wales, and Chester and Shrewsbury in England.

They have included everything from dishes, bowls, brooches, rings, and other jewelry, some made from gold or silver. These were expensive and precious items and were obviously not discarded or thrown here as rubbish; rather, devotees deliberately cast these items into the water as offerings. How do we know these devotees were Christians? Easy! Many such artifacts were inscribed with the Chi-Rho symbol.[17] The Chi-Rho (pronounced "kai-roe") was a monogram formed by the Greek letters *chi* and *rho*—X and P. They are the first two letters of the Greek word ΧΡΙΣΤΟΣ meaning "Christ." Before the cross was adopted in the later Dark Ages, this was the most widely employed symbol of Christianity. In fact, the practice of votive offerings still continues among Christians today who throw coins into holy wells as donations to particular saints. Among the general populace, the convention of casting money into wishing wells derives from this custom.

As I wandered the aisles of the National Library of Wales, I considered what I'd learned, so as to decide my next move. It seemed a reasonable possibility that a real lake had existed into which a historical Arthur's sword could have been cast, and in it there was an island upon which stood a sacred healing sanctuary where the fabled king might still lie buried. What I was looking for was either a surviving lake island or, as many ancient lakes had been drained for farmland, a hillock that had once been a lake island somewhere in what is now either England or Wales. But where was I to look? There might have been dozens of such sites scattered across England and Wales, most of them unrecorded and long forgotten. I could only assume that, as the Arthurian romancers asserted Morgan to be the person to whom Arthur was taken, the place I was searching for was associated with the goddess upon whom she was based—or at least someone considered to have represented the deity (as oracle). This deity, as I have argued, seems to have been Mórrígan. Mórrígan was the Irish name for the goddess—as were the names of her sisters: Badb, Macha, and Anann—but they might easily have had similar names in Celtic Britain, such as the examples cited above. Geoffrey of Monmouth, for instance, implied he took the name Morgan from an earlier

British text (see chapter 4). Perhaps if I located a shrine or temple where similar names were inscribed, it would be a place to start. As the National Library of Wales had archaeological archives including information on post-Roman sites in both England and Wales of the period I was investigating, I decided to see if anything in them struck a familiar chord. Back in the early 1990s, little in these archives was computerized—there was no database as such. (Such primitive times!) However, during a long-haul search though typed and handwritten index cards, I found nothing helpful in surviving Dark Age accounts or recorded on inscriptions found by archaeologists in mainland Britain. Perhaps the British equivalents of Mórrígan and her sisters had been known by *completely* different names. I had already seen that at Ireland's Lough Derg a water goddess was called Cliodna, and on Scotland's Loch Maree she was known as Slioch. Even one of the medieval Arthurian romancers, Layamon, refers to Morgan under a separate name: Argante. All the same, I could find no further Dark Age references to any of them either. Maybe Mórrígan and her sisters had inherited Roman monikers.

I already knew that, over the years, archaeologists had discovered various springs, pools, and lakes venerated by the Romano-Britons. When the Romans came they often adopted local gods and goddesses but called them by the names of equivalent Roman deities, and Celtic water goddesses, generally associated with healing, were usually regarded as Minerva, a Roman goddess of water and good health.[18] There were many examples of temples to Minerva being built over Celtic water goddess shrines, such as in the city of Bath in southwest England, where the geothermal waters were considered sacred, and at Minerva's Shrine in Chester, close to the Welsh border in west-central England. At Bath the Roman bathhouse still exists (after which the town gets its name), where people would bathe in the hope of being cured by the goddess, and in Chester the ruins of the original Roman temple to Minerva still survive. But although water goddesses were widely venerated throughout ancient Britain, and continued to be so by the Roman and post-Roman Britons, had there been a specific quartet of female deities comparable to Mórrígan, Badb, Macha, and Anann? I could find nothing pertaining to such at the National Library of Wales, but I did find reference to one of the most thoroughly excavated sites of a water goddess shrine in Roman Britain: at the Roman fort of Cilurnum on Hadrian's Wall in the far north of England. It seemed a good place to continue my search.

When the Romans invaded Britain in the first century AD, England fell fairly easily, but the wilder regions of Wales caused problems, which the Romans eventually overcame. Mountainous Scotland, however, proved much more difficult, and the Romans finally gave up trying to conquer it. The Celtic peoples of Scotland, whom the Romans called Picts (coming from the Latin *picti* meaning "painted," referring to their heavily tattooed bodies), continued to raid Roman settlements in northern England. In response, between the years 122 and 128, the Roman emperor Hadrian ordered a massive defensive structure to be built separating occupied Britain from Scotland. Known as Hadrian's Wall (see plate 7), it was ten feet wide and twenty feet high and stretched some seventy miles from coast to coast. (Much of it still survives, although in ruins, but some stretches have been painstakingly restored.) For the next three centuries, Hadrian's Wall marked the northernmost frontier of the Roman Empire. Along the rampart there were numerous defensive towers, and a series of forts, each occupied by between five hundred and a thousand soldiers. One of these, Fort Cilurnum, was situated halfway along the wall, near the present-day village of Walwick in the county of Northumberland, and consisted of barracks, bathhouses, and administrative structures. Just outside the fort a town soon grew up, housing those who made their living catering to the needs of the Roman army. There were never any official legions stationed on Hadrian's Wall, which was defended by auxiliary troops, many of them recruited from among the native Britons. By the mid-second century, many Britons had become accustomed to Roman rule—Britain had benefited from the new infrastructure—and in the north of England, in particular, most saw the Romans as a vital

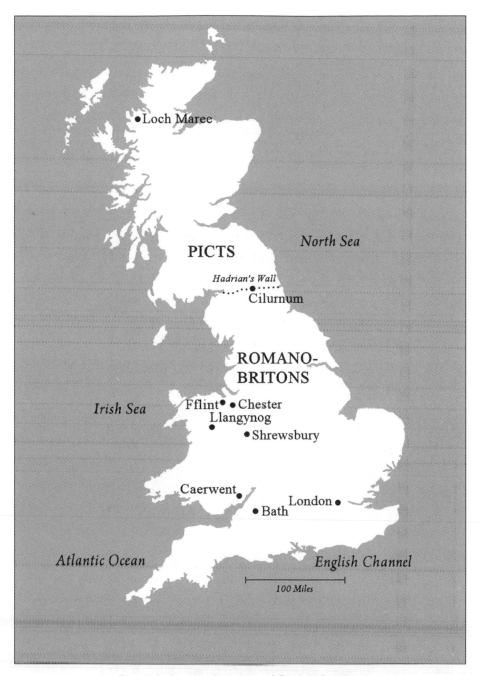

Fig. 5.2. Roman Britain and Pictish Scotland
separated by Hadrian's Wall.

defense from the hostile tribes of Scotland. So the "Roman" soldiers that manned forts like Cilurnum included many native Celts. It may come as something of a surprise to know that by the second century every freeborn Briton held Roman citizenship. Those who had fought the Romans had been enslaved, but those who capitulated—a significant majority—continued to live as free men and women. And it was the descendants of such people who lived in the town at Cilurnum. Accordingly, they still worshipped their own gods. So long as they obeyed Roman law and swore allegiance to the Roman Emperor, they could follow any religion they liked. It was around three miles from the town of Cilurnum that the Romano-Britons built a temple over an already existing shrine. It had originally been a pool, fed by a natural spring, considered sacred to a water goddess, into which votive offerings were cast. Originally, the shrine probably only consisted of a circle of standing stones surrounding the water, but the new structure was a grand Roman temple around forty-foot square. Archaeologists reckon that the pool itself had been turned into a square, brick-lined basin, some ten feet by ten, surrounded by a low stone wall. It was enclosed in a roofed, pillared building, at one end of which stood an altar and bas-reliefs depicting the goddess, complete with inscriptions dedicated to her.[19]

The foundations of the Roman fort still survive, and a museum stands at the site, displaying many of the ancient artifacts uncovered here. There had been hundreds of temples in Britain in Roman times, but very few have survived—even as ruins—and only a handful are shrines to a water goddess. These, such as those in Chester and Bath, are all dedicated to the Roman goddess Minerva, and their inscriptions reflect entirely Roman mythology. The temple at Cilurnum, however, is unique. It is the only excavated shrine from the Roman period known to have been dedicated exclusively to a Celtic water deity. There are other examples of Celtic sites sacred to water goddesses, as demonstrated by the votive offerings found in lakes, pools, and springs, from the pre-Roman, Roman, and post-Roman eras, but none of these incorporated elaborate brick-built constructions, surviving inscriptions, or statues and other ornamentation. Any shrines accompanying them were built chiefly from wood, which would have rotted away centuries ago. The Cilurnum shrine is different: it was created using long-lasting Roman architecture. As the only surviving example of such a water goddess sanctuary used by the native Britons, I hoped it would provide me with vital clues in my search for Avalon.

Cilurnum, today called Chesters (not to be confused with Chester), was first excavated as long ago as 1876 by the antiquarian John Clayton from the nearby city of Newcastle-upon-Tyne, and the museum at the site—now called Chesters Museum—was opened in 1903. Here I learned that the site of the shrine itself is now just a spring marked by a single standing stone in open countryside, the brickwork and artifacts discovered there having been moved into the museum. So, strictly speaking, although the shrine survives, it no longer exists in situ; rather, it is in pieces in a public gallery. Nevertheless, these artifacts revealed much. Many of the stone blocks that once formed the walls of the temple are inscribed with the goddess's name—Coventina (see plate 5). Various officers stationed at Cilurnum and other forts along Hadrian's Wall made these Latin inscriptions. For example, one read:

> To Coventina, [I] Aelius Tertius, prefect of the First Cohort of Batavi, willingly and deservedly fulfills a vow

A prefect was a military officer, roughly equivalent to a lieutenant colonel in the United States army, and a cohort was a Roman army unit consisting of around five hundred men, what we might now call a battalion. Aelius Tertius was, it seems, the fort commander. Some of the dedications were made on behalf of the entire cohort:

> To the goddess Coventina, the First Cohort of Cugerni . . . willingly placed this offering

The vow and offering referred to were clearly votive offerings, as literally thousands of such items were uncovered at the site of the pool: beads, glass and pottery utensils, pieces of jewelry, and an astonishing fourteen thousand coins. Because coins can be dated by the name of the emperor depicted on them, we know that the shrine was being used right through until the end of Roman rule. After the Romans left, the fort and town were abandoned as the Picts of Scotland surged south. Nonmilitary personnel also commissioned inscriptions:

> For the goddess Coventina, Crotus and his freedmen, fulfill [their vow] for the health of the soldiers

Freedmen—*libertas* in Latin—were originally former slaves who had been granted their freedom, but the term was ultimately applied to a general social class, often traders descended from freed slaves. In this case they were probably the native Britons from the Roman town. From inscriptions such as this, we can determine that the offerings were being made for continuing good health, for healing, or in the hope of cures. Coventina was clearly a goddess of water and healing, very similar to the Irish Mórrígan. It was when I saw the altar stones from the temple that I had to conclude that she was almost identical. The first was about two and a half feet high, one and a half feet wide, and six inches thick. It was a beige-colored, rectangular stone with a pointed top, like the gable end of a house, the upper half carved with a shallow recess in which was a depiction of the goddess in bas-relief, showing her reclining on a water lily and holding a leafed branch, the lower half bearing a Latin inscription naming her as Coventina. But it was the second of the altar stones that was particularly fascinating. Cut from the same type of stone, around three feet wide, one and a half feet high, and some six inches thick, it was also a bas-relief carving representing three rounded arches, separated by columns. Within each arch was depicted a bare-breasted woman reclining on a couch. Each of these three women held an urn, suggesting that they were also water deities or nymphs. There was no inscription on the stone, but staff at the museum told me that they were thought to represent Coventina in triplicate: a triple goddess was worshipped widely throughout the Celtic world, they said. As far as I was concerned, they were dead wrong about that. I had already come across this triple-goddess notion in my research and had discounted it early on.

Goddesses depicted in threes have indeed been found in early Celtic art, but the idea that they were a single deity in three guises is a modern concept. Many of today's Wiccans, pagans, and New Agers regard their chief goddess as having three forms: Maiden, Mother, and Crone, symbolizing the separate stages of the female life cycle. This, however, is a recent idea, popularized by the English writer and novelist Robert Graves in his book *The White Goddess* published in 1948.[20] Contemporary historians regard Graves's study of mythology as unreliable, as it was influenced heavily by the controversial early twentieth-century works on witchcraft by authors such as the English anthropologist Margret Murray[21] and the occultist Aleister Crowley.[22] In fact, since the 1940s, some authors have gone so far as to suggest that the Irish Mórrígan was actually a triple goddess, which they term *The* Mórrígan. It is maintained that "The Mórrígan" was actually one and the same as her sisters, Badb, Macha, and Anann, who were in reality her three aspects, Maiden, Mother, and Crone. Other Arthurian researchers, having equated Morgan with Mórrígan, maintain that the three queens in the Avalon story were the "three Morgans." As far as I could tell, there was no historical base for any of this. Although in Irish mythology their exploits occasionally overlap, probably due to confusion in later translations, Mórrígan, Badb, Macha, and Anann were completely separate figures with their own independent and distinctive stories. As for the three queens being aspects of Mórrígan in the medieval King Arthur stories, it just doesn't fit. They are all portrayed as young, not at different stages of life. One of them, the Lady of the Lake, even has her own literary résumé, which is totally different from that of Morgan le Fey.

From my perspective there had never been a triple goddess in the ancient Celtic world. But even if there had, there was no evidence whatsoever that the three goddesses depicted on the altar stone at the Chesters Museum were it (see plate 6). Based on discoveries made at the shrines to Minerva in Bath and Chester, as well as many intact examples of temples to goddesses worshipped by the Romans in Rome and elsewhere, archaeologists believe that the two altar stones were fixed to the wall above and behind the altar itself.[23] Because of its pointed top—or triangular tympanum, in architectural terms—the stone with the single goddess, identified by its inscription as Coventina, was set on the wall immediately above the stone depicting the three goddesses under their rounded arches. In effect, the two stones together represented a building in which Coventina sat in a gable window, while the other three figures sat in the colonnade below. In other words the scene depicted Coventina and three attendant goddesses, just like Mórrígan and her three sisters.

So was Coventina a name the Britons used for Mórrígan? Was this a depiction of the woman upon whom Morgan, the enchantress who tended to Arthur on Avalon, was based? And were the three goddesses the three Arthurian queens, one of them the Lady of the Lake herself? The site where the temple stood, now called Coventina's Well (although it was never actually a well), could not have been the lake in the Arthurian story; it was just a pool, around ten feet wide (see plate 4). Besides which, the area had been abandoned to the Picts when the Roman army left, almost a century before Arthur's time. But Coventina and her attendant goddesses did suggest that something very similar to the cult of Mórrígan did exist in Britain. It was certainly not confined to the north of the country, as images of three attendant goddesses to Minerva have been found elsewhere, such as in the Roman bathhouse in the city of Bath.[24] Unfortunately, Coventina has not been found on inscriptions other than those from Cilurnum, so it may have been just a local name for the deity. One of the staff I spoke to at the museum thought that Coventina might have been a Roman rendering of a Celtic water goddess called Covianna, a remarkably similar name to Vivanna, from which the name Vivianne, the Lady of the Lake, might have been derived. However, I could find no reference to an inscription bearing this name either. Nevertheless, that Coventina has not been found on any other contemporary inscriptions did not necessarily mean that the name was not used elsewhere, merely that no such inscriptions had been unearthed. There are only a handful of inscriptions bearing the name Minerva found in Britain, but we know from Roman records that she had dozens of temples and shrines in the country. It's simply that so few such artifacts have survived the wet British climate.

Whether or not the name Coventina was applied to this water deity elsewhere in Britain was basically irrelevant. Her shrine proved, to my satisfaction at least, that goddesses very similar to Mórrígan and her sisters had been venerated in Britain, confirming my conjecture that the Arthurian Avalon theme was based on early Celtic mythology. There was a Celtic tradition involving nine priestesses skilled in the art of healing who lived in isolation on lake islands; their leader, an oracle, apparently "channeled" a goddess. Nine sisters were said to live on the Isle of Avalon, and they had healing powers, while Morgan, their leader, seemed to represent the goddess Mórrígan. Besides Morgan, the most important of the nine sisters in the Arthurian saga were the three queens; from Ireland there was Mórrígan and her three sisters, and in Britain there was Coventina and her three attendants. Avalon appeared to have been an island in the lake into which Excalibur was thrown, and personal weapons such as swords were cast into sacred lakes as votive offerings. Such offerings were to a water goddess, such as Anann, upon whom the Lady of the Lake appeared to be based. I was convinced that the Arthurian story of Avalon, Morgan, and the Lady of the Lake had indeed derived from some early Celtic source, predating Geoffrey of Monmouth and the medieval romances by centuries. But was any of it actually real? Could a *historical*, mortally wounded warrior, upon whom the legend of King Arthur was based, have actually been taken to a lake, where his sword was cast as an offering in the hope of healing, and then transported to an island in the lake to be cared for by an oracle (or bard) and her female entourage? Such a scenario was certainly *possible* around the year 500: many of the old Celtic practices had been incorporated into the kind of quasi-Christianity prevalent in Britain at the time.

It was all good stuff. My problem was—as I stood in Chesters Museum, gazing at the depictions of Coventina and the three nymphs— I had no idea where to go next in my search for a historical Avalon. That was until I examined another exhibit I'd only previously glanced at: the top half of a human skull excavated from Coventina's Well. It was, I was told, the only human remain found there. It seemed unlikely to have been a sacrifice; if the place had been used for such rites, there would have been other human bones unearthed. It was certainly not someone who had fallen into the pool by accident, or the rest of the skeleton would have been discovered. It was probably, one of the museum staff explained, related to the Celtic practice of head worship. She was, of course, referring to the talking heads I discussed in chapter 4. It was most likely such a sacred head specifically associated with the Coventina shrine, with which the temple oracle would once have communed; perhaps the head of some ancient priestess or queen imagined to have personified the goddess. The skull dated from the period the site was abandoned, so it was thought to have been placed in the pool when the Britons fled south. Most probably it had previously been kept, possibly as a mummified head, upon the altar, but once the Picts invaded, it was considered appropriate to leave it in the goddess's hallowed waters.

It was while I was listening to the explanation of the skull that I was struck by something I had virtually overlooked. The most famous of such talking heads was the head of Bran, and it had close links with the story of the Grail. Bran was said to have been a onetime ruler of Annwn, upon which, in part, Avalon was based. Bran, as the magic cauldron guardian, seems to have been the character upon which the Arthurian romancer Robert de Boron based his Grail guardian Bron. Robert tells us that the Grail had been hidden in Avalon, a theme also employed by later medieval authors. The Welsh hero Peredur was the blueprint for the Arthurian Sir Perceval as portrayed by Chrétien de Troyes, and Perceval is the knight who finds the Grail. In Chrétien's account Perceval locates the Grail in the so-called Grail Castle, whereas in the earlier Welsh tale *Peredur,* in precisely the same circumstances, Peredur discovers what had to have been Bran's head in a castle in Wales (see chapter 4). I now had a new line of reasoning that might pinpoint the area where the lake island I was seeking could be found. If the Grail and the head of Bran were supposedly in the same place, and that place was Avalon, my next move would be to find where the *Peredur* tale actually located it. I almost laughed out loud. I was now not only searching for the mystical Isle of Avalon but on a quest for the Holy Grail.

6

The White Land

In the Welsh tale *Peredur,* the location of the castle where the hero sees the severed head is not revealed. However, if the relic was Bran's head, as I figured, then the most likely location the author had in mind would be a castle at the summit of a hill overlooking the town of Llangollen in northeast Wales. Known as Dinas Bran, or "Bran's Fort" in English, the ruins of the stone-built fortress, still to be seen, only date from the 1260s, but an earlier and more extensive citadel stood on the spot (see plate 9). Occupying the flat summit of the thousand-foot hill, the original fortification consisted of a single bank, some twenty feet high, and a surrounding ditch, encircling an area of about four acres. This hill fort, similar to the one at Cadbury (see chapter 2), consisting of a wooden stockade encompassing a fortified settlement, dated to around 500 BC.[1] Abandoned during Roman times, and reoccupied in the fifth century, it was certainly in use again at the time Arthur is said to have lived. The oldest surviving reference to the site is found in a medieval narrative called *Fouke le Fitz Waryn,* named after a local hero and written around 1250, which states that the ruins of an earlier castle had existed at this time.[2] According to the account the castle had been built by Bran himself, and Dinas Bran is also said to be where Bran's mystical talking head ended up.

In the Welsh tale *Branwen Ferch Llŷr* (Branwen, Daughter of Llŷr), Bran (Branwen's brother) asks for his head to be cut off as he is dying. After it has served as an oracle for many years, giving advice to the British leaders, the head of Bran is finally buried at a place identified as the White Hill.[3] The oldest extant copy dates from the 1300s, but literary scholars believe it to be very much older, perhaps originally dating in part from the post-Roman era. Fourteenth-century English copyists suggested that the White Hill had been the White Mount in London, where the Tower of London stood, but this would seem most unlikely for a tale where the action takes place in Wales. Besides, during the period in which the tales seem to have been composed, London was firmly under Saxon control. Welsh tradition, conversely, locates the White Hill at Dinas Bran, and with some justification. Not only is the place specifically linked with the legendary figure of Bran, but during the Middle Ages the hill on which the fort stands is recorded as Gwynfryn, Welsh for "White Hill."

In the Arthurian romances Arthur appears to be buried on or near Avalon, which is also the home of the Grail whose guardian is Bron. In turn, the Arthurian Grail seems to have been based to a large extent on the Welsh story of Annwn and the magic cauldron, and the magic cauldron's guardian was the almost identical-sounding Bran (see chapter 4). Dinas Bran, I decided, was well worth a visit. Today Dinas Bran is not only the name of the ruined castle but also the hill itself. This, though, is unlikely to have been the location for a historical Avalon. Not only is the hill huge, over a thousand feet high, it was also never surrounded by water. Nonetheless, I soon discovered that the immediate vicinity had firm links with the Welsh Arthurian tradition. Standing among the stark, gray-stone castle ruins—some of its thick walls over thirty feet high, complete with rounded arches and window openings long bereft of doors or glass—I could see for miles across the surrounding countryside: to the west, the mountains of Wales, and to the east, the plains of central England. Directly below, to the southwest, was the town of Llangollen, on the other side of the meandering River Dee; and just downstream were the magnificent ruins of the abbey of Valle Crucis.[4] During the fourteenth century this Cistercian monastery was where many of the Dark Age Welsh Arthurian tales were committed to writing in their present form (see plate 10).

Although the English invasion of Wales began as early as 1171, it was over a century before the country was fully conquered. Sometime around 1300 Welsh monks, realizing that much of their country's literary heritage was being lost, began to collect and copy Welsh tales, poems, and songs into single volumes. At Valle Crucis Abbey these were primarily Arthurian tales, preserved here during the turbulent years of the fourteenth century—the time of the Black Death—until they were copied into later manuscripts around 1400 that still survive, such as The Red Book of Hergest and The White Book of Rhydderch (both named after the color of their bindings). A number of these Welsh Arthurian stories were eventually translated into English by the Lincolnshire diarist Lady Charlotte Guest in the 1830s and eventually published under the collective title *The Mabinogion* (from the Welsh *mabinogi,* a name applied to old mythological tales), which is still widely in print today.[5] As well as these prose narratives, other Welsh mythology and chronicles were preserved in poetic form—in particular, in verses known as triads. Taking their name from the groupings of themes or characters into threes, the triads served as a mnemonic device, summarizing Welsh folklore and history. Not really poems in the true sense, they are basically lyrical outlines of what were obviously more detailed sagas and accounts; sometimes they consist of only a handful of lines.[6] They were committed to writing during the Middle Ages by various Welsh authors, and many of those that included the character of King Arthur were preserved by the monks of Valle Crucis. Although originally dispersed through many Welsh manuscripts, they were eventually brought together under the title *Trioedd Ynys Prydain* (Triads of Britain) in 1567 by the Welsh scholar William Salesbury. No doubt many Welsh Arthurian stories were lost to history, but thanks to the monks of Valle Crucis, we still have some of the originals, later adapted by authors such as Geoffrey of Monmouth, Robert de Boron, and Chrétien de Troyes. The question I needed to answer was this: Was it just a coincidence that the abbey was right next to Dinas Bran, the location that seems to have inspired the setting for the Grail Castle in the medieval romances, or was this particular area specifically linked with the early Arthurian legend? It was not long before I discovered that the district was deeply associated with the very oldest King Arthur traditions.

Before continuing I need to explain a little about the area at the time Arthur is said to have lived. We have seen how, after the Romans left Britain in AD 410, the country soon broke into separate kingdoms based on old tribal regions. The largest and most important of these were in western Britain, as the northern region was being harassed by the Picts and Irish, and the southeast and east were being invaded by the Anglo-Saxons. There were many small kingdoms, but the largest were Dumnonia in southwest England, Dyfed (pronounced "Dove-ed") and Gwent in south Wales, Gwynedd (pronounced "Gwineth") in north-west Wales, and Powys (pronounced "Powis"), which covered what is now middle England, together with central and northwest Wales. During the Dark Ages Dinas Bran was within the kingdom of Powys; in fact, from around 650 its fort seems to have become the kingdom's capital, when the Anglo-Saxons pushed into central England, forcing the Britons to retreat west. Today Gwent, Dyfed, and Gwynedd lend their name to Welsh counties, approximately covering the areas of the old kingdoms, but the modern county of Powys only comprises a small region in west-central Wales: the area to which the kingdom had been reduced by the early Middle Ages. The original Powys was much larger and was one of the most powerful kingdoms in post-Roman Britain, and it was in this kingdom that much of the action in the Welsh King Arthur tradition took place. Reading through English translations of early Welsh Arthurian tales and poetry in Llangollen's public library, I found that Dinas Bran was just one of the many sites in what had once been the kingdom of Powys to boast Arthurian connections.

I began by searching for local associations with the Celtic goddess quartet that my research suggested was linked with the tale of Avalon (see chapter 5). I did not initially discover a lake island in the vicinity, but I did find something of particular interest that may have been related to these ancient deities. A few miles to the southeast of Dinas Bran, just outside the modern town of Oswestry, was another pre-Roman hill fort reoccupied in the late fifth century.[7] Covering an area of some forty acres and consisting of several earthen ramparts, it was called Caer Ogyrfan (Welsh for the "Citadel of Ogyrfan") and was a similar, though much larger hilltop settlement to Dinas Bran. Not only was it also reoccupied around AD 500, but it too had Welsh Arthurian associations: local legend claimed it to be the birthplace of none other than Arthur's queen Guinevere. Guinevere is the name used by the medieval romancers for King Arthur's wife, but in the earlier Welsh stories, she is called Gwenhwyfar (pronounced roughly "Gwen-he-var"), such as in the tales of *Culhwch and Olwen* and *Peredur,* which we have already examined, and the *Lady of the Fountain* and *Geraint and Enid,* which also seem to have been composed during the Dark Ages.[8] All these tales were ultimately rehashed by the medieval romancers, but the Welsh versions were almost certainly the originals, as they interpolated purely Celtic mythological themes and names. Gwenhwyfar is one such example, whose name is Brythonic (post-Roman British) for "White Enchantress." In fact, the *far* element is the British equivalent of the Old French *fey,* "fairy," used by Chrétien de Troyes and subsequent romancers to described Morgan (see chapter 5). Not only is her name Celtic, but in Welsh tradition there are three Gwenhwyfars, bearing a great similarity to the three sisters of Mórrígan. Although, in the medieval Arthurian romances, Arthur has only one Queen Guinevere, in early Welsh literature Arthur had three queens *all* called Gwenhwyfar.[9] (This, incidentally, might explain why the cross the monks of Glastonbury claimed to have found in Arthur's grave is said to have referred to Guinevere as Arthur's second wife.)

Although these women are alleged to have had different fathers, they seem to have had the same mother as they each shared a common sister called Gwenhwyfach (pronounced roughly "Gwen-he-vak"), meaning "Little White."[10] (Some literary scholars have suggested that she was the inspiration for Snow White by the German brothers Jacob and Wilhelm Grimm, who in the early nineteenth century researched European folklore and mythology widely for their storylines. Although there are no "seven dwarfs" in Welsh legend, there are magic mirrors, poisoned apples, and a glass coffin.) Two things seemed evident to me.

The first was that the name Gwenhwyfar was probably not originally a personal name but a title; the second was that the three Gwenhwyfars—White Enchantresses—might have been linked to the three queens in the medieval Avalon theme. Along with their sister Gwenhwyfach, they may have been the Welsh equivalents to the Irish Mórrígan, Badb, Macha, and Anann and the northern Coventina and her three attendants (see chapter 5). Obviously, by the Middle Ages the three queens were different literary figures from Arthur's wife, but in the original version of the legend, Arthur appeared to have been portrayed as marrying all three of these mystical queens. I was hoping that the fort of Caer Ogyrfan—in legend said to be the home of at least one of the Gwenhwyfars—might prove to have once been surrounded by water. Sadly, however, the terrain could never have been an island in recent geological history.[11] All the same, the place was almost certainly associated with Gwenhwyfar in the early pre-romance Arthurian tradition. The Welsh triad *The Three Wives of Arthur,* for instance, not only refers to the three Gwenhwyfars, but one of them is said to be the daughter of Ogyrfan Gawr (Ogyrfan the Giant, a term often applied to tall warriors), the same man after whom the citadel was named.[12]

What I found especially interesting was the word *white* in what seemed to have been the title borne by Arthur's three queens in the legend. The *enchantress* part seemed obvious enough; they were thought to have magic powers. But why the *white* enchantress? Did this mean that they were considered good, like a white witch? Or was there something more? While looking through the local history collection in the Llangollen library, I found a number of references to the word *white* being associated with the kingdom of Powys, in places such as the White Hall, the White Castle, and the White Town. In fact Powys itself is referred to in medieval English accounts as the White Land. The meaning of the name Powys is something of a mystery. The Celtic tribe native to the area was called the Cornovii, so unlike kingdoms such as Dumnonia, named after the Dumnonii tribe, Powys did not derive its name from its people. It has been suggested that the name came from the Latin *pagus* meaning "the countryside," but I found no literary evidence to support this. Besides, it seemed quite a stretch from Pagus to Powys, and why call a kingdom simply "The Countryside"? There is no surviving reference to how the kingdom got its name, and no similar words to Powys are known in Welsh or Brythonic. As the only other name used for the kingdom is the White Land in medieval English texts, I could only assume that, that is what the now-forgotten word originally meant. There is no explanation in any of these works as to why the area was referred to as the White Land, but it was possibly because it had significant deposits of limestone, a light-colored, grayish-white rock used for building.[13] Many of the area's Roman towns had been constructed from local limestone, giving them a white, as opposed to the red, look of most cities of the time. If the kingdom had been called the White Land during the Dark Ages, then the title white enchantress might have been linked with the place where she (or they) were thought to have originated or ruled. Whatever the origin of the name, it was when I was reading one of the medieval works referring to Powys as the White Land that I was delighted to find reference to King Arthur himself actually living in the region.

The mid-thirteenth-century *Fouke le Fitz Waryn,* composed by an unknown author around 1250, concerns the exploits of a local baron named Fulk Fitz Warine: a historical figure that lived around AD 1200. In the work the area that had once been the kingdom of Powys is repeatedly called the White Land; for instance, when referring to Fulk, the narrative says, "In Britain the Great, a wolf will come from the White-Land."[14] (Fulk was known as the Wolf, a contemporary term for an outlaw, which Fulk had once been.) In fact the account, which frequently mentions Arthur, says that centuries before Fulk's time, the fabled king had actually dwelt in the White Land: "There King Arthur recovered his goodness and his valor, when he had lost all his chivalry and his virtue."[15] Furthermore, the narrative specifically tells us that the district had been called the White Land in Arthur's time: "For each of you may be sure that in the time of King Arthur that [the area in which Fulk lived] was called White Land."[16]

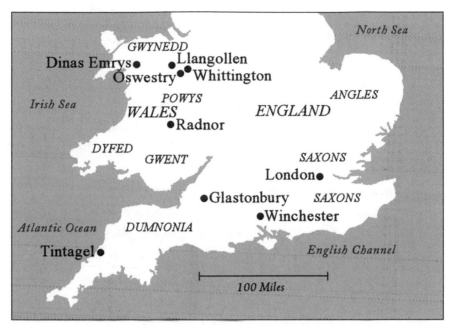

Fig. 6.1. The primary British and Anglo-Saxon kingdoms of the late fifth century, showing the locations discussed in this chapter.

Moreover, *Fouke le Fitz Waryn* even associates the area with the Holy Grail. When referring to Fulk's castle, the author explains that in legend the Grail itself foretold events there. Enigmatically, he uses the words "Thus the Graal tells us."[17] (Graal was a contemporary spelling of Grail.) Intriguingly, it seems that the Grail actually spoke, which might be related to the tradition of Bran's talking head. The implication seemed to be that the author believed the Grail was once said to be housed in or near Fulk's castle. (Unfortunately, we are not told what this particular Grail actually is: it could be a cup, a chalice, a dish, or even a severed head.)

Fulk was a historical figure who in 1204, after having been an outlaw for rebelling against England's King John, was pardoned and inherited his castle in the town of Whittington on the Welsh border in what is now the English county of Shropshire, just a couple of miles northeast of Oswestry. On first visiting Whittington I was transfixed by its beauty. Encompassed by a broad moat, upon which swam ducks, swans, and all manner of exotic waterfowl, the castle's towering ruins stood atop a hillock of soft green grass (see plate 11). Walls, turrets, and ramparts still survived, while the fortified gatehouse and moat-crossing bridge were almost perfectly preserved, with an arched entrance still carved with the coat of arms of the Fitz Warine family. In the sunlight the limestone brickwork shone brightly: the stronghold truly lived up to its local name as the White Castle. Although today its official name is Whittington Castle, historical records dating back to the time of Fulk Fitz Warine refer to it as the White Castle. Indeed, the *Fouke le Fitz Waryn* author initially calls it the White Tower, suggesting that only the central keep existed when Fulk inherited the place. The rest of it seems to have been built during Fulk's occupancy. In fact, the *Fouke le Fitz Waryn* narrative refers to it as the White Tower, in the White Town, in the White Land. The scenic little town surrounding the castle is still called Whittington, from the Middle English meaning "White Town," even today.

In a medieval Arthurian romance known as the *Didot Perceval* (Didot [pronounced "Dee-doe"] being the family name of the one-time owners of the manuscript), a White Castle is included as the place where the hero Perceval fights in a tournament just before he reaches the Grail Castle.[18] From the narrative it appears that the two locations are close to each other. Although the surviving work is anonymous, it seems to be a continuation of the works of Robert de Boron; indeed, some scholars believe that it was originally written by Robert himself as it dates from around the same time, AD 1200. If Whittington Castle is the setting for the White Castle in the romance, then it could, I decided, be regarded as further evidence that the nearby Dinas Bran was the location for the Grail Castle in the early Arthurian saga. As the *Didot Perceval* depicts Perceval as the grandson of Bron, the Grail guardian, then it would seem that, like Guinevere, Perceval was another character who was originally regarded as having come from what had been the kingdom of Powys.

For a while I speculated that the site of Whittington Castle might have been the place upon which Avalon was based. Not only was it an island, surrounded by a moat, but archaeology had revealed that earth-works on the spot, much older than the twelfth-century castle, dated from as early as the sixth century. However, when I discovered that the moat was an artificial construction dating from the late Anglo-Saxon period of the tenth or eleventh century, I had to abandon the idea. Interestingly, Whittington Castle did turn out to be associated with the Grail legend during the Middle Ages, but this was centuries after the period in which a historical Arthur may have lived; but all this was part of an investigation I conducted some years later, concerning the Holy Grail as it was perceived in medieval times.[19] Regardless of any later Grail connections, however, the site of Whittington Castle was clearly not the lake island I was seeking. Nevertheless, while I was reading *Fouke le Fitz Waryn,* I found reference to yet another Arthurian character: Merlin the magician. The author repeatedly states that Merlin had foretold the life of Fulk Fitz Warine, citing examples of his prophesies concerning the White Land. For example: "Merlin says that in Britain the Great, a wolf [Fulk] will come from the White Land" (see above); and "Out of the White Land, he shall [come and] have such great force and virtue. But we know that Merlin said it for Fulk Fitz Warine."[20]

Exactly where the author obtained these prophecies is unknown. The point was, however, that he was linking Merlin to what had been the kingdom of Powys, and Merlin was indeed connected with the kingdom in one of the very earliest Arthurian references to still survive. Geoffrey of Monmouth, in his *History of the Kings of Britain,* first introduces Merlin as a young boy. Believing that the child has visionary powers, the British king Vortigern captures Merlin and takes him to his hilltop fortress in Wales. The king had been having trouble constructing his fort; the foundations kept collapsing, and his magicians told him that to put things right he must sacrifice a child—and the young Merlin is chosen. However, just as Merlin is about to be killed, he has a vision of two dragons, one red, the other white, that fight each other in a pool in a cavern below the fort. This, he tells Vortigern, is why the building keeps collapsing. He tells Vortigern's men where to dig; the pool is found and the dragons released. The king is so impressed that he spares Merlin, appointing him as one of his advisors and rewarding him with land.[21] Although this is clearly a mythological anecdote, it actually predates Geoffrey of Monmouth by some three hundred years. The same story is found almost verbatim in the writings of the ninth-century monk Nennius who came from Radnor in southwestern Powys.[22] Nennius wrote the Latin *Historia Brittonum* (The History of the Britons) around the year 830.[23] The work outlines a history of Britain compiled from various monastic texts. While it contains many known historical events, it also includes assorted myths and legends from around the country that the author considered worthy of preservation. One such legend was the same story that Geoffrey later recounted concerning the boy threatened with sacrifice by Vortigern and exalted after he reveals the two dragons in the pool below the king's fortress.[24] Not only was Nennius from Powys, but the place where the legendary event was said to have taken place was also in the kingdom. Called Dinas Emrys, the hill lies around forty miles west of Dinas Bran and is situated on what was once the border between Powys and the north Welsh kingdom of Gwynedd. (An early Welsh tale called *Lludd and Llevelys,* preserved in The Red Book of Hergest, refers to the two dragons first being confined to the cavern pool at a place later called Dinas Emrys.)

Close to the village of Beddgelert, the rocky hillock is around 250 feet high and mainly covered by woodland, but during the Dark Ages it was probably treeless, providing a clear view of the surrounding terrain. On its summit there can still be seen the remains of stone fortifications dating from the thirteenth century, but excavations in the 1950s, by the archaeologist Hubert Savory of the National Museum of Wales, revealed that the site had been occupied and reconstructed on several occasions, including the mid-to-late fifth century when the story of Vortigern and Merlin is set.[25] Remarkably, the excavations discovered that there was indeed a pool beneath the hill fort, just as described by Nennius and Geoffrey of Monmouth. The fort was perfectly positioned to guard a pass through the Snowdonia Mountains joining Gwynedd and Powys, so it was a location of vital strategic importance as the accounts relate. The most astonishing thing I discovered was that unlike Bran and Gwenhwyfar, who appear to have been mythological characters at some point interpolated into the King Arthur legend, Vortigern was a historical figure. He is named as the most powerful British leader of the mid-fifth century in the *Welsh Annals,* compiled from earlier monastic records around 950,[26] and the Anglo-Saxon Chronicle, an Anglo-Saxon history assembled in part from older military accounts in the late 800s.[27] Moreover, he is also recorded by Gildas, a British monk who wrote around the year 545, within living memory of the time Arthur is said to have lived[28] (more about Gildas later). There can be little doubt that Vortigern was a historical king of Powys, as his name was inscribed on a stone pillar dating from around AD 850, listing the rulers of the kingdom. Standing on high open ground overlooking Valle Crucis Abbey in Llangollen, the pillar was originally a stone cross, some twenty feet high, and it was from it that Valle Crucis gets its name: Valle Crucis means "Valley of the Cross" in Welsh. Now called the Pillar of Eliseg—named after the man it was erected to commemorate—only parts of its original inscription remain legible (see plate 12), but before it had weathered the still visible lines were recorded by the Welsh antiquarian Edward Lhuyd in 1696.[29] Although the names of all the Powys kings were not discernible even then, many did survive, and Vortigern was recorded as the first of them. (Today, a replica of the pillar can be found in the Llangollen Museum, along with the inscription recorded by Lhuyd.)

More incredibly still, and as unlikely as it might first sound, Merlin also appears to have been based on a historical figure. Geoffrey of Monmouth gives his full name as Ambrosius Merlin, and in Nennius's earlier account the boy who reveals the dragon pool to Vortigern is called simply Ambrosius. Nennius's account is almost identical to Geoffrey's, so there can be little doubt that they are both referring to the same person. Like Vortigern, this Ambrosius was a real historical character. Gildas refers to him as the man who went on to lead the Britons in their struggle against the Anglo-Saxons in the late 400s. Ambrosius also appears in various early accounts from

Wales, where his name is rendered in Welsh as Emrys. (Ambrosius became shortened to Ambrose in English, and Emrys is the Welsh pronunciation of Ambrose.) In English, Dinas Emrys, the place where the fabled meeting between Merlin and Vortigern occurred, translates as the "Fort of Ambrosius": Nennius suggests that Ambrosius took over the fort following Vortigern's demise. Clearly, the story of the two dragons was merely legend, but an encounter between Merlin and Vortigern does seem to have been regarded as a historical event in the very early Arthurian tradition. Whether or not Merlin was attributed with special powers, as he is in the medieval romances, is something we shall return to later when examining him and Vortigern in more detail. For now, however, what's important is that I had found two more Arthurian characters firmly associated with the kingdom of Powys.

In the medieval Arthurian saga, the story is usually set in southern and southwest England. For example, Arthur is born at Tintagel in Cornwall, his capital is in Winchester, and his grave is in Glastonbury. I had discovered that all such connections were late interpolations from the Middle Ages, starting in the 1100s. However, Arthur was certainly not invented by medieval authors as he appears in earlier Welsh accounts, some dating from three centuries before. Furthermore, many of the seemingly fanciful themes in the romances originated with genuine mythology of the Dark Ages, such as Avalon, Excalibur, Guinevere, Morgan le Fey, the nine maidens, and the three queens. Whether or not Arthur was a historical figure, his legend was truly much older than the stories familiar today. I was, of course, searching for a historical character behind the legend, and if he *did* exist, I hoped to find his grave. I had traveled all over the British Isles, but now I finally had a specific area to concentrate my search. The oldest Arthurian traditions all seemed to focus on what had been the kingdom of Powys. The Grail legend, exemplified by Dinas Bran and the nearby White Castle, was associated with the region; Guinevere was said to have been born here; Vortigern ruled the kingdom; and Merlin makes his home in the area. And all these traditions appeared to predate the Arthurian links with the south and southwest of England by centuries. Was the post-Roman kingdom of Powys where the Arthurian story first began? An exhilarating notion occurred to me: Had previous researchers failed to find a historical King Arthur because they had been looking in the wrong place?

7

Last of the Romans

My search for the origins of the Arthurian legend had led me to the British kingdom of Powys. Its exact size in the late fifth and early sixth centuries is unknown, but it seems to have covered approximately what are now the West Midlands of England, together with central and north-central Wales. From the time of Geoffrey of Monmouth's writings in the 1130s, Arthur is referred to as *King* Arthur and is usually depicted as king of all Britain, or in some cases as king of England. Much to the annoyance of the Welsh, "England" was often used to refer to both England *and* Wales from the time the English began invading their country in the twelfth century. It can be a bit confusing, even for us British, so I should probably pause and explain a bit more concerning the geopolitical setup of the British Isles. Strictly speaking, the term *Britain* refers to just England and Wales; it derives from *Britannia,* the Latin name for the province established by the Romans, which covered the parts of the British Isles they occupied. Wales became a separate country inhabited by the Britons after the Anglo-Saxons fully invaded the north, east, and south of Britain, establishing a unified kingdom of England by the mid-950s. Ultimately, Wales came under English rule after 1282 and today retains its semiautonomy as a British principality. "Great Britain," which includes Scotland, did not exist as a single nation until 1707, while the "United Kingdom of Great Britain and Ireland" came into existence in 1801, after the British annexed Ireland. From the time Southern Ireland gained its independence in 1922 and formed the Republic of Ireland, the United Kingdom—or UK for short—now consists of England, Wales, Scotland, and Northern Ireland. (United Kingdom is actually the shortened form of "United Kingdom of Great Britain and Northern Ireland.") Oh, and by the way, the term *Brits* can refer to a citizen from any part of the UK, or just a part or parts of it, depending on your political point of view. Anyway, enough said! The point is that during the Middle Ages, when Arthur was perceived as having once been king, Britain referred to what had been Roman Britain: England and Wales. But as we have seen, around the year 500 when Arthur is said to have lived, Britain had fragmented into many separate kingdoms. So if he existed, what would Arthur really have been king of? Presumably, just one of these kingdoms—at least, initially! Had that been the kingdom of Powys?

Before I could begin to answer this question, I needed to examine in more detail the history of post-Roman Britain. As my research during this next phase consisted principally of reading, interviewing historians and archaeologists, and seeking out ancient manuscripts, I will keep things easy. I shall explain simply—hopefully—what is known concerning this period. When I say "known," I should probably say "generally thought," as much of post-Roman history is derived from fitting together diverse pieces of evidence, both historical and archaeological, and a certain amount of guesswork. Besides which, scholars often disagree on various matters concerning the era. The events throughout mainland Europe are pretty well understood, as they can be reconstructed from various Roman sources. Exactly what occurred in Britain, isolated from continental Europe, however, is much less certain. I'll begin by explaining the collapse of the Roman Empire in the West.

The city-state of Rome in Italy began its expansion to become a Roman domain during the fifth century BC, which continued to grow over the next few hundred years. Until 27 BC it had been a republic, governed by a senate, but in that year Augustus became the first Roman emperor. (It's a common misconception that Julius Caesar, who died in 44 BC, had been an emperor. He wasn't. He was a general whom the senate installed with what, for all intents and purposes, were absolute powers.) From that time the territories ruled by Rome became known as the Roman Empire, which reached its greatest extent in the second century AD and included territories all around the Mediterranean Sea, as well as Western Europe and parts of the Middle East. In 395 the Roman Empire split in two, when the Emperor Theodosius I divided it between his two sons upon his death. The Western Empire, still ruled from Rome, included much of Western Europe and a part of northwest Africa, while the Eastern Empire, ultimately ruled from Constantinople (modern Istanbul), came to be known as the Byzantine Empire. Remarkably, although it was much reduced in size after the Muslim conquests of the seventh century, the Byzantine Empire survived until Constantinople fell to the Turks in 1453. The Western Empire fared far worse. Significantly weakened by the split, it endured for less than a century. And *endured* is just the right word. From the start it was harassed by what the Romans called barbarians.

Barbarian was a term for any people the Romans perceived to be uncivilized—in this case those from the immediate east of the empire. The long northeastern frontier of the Western Empire was marked by the Rhine and Danube Rivers, which became increasingly indefensible, and the huge barbarian tribes from the east of this geographical boundary are collectively known as the Goths. (The word *Gothic,* as in a style of architecture during the Middle Ages, has no connection with these tribes. Neither does the term *Goth* for the contemporary subculture: the so-called Gothic Revival of the nineteenth century, named after a reintroduction of a Gothic style of architecture, also saw the popularity of the horror and "dark" genres in literature, from where the modern Goths get their name.) What began as incursions of plunder by the Goths soon turned into full-scale invasions, and it was all caused by the weather. In what is now the Ukraine, a particularly fertile area, lived a massive ethnic group called the Huns, descendants of the Mongols from central Asia. (These people had no connection to the Germans as they were called by the British during the First World War. The term

Hun, in this context, derived from the spiked helmets worn by the German forces, similar to those depicted in contemporary illustrations of the ancient Huns.) Ironically, around the same time that the Roman Empire split in two, the Ukraine suffered years of low rainfall, leading to a series of disastrous crop failures. Impelled to migrate westward in search of food, the Huns surged toward the lands occupied by the less powerful Goths, who were in turn driven further west. Consequently, the vanquished Goths crossed the Danube and Rhine. But it didn't stop there. With Rome on the defensive, its armies tied up fighting the Goths, other peoples broke through the frontiers of the Western Empire, and the North African provinces were lost. Eventually, the situation in Europe became so bad that the Western emperor, Honorius, moved his capital to the city of Ravenna in northeast Italy, and in AD 410 the Visigoths—the West Goths—seized Rome itself; the first time in eight centuries that the so-called Eternal City had fallen to foreign invasion. It was to bolster his forces to retake Rome that Honorius withdrew the troops from Britain.

Britain had been part of the empire for three and a half centuries, the fabric of its government reliant on Rome's military support. This had provided stability for longer than anyone could remember. Now, suddenly, it was gone, and anarchy threatened the land. Every freeborn Briton had long been a Roman citizen, and few would have danced in jubilation on the beaches as the last boatload of soldiers disappeared over the horizon. You can imagine the turmoil: How many countries, even today, would remain intact and peaceful if all the police and armed forces suddenly disappeared? Precise records during this period of British history are few and far between, but an overall picture can be gleaned from Germanus, the bishop of Auxerre in Burgundy, who visited Britain in 429 as an envoy of the Catholic Church. According to his biographer, Constantius from Auvergne in modern-day France, writing around 480, "although there were serious troubles in the north, an organized Roman way of life persisted in the numerous British towns."[1] Even so, matters grew progressively worse, and over the following

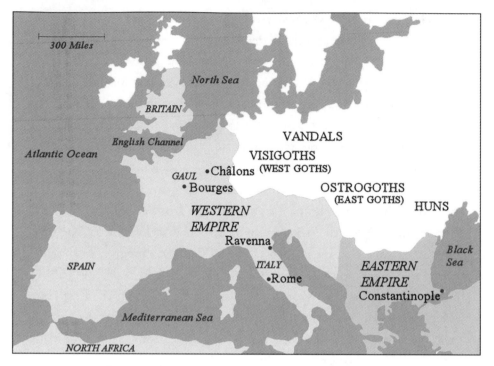

Fig. 7.1. The Western and Eastern Roman Empires
around AD 400.

decade, central administration seems to have collapsed. In many parts of the country, the Britons reverted to tribal allegiances, and local warlords soon established themselves as regional monarchs, setting up a number of separate kingdoms. With continual territorial squabbles, the island slid inexorably into chaos and the Dark Ages.

In these troubled times few records were kept, and almost none have survived for us to examine today. The principal reason that so little is known of this period of British history is that the break from Rome removed Britain from the field of Mediterranean writers from whom we acquire much of our earlier information. It is therefore far from certain exactly what took place during the mid-fifth century. There is, therefore, considerable academic disagreement about post-Roman British history. For the rest of this chapter, we will often find ourselves in the realm of historical detective work. So, to be accurate, I will be describing the events as I personally came to interpret them from my research. Accordingly, rather than merely outline what seems to have occurred, it is important to say *how* I—or anyone else for that matter—reconstructed mid-fifth-century British history. Principally there are the historical sources, which are records, writings, and other documentation composed *closest* to the time being investigated, as opposed to primary sources, which are works contemporary with the events described. Unfortunately, no written works survive from mid-to-late fifth-century Britain, so the historical sources in this case were compiled sometime later. They do, though, appear to be based on earlier material committed to writing closer to or during the period in question. Other than Welsh tales and poems and fragments of other British war sagas—a number of which we have already examined—the key historical sources are limited to the works of the British monks Gildas and Nennius, the Saxon historian Bede, together with the *Welsh Annals* and the Anglo-Saxon Chronicle. As these Dark Age writings will play a crucial part in our examination of the case for Arthur's historical existence, it is well worth providing a brief summary of them here.

- Gildas, who lived from around 500 to 570, was a British monk from a monastery in Glamorgan in South Wales. He wrote a Latin work around the year 545 that concerned the late fifth and early sixth centuries titled *De Excidio et Conquestu Britanniae* (On the Ruin and Conquest of Britain). (The oldest complete copy of Gildas's work is kept in Cambridge University Library in England, where it is cataloged as MS Dd. I.17.)[2]
- Nennius, as we have seen, was a monk from Radnor, in what had been the kingdom of Powys, now in west-central Wales. His dates of birth and death are unknown, but he is attributed with having written a Latin work titled the *Historia Brittonum* (The History of the Britons), compiled from both legendary and earlier historical sources around AD 830. (The *Historia Brittonum* is preserved in the British Library, London, in a manuscript cataloged as Harleian MS 3859.)[3]

- Bede, or the Venerable Bede as he is often called, was yet another author monk. Unlike Gildas and Nennius, he was Anglo-Saxon, coming from a monastery at Jarrow in northeast England. He lived from 673 to 735, and in 731 finished his Latin *Historia Ecclesiastica Gentis Anglorum* (The Ecclesiastical History of the English People). This work transformed the rough framework of existing material from ecclesiastical documents into an actual history book. (The earliest copy of the *Historia Ecclesiastica Gentis Anglorum* is in the National Library of Russia, in St. Petersburg, cataloged as lat. Q. v. I. 18.)[4]

- The Anglo-Saxon Chronicle, written in Old English (the Anglo-Saxon language), was not composed by a sole author but was a collection of Anglo-Saxon monastic records brought together into a single manuscript between the years 871 and 899 under the supervision of the English king Alfred the Great. It lists events in Britain from 449 to Alfred's time in chronological order, prefixed with the relevant year AD. Later copies of the Anglo-Saxon Chronicle included further events up until the time of their writing. (The oldest copy of the Anglo-Saxon Chronicle is in London's British Library, where it is cataloged as Cotton MS Tiberius B.i, f. 128.)[5]

- The *Welsh Annals*—or *Annales Cambriae* in the original Latin—is a register of events from 447 to 954 compiled from records kept at Saint David's Cathedral in southwest Wales. It is not a detailed record by any means but rather a chronological list of dates coupled with brief notations of significant events that occurred in each year, accompanied by an appendix of genealogies of certain Dark Age royal families. Despite its name the document not only concerns events in Wales but throughout the British Isles. It is thought to have been committed to writing in its present form around 954, as this is the last year recorded. (The *Welsh Annals* is preserved in the same manuscripts as Nennius's *Historia Brittonum* in Harleian MS 3859 in the British Library, London.)[6]

Plate 1. Glastonbury Abbey in southwest England, where twelfth-century monks claimed to have discovered King Arthur's grave. Photo by Deborah Cartwright

Plate 2. The ancient ruins of Tintagel Castle in the English county of Cornwall, the traditional birthplace of King Arthur. Photo by Deborah Cartwright

Plate 3. The London Stone, said to have been the very stone from which the young Arthur pulled his sword of power. Photo by Deborah Cartwright

Plate 4. The isolated pool known as Coventina's Well near Newcastle. Its once revered waters preserved vital secrets concerning the Lady of the Lake. Photo by Deborah Cartwright

Plate 5. Roman altar stone in Chesters Museum, near Newcastle, showing the water goddess Coventina, the original Lady of the Lake in British mythology. Photo by Deborah Cartwright

DEDICATION TO THE GODDESS COVVENTINA BY TITUS D. COSCONIANUS, PREFECT OF THE FIRST COHORT OF BATAVIANS. THE GODDESS HOLDS A WATER LILY LEAF IN HER RIGHT HAND, AND WATER FLOWS FROM A PITCHER BY HER LEFT ELBOW

RIB 1534

B90 CH267

CARRAWBURGH, COVENTINAE WELL 1876

Plate 6. Inscribed relief from Chesters Museum, depicting the three Celtic water nymphs that may have inspired the Arthurian theme of the queens of Avalon. Photo by Deborah Cartwright

RELIEF OF THREE WATER NYMPHS, HOLDING BEAKERS AND POURING WATER FROM PITCHERS. IT MAY ORIGINALLY HAVE COME FROM THE SHRINE DEDICATED TO THE NYMPHS

CARRAWBURGH, COVENTINAE WELL 1876

CSII

Plate 7. The remains of Hadrian's Wall in the far north of England. This astonishing seventy-mile-long Roman structure was the northern border of Arthur's Britain. Photo by Deborah Cartwright

Plate 8.
Reconstructed
Roman fort of
The Lunt, near
Coventry. This was
the typical style of
fortification used at
the time Arthur is
said to have lived,
around AD 500.
Photo by
Deborah Cartwright

Plate 9. The Dark Age hill fort of Dinas Bran in central Wales, the resting place of the Grail in the Welsh Arthurian tradition. Photo by Deborah Cartwright

Plate 10. Valle Crucis Abbey, where the 1500-year-old story of King Arthur was preserved by monks to survive to this day. Photo by Deborah Cartwright

Plate 11. Whittington Castle in the English county of Shropshire, the Grail Castle depicted in the Arthurian romances of the Middle Ages. Photo by Deborah Cartwright

Plate 12. The Pillar of Eliseg near Llangollen in north-central Wales. Its Dark Age inscription revealed the bloodline of the historical King Arthur. Photo by Deborah Cartwright

Plate 13. Caer Ddegannwy towers above the coast of North Wales. On this impregnable rocky outcrop stood the fort of the historical Uther Pendragon, King Arthur's father. Photo by Deborah Cartwright

Plate 14. The ruins of Viroconium in central England, the capital of early Dark Age Britain. The last functioning Roman city in the country, it may have been the inspiration for the legendary Camelot. Photo by Deborah Cartwright

Plate 15. View from the northern end of Lake Bala in central Wales. It was here, in a seventh-century monastic community, that the manuscript was composed to reveal the true identity of the historical King Arthur. Photo by Deborah Cartwright

Plate 16. Warwick Castle, one of the locations believed during medieval times to have been the magnificent citadel of Camelot. Photo by Deborah Cartwright

Plate 17. The winding River Camlad in Shropshire, as seen from Shiregrove Bridge. According to ancient Welsh tradition, this was the scene of Arthur's last battle and his death. Photo by Deborah Cartwright

Plate 18. St. Illtyd's Church at Llanhilleth in southern Wales, the burial site of the seventh-century poet Heledd, the British princess whose writings finally revealed the whereabouts of King Arthur's lost tomb. Photo by Deborah Cartwright

Plate 19. The ancient earthwork known as The Berth in Shropshire, central England. Could this be the true final resting place of the historical King Arthur? Photo by Deborah Cartwright

From these historical sources we can reconstruct a general outline of mid-fifth-century Britain. Although specific details are often lacking, the basic picture appears to be that the north was suffering repeated incursions from the Picts of Scotland, while the West was being partially invaded by the Irish, but the greatest problems for the majority of the Britons were due to the struggle for regional supremacy between their own native chieftains. And it was into this beleaguered and fragmented country that the Anglo-Saxons came.

Because of the attack by the Huns on the Goths, there were mass migrations westward right across Europe—an unprecedented domino effect that ultimately destroyed the Western Empire. As a result of this general move westward, coastal dwellers from what is now North Germany began to cross the North Sea to settle in eastern Britain. These people were the Angles from what is now Schleswig-Holstein, the northernmost state of modern Germany, and the Saxons to the immediate south of them, from what today would be the coastal north of the German state of Niedersachsen. Initially, these migrants settled just the coastal areas: the Angles in the east and northeast, and the Saxons in the southeast. There may have been local skirmishes with these newcomers, but rather than attempt to repel them, the British chieftains began to enlist their services as mercenaries to fight not only the Irish and Picts but also each other. Payment included land on which they could settle. (Ironically, this is exactly the kind of deal the Anglo-Saxons themselves later made—with disastrous consequences—with the Vikings who began to arrive in Britain in the late eighth century. But that's another story.)

From what can be gathered from the historical sources, by the mid-fifth century one British chieftain organized a massive new influx of Angles and Saxons, additionally recruiting a people known as the Jutes from modern Denmark, settling entire tribes in parts of the east and southeast of what is now England. Bede and the Anglo-Saxon Chronicle give the year of this considerable Germanic immigration as 449, an event that early historians refer to as the Saxon Advent. (By the late Dark Ages, *Saxons* was the term applied to the Anglo-Saxons as a whole [see chapter 3]. Strange really, as Angles would seem to be more appropriate: ultimately, the united Anglo-Saxons referred to their country as *Engla Land,* "Land of the Angles," from where the modern name England comes.) Archaeology supports the Dark Age sources regarding these migrations. For example, distinctive Angle-style pottery, unearthed during excavations in the northeast and east of England, reveals that the Angles began settling in what are now the counties of Yorkshire, Lincolnshire, Norfolk, and Suffolk around the year 450. The same applies to the Saxon settlements in what is now the county of Essex, and the Jute settlements in the county of Kent, both in the southeast, where characteristic styles of their pottery have been found.[7] During the 1990s, when I was first investigating the Arthurian tradition, the primary method of dating pottery was by ceramic sequencing. Ceramic sequences are chronological lists of ethnic earthenware styles: their fashion and techniques of manufacture change over the years, and the dating of a particular trend is made possible by datable items found alongside such objects unearthed at other sites. These days, a scientific method called rehydroxylation dating is also used, which can chemically estimate how long ago a ceramic artifact was fired (hardened in the kiln). It is accurate to within around thirty-five years either way, and by testing a number of samples of pottery, tiles, or bricks, a more precise date can be determined. Using such a technique, modern estimates agree with the dating of the Saxon Advent made by ceramic sequencing of the early Angle, Saxon, and Jute pottery finds.

As a consequence of the ambitious British chieftain employing huge numbers of foreign mercenaries, a large part of Britain came under his control. Gildas calls him simply *tyrannus,* Latin for "absolute ruler," Bede uses the Latin name Vetigernus, while the Anglo-Saxon Chronicle and Nennius call him Vortigern. Yes, the same man who was allegedly helped by the young Merlin. We know from references such as the inscription on the Pillar of Eliseg (see chapter 6) that Vortigern was king of Powys, but with the help of his overseas allies, he seems to have become pretty much the king of all Britain for a while.

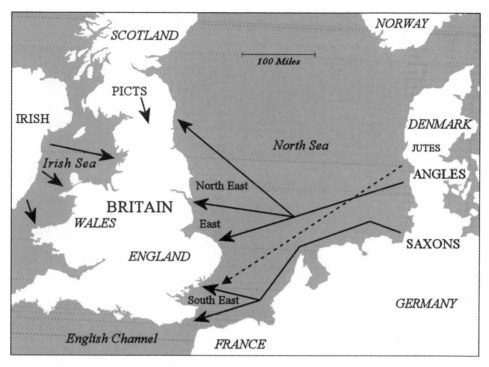

Fig. 7.2. The invasions of Britain
in the mid-fifth century.

In many ways the Angles, Saxons, and Jutes were closely related, the area from which they originated being no larger than modern Wales. For most purposes, therefore, the term *Anglo-Saxon* can safely be applied to the entire culture, including the Jutes, who soon after their arrival lost their individual identity and merged with the Saxons in Kent.[8] Indeed, the differences between them were tiny compared to the massive cultural gulf separating them from the Romanized British, many of whom were practicing Christians (albeit in a peculiarly Celtic way, see chapter 5). The pagan newcomers had their own religious customs, which the majority of the Britons would probably have found abhorrent. In Roman terms the Britons were civilized, the Anglo-Saxons were barbarians. With such a culture gap, problems were bound to arise. And they did.[9]

Trouble began around 455, when the Saxon colonies in the southeast revolted against their British overlords. There were doubtless many reasons for the rebellion, although Gildas informs us it arose over a question of payment for the mercenaries. He provides no details but does explain the severity of the insurgence, saying that cities were destroyed and their British inhabitants killed, enslaved, or forced to flee.[10] Bede gives the same account, although he adds the names of the revolutionary leaders: two brothers called Hengist and Horsa. The Angles in the north also joined the rebellion. Bede writes that they swapped sides, formed an alliance with the Picts, and attacked the Britons.[11] The extent of any overall organization of the Anglo-Saxon revolt is difficult to ascertain; what is certain is that the Britons were completely unprepared. The rebellion appears to have begun with the Saxon overthrow of a British contingent in the extreme southeast of England, which the Anglo-Saxon Chronicle records for the year 455. It was a crucial turning point in the history of post-Roman Britain, as the successful revolt saw the establishment of the first Saxon kingdom in the country: the kingdom of Kent, after which the modern county is named. The Chronicle also tells us that Horsa died in the conflict, leaving his brother Hengist as king, and that Vortigern's general, his son Cateyrn, also died in the conflict. The Saxon victory and the disarray of the British forces in the area immediately prompted a wider revolt throughout the southeast. The Britons were routed, and the Saxons set up other kingdoms: Essex (meaning "East Saxons"), to the north of the River Thames, and Middlesex (Middle Saxons), around London. Southeast England was firmly under Saxon control. To the immediate north the Angles quickly followed suit, seized even more land, established their own kingdoms—Suffolk (South Folk, from the Germanic *fulka* meaning "tribe"), and Norfolk (North Folk), both still lending their names to the modern counties of those districts— and pushed west into what is now the county of Cambridgeshire. In the northeast, with the help of their Pict allies, the Angles also seized a huge area, reaching as far south as the modern county of Lincolnshire.[12] By 460 virtually the entire eastern part of Britain was in Anglo-Saxon hands. The fate of the British leader Vortigern is something of a mystery, but he seems to have been overthrown by his own people. Nennius, who is the only source to provide any details of Vortigern's demise, tells us that he was so hated by the Britons for inviting in the Anglo-Saxon mercenaries that he was deposed, forced to flee, and "wandered from place to place until . . . he died without honor."[13]

Gildas and Bede both relate how something of a stalemate then transpired for about a decade. It is reasonable to assume that this occurred sometime from around 465, as the Chronicle (Anglo-Saxon Chronicle) lists no battles between 465 and 473. The two monks explain how this relatively peaceful period gave the Britons time to gather strength, also that they found a new and altogether different kind of leader: a smart, military strategist called Ambrosius. This is the same man who as a boy found favor with Vortigern and, going by what Nennius and Geoffrey of Monmouth reveal, seems to have been the man behind the legend of Merlin. If this is right, then the wise old Merlin had once been a mighty warrior.

The eight-year period between 465 and 473 seems to have allowed the native British to reorganize their forces. Of this time, Bede says that "the Britons began by degrees to take heart, and gather strength." He attributes this to Ambrosius's leadership: "They had at that time for their leader, Ambrosius Aurelius, a modest man, who alone among the Romans had survived the storm."[14] (The "storm" referred to the Anglo-Saxon rebellion.) Gildas also explains that Ambrosius was the man responsible for strengthening the Britons, and like Bede, he describes him as a Roman, "a gentleman who perhaps alone of the Romans had survived."[15] We shall examine the Merlin connection shortly, but for now we need to establish exactly who this Ambrosius Aurelius was.

Well, for a start, he seems to have been a Roman. However, that Gildas and Bede both refer to Ambrosius as the *last* of the Romans is somewhat confusing. By the time the Roman legions departed Britain in 410, every freeborn Briton was a Roman citizen. It had been centuries since only inhabitants of Rome or even Italy had been exclusively referred to as Romans; even many of the later Roman emperors had originated from places outside Italy, such as Spain, Africa, Syria, France, and even Britain, to name just a few. The Roman Empire had been an ethnic melting pot. Although by the 460s Britain had not been a part of the Roman Empire for half a century, the Western Empire still existed, and there were probably many people in Britain, especially among the more privileged classes, who continued to regard themselves as Romans, particularly the Christians. So why refer to Ambrosius as the last of the Romans? The answer seems to be that the authors regarded him as the last of the Roman elite. Gildas tells us that Ambrosius's "parents had worn purple," which was the color special to the Roman emperors.[16] Something Bede also makes clear when saying that Ambrosius's parents "were of the royal race."[17] So Gildas and Bede seem to be telling us that Ambrosius was a distinctly high-status Roman, descended from an emperor. Nennius provides us with additional information. When the young Ambrosius first meets Vortigern, the king questions him concerning his background, and the boy answers: "A Roman consul was my father."[18] Nennius offers no date for the episode, but by cross-referencing the events he describes with the other sources, it would seem to have been set somewhere around the year 450, and just four years earlier there had indeed been a Roman consul with the same family name: one Quintus Aurelius.

During the time of the Roman Republic, a consul was the highest elected political office (Julius Caesar had been one), but by the fifth century it was merely an honorary position by appointment of the emperor. There were usually two consuls who served for just one year, but though officially something akin to modern vice presidents, in reality they had no actual power. Very few consuls inherited imperial office upon the death of their emperor. Well, not for long—particularly as there were two of them, plus a number of far more powerful generals who wanted the job. Quintus Aurelius is recorded as having been consul in Rome in 446, and since there hadn't been an Aurelius as consul for over half a century, Quintus was presumably Ambrosius's father that Nennius had in mind.[19] This would also fit with what Gildas and Bede say about his ancestor seemingly being an emperor, as the powerful Aurelius family was descended from Marcus Aurelius, who reigned from 161 to 180. He was an especially respected ruler, who was also a scholar, writer, and philosopher: the "good emperor" portrayed by actor Richard Harris at the start of Ridley Scott's blockbusting movie *Gladiator.*

When I first proposed that Ambrosius was a member of this imperial line, some scholars questioned my theory, saying that there was no archaeological evidence that members of the Aurelius family had ever settled in Britain. But in 1992, later in the very same year that my book *King Arthur: The True Story* was published, they were proved wrong. On November 16 the biggest single collection of Roman gold and silver artifacts ever discovered in Britain was unearthed in a field near the village of Hoxne in the county of Suffolk in eastern England. Known as the Hoxne Hoard, it consisted of almost fifteen thousand coins, and around two hundred items of exotic tableware and jewelry, which are now on display in London's British Museum. Archaeologists established that these valuable treasures had been buried in a box sometime during the early fifth century—probably by the fleeing Romans, in the hope of later recovery, when the Angles raided the area—and many of them were inscribed with the family name Aurelius.[20]

So there was a consul named Aurelius who was alive at just the right time to have been Ambrosius's father, and members of the Aurelius family had been in Britain by the early 400s—shortly before Ambrosius appears on the scene. Who Ambrosius was and that he historically existed can be in little doubt. The first encounter between Ambrosius and Vortigern is, it seems, partially legend, but that the two met and that Ambrosius succeeded Vortigern as king, or at least some kind of overlord of the tribal chieftains of Britain, is also fairly certain. Not only does Nennius say that after Vortigern's death Ambrosius became "the Great King among the kings of Britain," but he also had the authority to appoint Vortigern's surviving son Pascent as ruler of provinces in the west.[21] Moreover, his leadership of the Britons is confirmed by both Gildas and Bede (see chapter 7).

Other than this we know very little about Ambrosius's period of leadership. Gildas says simply that under him the British regained strength and "battled their cruel conquerors,"[22] while Bede says virtually the same: "the Britons revived and offered battle to the victors."[23] (Note that Gildas, a Briton, refers to the Anglo-Saxons as "cruel conquerors," whereas Bede, an Anglo-Saxon, calls them the "victors.") Ambrosius's forces seemed to have first advanced deep into the occupied southeast: as the Chronicle says they fought against Hengist, the Saxon king of Kent. However, the Britons were beaten back, as an entry in the Chronicle for the year 473 states that "Hengist and his son Oisc fought against the Britons and captured innumerable spoils, the enemy fleeing from them as they would from fire." From the archaeological evidence, it seems that the Saxons pushed along the Thames Valley, as far west as the modern county of Berkshire. The Britons seem to have held the advance at this stage, demonstrated by the defensive earthworks they built (see pp. 130–31), and there appears to have been an uneasy standoff in the southeast for the next decade.[24] The war then shifted to another front, in both the north and east, against the Angles. (The campaigns against the Saxons and Angles might actually have been fought simultaneously, as we shall examine in the next chapter.) Here the fighting appears to have gone very much in favor of the Britons. Archaeology indicates a renewed British presence throughout the entire northern part of England and in the east, in the modern counties of Cambridgeshire and Lincolnshire. The evidence, for example, are distinctive British ceramics and modes of burial recurring here from this time.[25] So how exactly did Ambrosius manage so successfully against the Angles? Where, for instance, did he get such well-trained warriors to do the job, when just a few years earlier the Britons had been an incompetent rabble? His advance seems to have occurred in the mid-470s, and this coincides precisely with the end of the Western Roman Empire. Was there a connection? Let's see how the Western Empire finally collapsed.

From now on, for convenience sake, I will refer to the Western Empire as the Roman Empire, as Rome had been its capital; it was also where the Roman Catholic Church was administrated and the pope was based. For all intents and purposes, it is the only one of the two empires that has any direct bearing on our investigation into King Arthur. Similarly, I shall refer to the Eastern Empire as the Byzantine Empire. This was actually the term applied to it many years later—named after its capital, Constantinople (modern-day Istanbul in Turkey), which was originally known as Byzantium—but it makes things much easier. (Incidentally, although the Byzantine Church was originally Catholic, it became what we now call the Eastern [or Greek] Orthodox Church.)

This, then, is how the "Roman Empire" finally ended. By the mid-440s the Huns, who started the barbarian invasions by moving west from the Ukraine, had pushed through the Goth regions of Germany and crossed the Rhine into Roman Gaul (which included modern France, Belgium, and Luxembourg, as well as parts of the Netherlands and Switzerland). Led by their infamous, fearsome leader Attila, the Huns devastated everything in their path. Ultimately, the Romans formed an alliance with the Visigoths and eventually defeated Attila at the Battle of Châlons in northeast France in 451. The man who led the joint army to victory was the Roman general Flavius Aetius, who became so popular that the emperor Valentinian III saw him as a threat to his power and murdered him in a fit of jealousy three years later. On March 16, 455, Valentinian was himself assassinated by two of Aetius's officers to avenge their general's murder. If one single act could be said to have been the death knell for the Roman Empire, it was this. Valentinian had been emperor for thirty years and was just about the only thing holding the empire together. Within days of his death, civil war erupted between various claimants to the imperial throne, leaving the empire totally exposed. Just eleven weeks later Rome itself fell to a Germanic tribe called the Vandals (originally from what is now Poland), who pillaged and sacked the city so brutally that their name has become synonymous with acts of mindless carnage. The emperor's widow, the empress Licinia, and her daughters were raped and dragged away into slavery, and those who failed to flee the city were butchered in the streets. The Roman Catholic hierarchy, however, managed to survive. The resourceful pope, Leo I, managed to negotiate a safe passage for the Church leaders from the city, and the papal administration returned to Rome once the Vandals had moved on.[26]

Extraordinarily, even the sacking of the ancient capital failed to bring the warring Roman factions together. Throughout Europe various commanders assumed the title of emperor and fought each other to a standstill while the Goths, Vandals, and other Germanic tribes surged between the last of the Roman legions, plundering towns and cities as they went. The Roman civilization that had dominated Western Europe for centuries crumbled to ruins in a matter of months. Roman Italy held together for a few years, while a general named Ricimer tried to save the empire by installing a series of puppet emperors at the new capital of Ravenna on the Adriatic coast, 170 miles northeast of Rome. Ricimer, who was actually half Visigoth, effectively ruled what remained of the empire from 456 until his death from natural causes in 472. However, his authority did not extend much outside Italy; northwestern Europe beyond the Alps had collapsed into chaos, though scattered Roman forces continued a valiant but futile struggle. With the powerful Ricimer gone, a succession of weak emperors came and went over the next three years, until 475 when a general named Flavius Orestes assumed control of the empire—now pretty much just Italy—and appointed his twelve-year-old son Romulus as a puppet emperor. Orestes spent the next ten months fighting the Goth king Odovacer, who eventually defeated him at Piacenza in northern Italy. With the campaign lost Orestes was swiftly executed. A few weeks later, in the fall of 476, Ravenna was captured, Romulus was deposed, and Odovacer appointed himself king of Italy. Odovacer was in no way what the Romans called a barbarian, and he was nothing like the brutish Vandals. Being a Christian, he allowed the Roman Catholic Church to survive, and he spared the life of the boy emperor. Romulus, or Romulus Augustulus (Little Majesty) as he is sometimes known, was sent to live comfortably in a villa in southern Italy. All the same, the Roman Empire—the Western Empire that is—was complexly finished.[27]

It was at this very time that Ambrosius appears to have gone on the offensive against the Angles. The mounting of his victorious campaign into Angle-held territory, and the muscle to hold the gains and construct huge defenses (see p. 130–31), implies that he commanded the kind of professional force that had previously not existed in post-Roman Britain—a properly trained and equipped army. Where did it come from? Because of the final collapse of the Roman Empire at this time, the troops may well have come from across the English Channel. During the last few years of the empire, although Gaul was in a state of chaos, various contingents of the Roman army scattered across the province attempted to hold their ground against the various Germanic tribes. By the end of 476, once there was no longer an empire to fight for, what happened to these forces? They may simply have dispersed or changed sides, but it seems likely that some, at least, made for the north coast of France and escaped to Britain.

In his *De Origine Actibusque Getarum* (The Origin and Deeds of the Goths), the Byzantine historian Jordanis, writing in Constantinople during the mid-sixth century, records that a sizable Roman force led by a general named Riotimus had a direct link with Britain in the 470s. He tells us that "Riotimus came with twelve thousand men to the land of the Bituriges." This was an area around modern Bourges in central France. All did not go well, however, because "Euric, king of the Visigoths, attacked them with a vast army and after a prolonged struggle routed Riotimus." Riotimus managed to retreat to the area occupied by an adjacent Germanic tribe allied to the Romans. This seems to have occurred in 472, as Jordanis refers to the death of the emperor Anthemius who died in that year. What happened to Riotimus after this is unrecorded, but Jordanis tells us that he had retreated with "all the men he could gather," so he may still have had a sizable army. What's interesting is that Jordanis refers to Riotimus as *Rex Britannorum*—King of the Britons.[28] Clearly Riotimus could not have been the overall king of the Britons; all the British sources suggest that Ambrosius was the overlord or principal king of Britain at this time. But, as we have seen, Britain was divided into many regional kingdoms by the 470s, so Riotimus could have been king of one of these. Jordanis, however, was writing almost a century later and close to fifteen hundred miles away. He, or his source, can be forgiven for some minor confusion. In fact, although Jordanis suggests that Riotimus was a British king when he led the Roman forces, he may not actually have become such until later.

It's only speculation, but it is possible that by the time the Roman Empire finally collapsed in 476, Riotimus and his surviving army made their way north and crossed the English Channel into the less hostile Britain—at least the parts of it controlled by Ambrosius. Jordanis also implies that the twelve thousand men originally under Riotimus's command had themselves come from Britain to aid the struggle in Gaul. This is certainly most unlikely. Twelve thousand men would be more than two entire legions! A legion consisted of approximately five thousand soldiers. If there had still been two functioning Roman legions in Britain in the 470s, then the Anglo-Saxons would probably have been kicked out of the country altogether. It had only taken four legions for the Romans to conquer and occupy the whole of Britain in the first place. It is a far more reasonable assumption that these twelve thousand troops were what survived of the bulk of the Roman army in Gaul. A possible scenario is that the remnants of this army arrived in Britain to aid Ambrosius, and that Riotimus himself was established as a king in a particular region, perhaps the retaken areas of eastern England.

Whoever they were, archaeology certainly supports the fact that a functioning Roman army was present in Britain during the mid-470s. Distinctive Roman military items have been found at British defenses from this period. Long stretches of earthen bank and ditch fortifications were constructed in the mid-to-late fifth century by the Britons in the eastern and southern parts of England. The Britons were known to have dug ditches, called linear defenses, along embankments facing Anglo-Saxon occupied regions, to impede attack from that side. (These embankments were often pre-Roman earthworks, modified at this time.) An interlinked series of such linear defenses

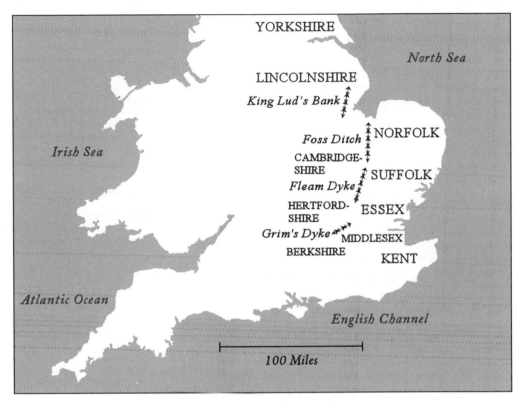

Fig. 7.3. British linear defenses of the 470s.

include: Foss Ditch and Fleam Dyke, which respectively cut off much of Angle-occupied Norfolk and Suffolk from the British west; King Lud's Bank, in the modern county of Lincolnshire, that prevented fresh incursions inland; and Grim's Dyke to the northeast of London, which separated Saxon Middlesex from British-held Hertfordshire. In effect, these earthworks confined the Anglo-Saxons to the central east and southeast of England. Such defenses would, of course, be useless unless they were patrolled, and from the 470s those guarding them appear to have been Roman soldiers. Evidence of Roman armor being worn by these defenders are such items as military buckles, clasps, and hobnails from Roman boots, unearthed at archaeological excavations at these sites and dated (by ceramics found alongside them) to the mid-to-late fifth century.[29] This was over half a century since the Roman army officially left Britain, and after the Roman Empire in the west had totally collapsed. Accordingly, a considerable Roman force of some kind must surely have come from continental Europe to join Ambrosius when the empire ceased to exist.

So, by around 480 the Anglo-Saxons were confined to the southeast and east, and the Britons were firmly in control of the rest of the country. And the man in overall control of the Britons was Ambrosius, the historical figure who appears to have been behind the Merlin legend. We are now very close to the period that Arthur appears on the scene, with Merlin—in the medieval romances, at least—as his trusty advisor. Before finally coming to examine the historical evidence for King Arthur's existence, we need to know how Ambrosius, the "last of the Romans," British high king, and mighty general, became the fabled wizard of legend.

8

Merlin the Bard

Ambrosius Aurelius was almost certainly a historical figure. But was he the real Merlin? To answer this question let's start with a brief outline of the story of Merlin as related by authors of the Middle Ages.

One thing that might not be known to younger readers, familiar with the popular TV series *Merlin,* is that in the traditional Arthurian saga, Merlin and Arthur are not portrayed as being of the same generation. When Arthur ascends the throne, Merlin is an old man. In fact, he is already quite old during the reign of Arthur's father, Uther Pendragon. (One way to envisage the Merlin of the medieval romances is something like Gandalf in *Lord of the Rings*.) Having the gift of prophecy and knowledge of the mystic arts, Merlin is Uther's advisor. A once good king of the Britons, Uther Pendragon eventually brings the nation to ruin through his lust for Igraine, the wife of Gorlois the Duke of Cornwall. Civil war ensues between the king and the duke, during which Gorlois is killed and Igraine becomes Uther's queen. With the country in turmoil, the disillusioned Merlin leaves the court, stealing away with the infant Arthur, Uther and Igraine's newborn son. After leaving the baby to be brought up in secret by the trusty Sir Ector, Merlin disappears into the wilds where he remains for many years, dwelling for a time on the Isle of Avalon where the Lady of the Lake forges Excalibur on his request. Meanwhile, Uther dies and Britain languishes without a king, beset with internecine strife and harassed by foreign invaders. When Arthur comes of age and pulls the sword from the stone, Merlin returns to reveal the youth to be Uther's son and rightful heir to the throne. Merlin then becomes King Arthur's mentor and helps him unite the kingdom. He takes the new king to the Lady of the Lake to receive Excalibur, then oversees the building Camelot and establishes the knightly Order of the Round Table. When Arthur falls sick and pestilence plagues the realm, the wise old wizard inaugurates the quest for the Holy Grail to cure the king and heal the land. Ultimately, Britain is again drawn into civil conflict, after a rebellion led by Arthur's treacherous nephew Modred. Before the rivals fight to the death at the Battle of Camlann, Merlin departs in dismay, ultimately ending his life as a forest-dwelling hermit, driven mad by the tragic plight of the Britons.

This, in essence, is the account of Merlin's life as it appears in the medieval Arthurian romances. There are various renditions that include additional anecdotes, such as Merlin's love affair with the Lady of the Lake and his feud with Morgan le Fey, and some include the episode where the young Merlin encounters Vortigern at Dinas Emrys, but the central theme adhered to by all the authors is that Merlin is not only a learned councilor but also a prophet, poet, and magician. The first author known to have portrayed Merlin in the role as Arthur's royal mentor is Geoffrey of Monmouth in the mid-twelfth century, but he appears in older Dark Age literature under the original Welsh rendering of the name Myrddin (pronounced "Merthin"). However, in these narratives he is not associated with Arthur but acts as advisor to various other British chieftains. If the later romancers took their storylines of Merlin as the real power behind King Arthur's throne from earlier Welsh sources, then these have not endured for us to examine today: the surviving Welsh tales appear to concern only Merlin's later life, after Arthur's death. Like Merlin in the medieval romances, Myrddin of Welsh literature is depicted as a mystic, although in this case he is said to be a bard.

The medieval story of the boy Merlin meeting Vortigern was undoubtedly based on the legend of the young Ambrosius: we have seen how Geoffrey of Monmouth refers to the episode, as did Nennius in the early ninth century, and that here the youth in the incident is identified as Ambrosius. But it is not only with Nennius that we find Merlin and Ambrosius linked as the same person. In chapter 6 I mentioned how the shortened form of the Latin Ambrosius is Ambrose (just as Marcus is Mark, and Antonius is Antony), and that the Welsh rendering of Ambrose is Emrys. (Nennius himself explains that Ambrosius was known as Embres in the language of the Britons, so we can see how the name evolved from Ambrose in Latin, to Embres in Brythonic, to Emrys in Welsh.[1]) It is under this name that Ambrosius is included in early Welsh literature—for example, in two of the Welsh triads (see chapter 6), the *Three Skillful Bards* and the *Three Disappearances*—where he is referred to as *Myrddin* Emrys: in other words, Merlin Ambrosius.[2] So we have confirmation that early Welsh authors considered Ambrosius and Merlin to be one and the same. Furthermore, they all suggest that at some point he became a bard; the *Three Skillful Bards,* for example, relates that Myrddin Emrys was one of the three most distinguished bards in Britain. As we saw in chapter 5, Dark Age bards were not only poets but were attributed with prophetic, healing, even magical powers. Moreover, some acted as advisors to the British kings. Accordingly, they were regarded pretty much as Merlin is in the romances of the Middle Ages. To place him in a historical context of post-Roman Britain: for "Merlin the Magician" we should perhaps read "Merlin the Bard." Regardless of any associations with King Arthur, literary scholars are divided on the subject of the Myrddin of Welsh tradition as a historical figure. Was he, they ponder, a real or fictitious Dark Age bard?

One particular manuscript suggests that he had indeed been a real-life individual. *Lly du Caerfyrddin* (The Black Book of Carmarthen) is a collection of early Welsh works compiled into one volume during the early thirteenth century, but many of the poems in the manuscript have been dated to very much earlier. Now preserved in the National Library of Wales (where it is cataloged as Peniarth MS 1), The Black Book of Carmarthen contains two poems that appear to have been composed in the sixth century: "The Greetings" and "The Apple

Trees," which are said to have been composed by Myrddin himself.[3] They both involve a battle at a place called Arfderydd in northern England, after which the author claims to be living as a hermit in a nearby forest. Another, seemingly contemporary poem in the manuscript, titled "The Conversation of Myrddin and Taliesin," concerns Myrddin and another bard discussing this same battle. First, these works all imply that the romance Merlin was based in part on the Myrddin of the poems: he is living a reclusive forest existence, having lost his mind, exactly like the Arthurian Merlin. Second, they suggest that Myrddin was a historical figure: the Battle of Arfderydd appears to have been a genuine event, as it is recorded in the *Welsh Annals.* In fact, the *Welsh Annals* actually records Myrddin in reference to this battle: "The Battle of Arfderydd [in the kingdom of Rheged in northwest England] . . . in which Gwenddolau fell and Myrddin went mad." (Gwenddolau was king of Rheged.) However, there's a big problem. The date given for the event is 573. If this Myrddin was alive in the period Arthur is said to have lived, he would have to have been well over a hundred years of age. Okay for a fabled Arthurian wizard, I suppose, but not very likely in reality.

The Arthurian theme of Merlin ending his life insane as a hermit in a forest does indeed fit with the Myrddin recorded in The Black Book of Carmarthen. And he is someone who, going by the *Welsh Annals,* was a historical figure. However, this forest-dwelling Myrddin could not have been associated with a real King Arthur. Ambrosius, on the other hand, lived in the right era to have been an elderly man during Arthur's time. (Ambrosius seems to have been a boy of about ten when he meets Vortigern around 450, which would make him say thirty around 470 when he became leader of the Britons. Accordingly, if still alive, he would be about fifty when Arthur first appears on the scene sometime around 490: a reasonably old man for a Dark Age Briton.) It would seem, therefore, that the medieval Merlin was a composite character based on two separate figures with the same name that lived a hundred years apart. Welsh literature usually refers to the later of them as Myrddin *Wyllt* (the Wild) to avoid confusion.

The question that aroused my interest was why Ambrosius, evidently of Roman Italian lineage, had been called Myrddin. Myrddin is obviously a Brythonic rather than a Latin name, although nothing survives to directly reveal its derivation. It's possible that Ambrosius assumed a British name to appeal to the native Britons. However, there seemed to be more to it. The only people recorded with the name Myrddin during the early Dark Ages were all bards. Besides Myrddin Emrys and Myrddin Wyllt, old Welsh literature, such as the *Three Skillful Bards,* records another bard bearing the name during the sixth century: Myrddin, son of Madoc Morvryn. He is the subject of two works in The Red Book of Hergest (see chapter 6): *The Conversation of Myrddin and Gwenddydd,* a poem about the bard and his sister, and *The Lament of Myrddin in his Grave,* which purports to be the bard's dying words.[4] So in the period of one century, three illustrious bards all shared the same name. Could it have been a title of some kind? Like Ambrosius, Myrddin Wyllt also seems to have adopted or been given the name Myrddin as an epithet, as it does not appear to have been his birth name. He is recorded in a work written in the mid-1100s by a monk called Joceline from Furness Abbey in Scotland. Preserved in a manuscript cataloged as the Cotton Titus A. XIX in the British Library, Joceline's *The Life of Kentigern* refers to a mad, reclusive bard who lived in a forest on the English-Scottish border in the late sixth century.[5] As he is said to have been driven insane after witnessing the slaughter at the Battle of Arfderydd, this is clearly a reference to Myrddin Wyllt. However, Joceline does not call him Myrddin but Laleocen (pronounced "Lailoken"). I ultimately concluded, therefore, that Myrddin was probably an appellation given to a chief, or perhaps the leading bard of the time.

As far as I was aware, no Arthurian researchers had previously worked out what the name Myrddin actually meant. However, in The Red Book of Hergest, I found a poem called "The Prophesy of the Eagle," in which, although Myrddin is not mentioned by name, the speaker (the one doing the prophesying) appears to be the same forest-dwelling recluse in the other works concerning Myrddin Wyllt.[6]

Accordingly, Myrddin Wyllt is the eagle referenced in the title. It is, then, possible that Myrddin means "eagle"? Eagle is *eryr* in modern Welsh, but this derived from the Middle English *egle,* so would not have been the older Brythonic word for the bird, which is actually unknown. The Celts were fond of giving important individuals the epithet of an animal, usually representing their disposition, stature, or prowess. For example, the Irish saint Columba was called *Colm Cille* (Church Dove), for his gentleness; Maelgwn, an important Welsh chieftain, was known as *Maglocunus,* the Great Hound, for his size; and the warrior queen Boudicca was known as *Llewes,* the Lioness, for her ruthlessness in battle. By the same token the title "the Eagle" may have been bestowed on a leading bard, as the bird was associated with foresight and prophecy. In fact, such animal titles were often inherited. For example, the Celts also used mythical beasts as honorary titles, and the best known of them has to be the Welsh Dragon, still depicted on the national flag of Wales. It was originally the emblem of the kingdom of Gwynedd in North Wales (whose influence eventually extended throughout much of the country) and was derived from its kings who held the title "the dragon," which was passed on to successive rulers.[7] Likewise, Myrddin could have been a title for the head bard handed down through the sixth century: from Ambrosius, to the son of Madoc Morvryn, to Laleocen. One way or the other, it is the first of them that concerns us here. He is the only one who might have been a contemporary of a historical King Arthur.

As discussed, in post-Roman Britain bards were not only poets but were thought to possess prophetic insight, were renowned as healers, and were regarded as having magical powers. So how come a king, or at least the supreme commander of the British forces, ended up being portrayed as a bard? None of the Dark Age historical sources reveal what happened to Ambrosius the warrior. By the late 470s Ambrosius had done a fantastic job uniting the British kingdoms, neutralizing the Pict and Irish threats, and confining the Anglo-Saxons to the extreme east and southeast of England. But then he simply disappears from record. He is not referenced again by Nennius; the *Welsh*

Annals don't mention him at all, while Gildas and Bede provided no details of the next couple of decades, other than a single line each. According to Gildas, "at times our countrymen and at others the enemy triumphed in the field."[8] And according to Bede, "sometimes the natives and sometimes their enemies prevailed."[9] This might seem strangely vague, but we have to appreciate that these two authors were both monks, writing primarily about ecclesiastical matters, and military events took something of a secondary role in their narratives. The Anglo-Saxon Chronicle is different, as it was compiled to an extent to celebrate the invaders' triumphs in battle.

Although the Chronicle fails to refer to Ambrosius by name, we can gather that regardless of his achievements in uniting the various British factions against the invaders in the mid-470s, he seems to have been waging a losing struggle. Despite their initial successes the British forces were slowly being whittled down, whereas the Saxons could count on reinforcements from Germany. The Anglo-Saxon Chronicle records that in the year 477 a new wave of Saxons arrived in southern England, led by a man named Ella. They landed at a place called Cymenshore, believed by historians to be Selsey in the modern county of West Sussex, driving the Britons inland. Ella's forces continued to advance over the next few years, defeating the Britons at the Battle of Mercredesburne in 485, thought to be a pre-Saxon fortification known as Town Creep near the village of Ashburnham in modern East Sussex, and taking the Roman town of Anderida (modern Pevensey) in 490, which appears to have been the British capital of the region. By this time the Saxons had secured control over a large area and founded the kingdom of Sussex (South Saxons), from which today's counties of East and West Sussex get their names, with Ella as its first king. According to the Chronicle, in 495 a new influx of Saxons arrived farther west, landing near modern Southampton almost halfway along the southern coast of England. Although their leader Cerdic died in battle with the Britons, the Saxons won, and his son Cynric established a new kingdom in the area, later to be called Wessex (West Saxons). So although the Britons seemed to have retained control of the north and west of Britain, by the 490s the Anglo-Saxons had not only consolidated their hold on the southeast, they were also advancing inexorably westward.[10]

As Ambrosius is not so much as mentioned during this period, we can only assume that he was either dead, or had for some reason abdicated, retired, or been removed from office. If he was still alive to become the inspiration for the Arthurian Merlin, then obviously it was not the first of these possibilities. The historical sources do not reveal directly who led the Britons at the time. Historians generally assume that with Ambrosius no longer in command, British unity fell apart, and the regional kingdoms reverted to autonomy and territorial squabbling, which would certainly explain the renewed Anglo-Saxon success. However, according to the medieval Arthurian romances, the Britons did eventually elect an overall leader: Uther Pendragon. None of the pre-romance sources refer to Uther Pendragon, but there was, I discovered, a historical figure upon whom he may have been based. Like Myrddin, the name Uther Pendragon seems to be a title. Remember how the kings of Gwynedd in north Wales bore the title the dragon. Well, in Welsh the word *uthr* (pronounced "oo-ther") means "terrible," as in mighty, and the word *pen,* means "head," as in leader. So *Uthr Pen Dragon* means "Terrible Head Dragon." Surely this could not be coincidence. The romance Uther Pendragon might, it seemed reasonable to suppose, have been based on someone who had been chieftain of the kingdom of Gwynedd in North Wales.

The oldest known king of Gwynedd was one Enniaun Girt (meaning "the Impetuous"). Enniaun (pronounced "Ennion") is recorded in the genealogies attached to the *Welsh Annals*—known as the Harleian genealogies—as the son of a mercenary named Cunedda who came from northern Britain to help repel the Irish.[11] This was probably by invitation of Vortigern in the mid-fifth century, at the same time as he had recruited aid from the Anglo-Saxons. Gildas, writing around 545, refers to his contemporary king of Gwynedd as a powerful ruler named Maelgwn, while the Harleian genealogies also list Maelgwn as ruler of Gwynedd, recording him as the grandson of Enniaun. Accordingly,

Fig. 8.1. Locations discussed in the search for Merlin.

Enniaun, two generations earlier, would appear to have reigned during the late 400s, either at the time Ambrosius was supreme commander or immediately after. The Gwynedd kings certainly bore the title the dragon by the early sixth century, as Gildas refers to Maelgwn by that very appellation,[12] and we also know that the title was inherited. We saw above how throughout the Dark Ages the kingdom of Gwynedd extended its influence widely in Wales, its leaders continuing to use the dragon epitaph, which eventually became the dynasty's emblem and which still survives as the red dragon depicted on the Welsh national flag. So it seemed to me a reasonable assumption that Enniaun would previously have held the title. If he was indeed the first king of Gwynedd, he was presumably the first to bear the name. (Incidentally, according to Geoffrey of Monmouth, Uther gained his epithet Pendragon, after the appearance of a huge comet in the shape of a dragon, which inspired him to use the dragon as his emblem on flags, banners, and shields.) My conclusion: if any historical figure had been called *Uthr Pen Dragon*—the Terrible Head Dragon—immediately before Arthur's time, then it would be Enniaun Girt.

Besides Uther Pendragon the early medieval romances also include Ambrosius Aurelius, the first author to interpolate him by that name in the Arthurian saga being Geoffrey of Monmouth (although he calls him Aurelius Ambrosius). However, in Geoffrey's twelfth-century work, he is depicted as a separate character to Merlin, as he is by the Arthurian authors who followed his lead. In my opinion, however, he was clearly wrong. Recall, Geoffrey asserts that Merlin had been the psychic boy brought before Vortigern, while Nennius—three hundred years earlier—records precisely the same episode, identifying the youth as Ambrosius. By the 1300s Ambrosius had obviously been confused as two separate figures: Ambrosius Aurelius and Merlin—understandably, as Ambrosius was a warrior king while Merlin was a wizard. But, as we have reasoned from both Nennius and early Welsh literature, Merlin and Ambrosius Aurelius were originally considered to be one and the same. We have to remember that in Geoffrey's time the various historical sources available to us today would still have been scattered throughout various uncataloged and uncollated manuscript collections all over the British Isles. During the twelfth century there was certainly much confusion concerning post-Roman British history. Some things Geoffrey got right; others he got completely wrong. One example of a glaring inaccuracy is in reference to Ambrosius's parentage. According to Geoffrey, Ambrosius's immediate predecessor as king of the Britons was his brother Constans, the son of a British king called Constantine. Constans, he tells us, had been a monk, but on the death of his father, he was persuaded to leave his monastery and accept the crown. Geoffrey is right in as much as such a man really existed. The Roman emperor Constantine III had a son called Constans; ordained a monk, he reluctantly gave up the cloth to become emperor when his father died. However, neither had anything to do with Britain, and Constans died in 411, over half a century before Ambrosius's time,[13] besides which we have seen how Ambrosius was almost certainly the son of the consul Quintus Aurelius. So Geoffrey's confusion concerning Ambrosius and Merlin as two separate characters fits with his handling of other historical figures of the late and post-Roman eras.

Returning to Uther Pendragon, in his *History of the Kings of Britain* of 1136, Geoffrey depicts Uther as ruling Britain immediately after Ambrosius. According to Geoffrey, Ambrosius was poisoned by the Saxons; although, as we have seen, none of the older sources reveal how or when Ambrosius died. So Geoffrey's assertion that Ambrosius was succeeded by Uther, who was in turn succeeded by Arthur, became the version of events adopted by the subsequent medieval romances. Uther, therefore, is envisaged as having reigned somewhere around 480. And this is precisely when Enniaun Girt was king of Gwynedd. Whether he succeeded Ambrosius as high king of the Britons, if indeed they had one at all during this time, is unknown. However, it is certainly possible. By the time Gildas was writing, Enniaun's descendants ruled much of western Britain, suggesting that he had been a particularly powerful and influential king (see chapter 9). When I was researching all this back in the early 1990s, no one had previously identified a plausible contender for a historical Uther Pendragon. Nor have they since, as far as I can tell. So, as there is no historical record of anyone with the personal name Uther, or anything like it, having lived in the late fifth century, I stand by my original conviction: if Uther was based on anyone who really existed, then Enniaun Girt is by far the most likely candidate.

The big question I had to address next was: How did Ambrosius the warrior become Merlin the bard? As noted, what ultimately happened to Ambrosius Aurelius is a historical unknown. However, if he were one and the same as Myrddin Emrys, then he must have retired as overall British commander. He might have been injured, ousted, or was simply too old to continue. It was only guesswork, but I reckoned that he was no longer in office by 477, as in this year the Anglo-Saxons renewed their advance. Enniaun may have taken over right away or at some point over the next few years, with Ambrosius, now known as Myrddin, acting as royal advisor. With his experience it would make sense for him to act as royal councilor on military and political matters, but what about him reemerging as a mystic? Again just a guess, but perhaps unable or unwilling to continue as a warrior, Ambrosius had some kind of epiphany and took up the calling as a bard. If so, he would not be alone. Throughout the world there are many historical examples of warriors, princes, and kings abandoning their former lives to seek enlightenment, or to become gurus, shamans, and monks: the knight Galgano we encountered in chapter 3, to name but one. If so, then what would being a bard have actually entailed?

By the later Dark Ages, with the adoption of the strict practices of the Roman Catholic Church in Britain, bards had become relegated to mere poets. They were often paid by a high-status individual, usually a regional chieftain, to compose poems praising their patron's virtues and achievements—the reason being that few Dark Age warlords or their courtiers, let alone the common people, could read or write. Even if they could, there was very little to write on. Parchment manufacture was virtually nonexistent in early Dark Age Britain. So to get your propaganda across, you needed someone to compose poetry that could be remembered and recited by others: hence the need for bards. However, although this was one function of the bards in the fifth and sixth centuries, before the reintroduction of Catholic Christianity in the seventh century, they were also regarded as healers, prophets, and wonder workers. As such they were employed by various British kings as advisors. For example, during the late sixth century, the bard Aneirin was advisor to King Urien of Rheged, a kingdom in northern England, and in the mid-sixth century the bard Taliesin similarly served the kings of Powys: Brochwel and his successor Cynan (pronounced "Cun-an").[14] Likewise, in the late fifth century, Ambrosius may have been councilor to a historical Uther Pendragon—perhaps Enniaun of Gwynedd—and subsequently to King Arthur.

If Ambrosius, under his new bardic title Myrddin (possibly meaning "the Eagle"), was advisor to a Gwynedd king, then his training as a bard probably took place at the aptly named Bardsey Island, meaning literally "Island of Bards," some two miles off the coast of the Llyn Peninsula in western Gwynedd. Various Dark Age poems and tales refer to it as the burial site of important holy men and women and the last resting place for hundreds of British bards. After a monastery of the Celtic Church—the quasi pagan-Christian religion followed by the post-Roman Britons (see chapter 5)—was founded there in 516, a cross was erected to celebrate the twenty thousand saints said to be buried on the island: the early Celtic Christians referred to the bards as saints. (The original cross no longer survives, but a medieval replacement still exists today.) This is clearly a gross exaggeration, but it does demonstrate how closely Bardsey Island was associated with the bardic tradition during the period Merlin is thought to have lived. We have seen how the bards, like their druid forbears, used sacred islands as the locations for sanctuaries, similar to monasteries, where they lived in seclusion to learn and observe their practices, so Bardsey Island is the most likely location in Gwynedd for a new bard to be trained.

Sadly, precisely what such training involved has gone unrecorded. Or at least nothing has survived in writing for us to examine today. We do, however, know something about the ancient druids (thought to derive from an ancient Celtic word for "seer"), whose practices were probably similar. There can be little doubt that the bards were related to the earlier druids. The ancient Greek writer Diodorus Siculus, in his work the *Library of History* of 36 BC, referred to a druidic caste renowned as poets whom he calls the bardous,[15] as did the Greek historian Strabo in his *Geography,* written around AD 20,[16] which some linguists suggest meant "sacred speakers," which is almost certainly where the later name "bard" originated. As the pre-Roman Celts had no form of writing, their history, religion, even their practical skills, such as metallurgy and agriculture, had to be committed to memory. For this reason, certain members of a tribe were chosen to be trained in particular memory techniques, which included rhyming and poetry as aids to recall. These special individuals were not only the librarians of Celtic culture, but they were also the actual "libraries." The poems and sagas they kept in their heads were the archives of the civilization's knowledge and history. When the Romans brought writing to the Celts, these people soon became obsolete in that role. Although poetry and storytelling retained their prestige in Celtic society, it was the druids' function as priests and scholars that assumed precedence. There are a number of groups in Britain today calling themselves druids, such as those who perform ceremonies at Stonehenge on midsummer's day, but they can be traced back only to the eighteenth century when it became fashionable to form mystical societies and reenact ancient rites. Unfortunately, besides their poetic talents, little is known of the original druids. We are told, however, that they possessed remarkable powers of the mind. Just over two thousand years ago, Julius Caesar encountered the druids in Gaul, referencing them in his work the *Gallic War,* completed around 50 BC. He refers to them as a class of their own, who lived something of an exalted existence apart from the rest of society. They were not only priests, he explains, but also acted as judges, "determining awards and penalties," and were highly revered even by the ruling elite, as "all men move out of their path" when they approach.[17] Although Caesar was writing of the druids in Gaul, he tells us that they originated in Britain, where they still enjoyed a privileged status: "It is believed that their rule of life was discovered in Britain and transferred hence to Gaul; and today those who would study the subject [druidism] journey to Britain to be trained."[18] (This was a century before the Romans invaded Britain.)

Caesar goes on to provide a tantalizing insight into this training. For instance, he tells us they mastered sophisticated memory techniques,[19] what we might now call mnemonics: aids to recall, such as rhyming verse, acronyms, and allegories, as well as complex visualization techniques, like those employed by modern mentalists to remember the order of multiple packs of playing cards or recite astonishing lists of numbers. The druids, it seems, were also astrologers, philosophers, and naturalists, all these disciplines being taught in isolated sanctuaries that were off limits to the general population. Caesar's contemporary, the Roman writer Cicero in his *On Divination,* recorded additionally that they were skilled in the art of premonition and were renowned as healers with knowledge of herbal remedies and human physiology.[20] In many ways, it seems, druidic instruction was not dissimilar to that of Tibetan Buddhism or Japanese Zen. When the Romans invaded Britain, they saw the druids as a threat to their authority and wasted no time in an attempt to eradicate them. However, if Dark Age Celtic poetry is to be believed, individual druids survived in secret as the bards. Once the Romans left, these shamanlike bards reemerged as both tribal court poets, to record and promote the exploits of kings, and to act as advisers on various affairs. Like the druids, they were also credited with the gift of prophecy and magical powers and were often referred to as *dewin,* the Welsh word for "wizard."

It was another guess, but I decided that Ambrosius may have spent some years being trained as a bard, perhaps on Bardsey Island, before returning to act as councilor to the Gwynedd king Enniaun, sometime around 480. Whether or not three years' training would be sufficient to fully qualify as a bard is unknown. We do know from Julius Caesar that the ancient druids were chosen as children and underwent many years of instruction, but times had changed. What is interesting, though, is that if there is any truth in the legend that the young Ambrosius was considered to have some kind of psychic abilities when he first met Vortigern, then he may have been considered eligible for fast tracking, particularly considering his former status as a ruler and military commander.

There was, I decided, enough circumstantial evidence to suggest that Merlin and Uther Pendragon were based, to some extent at least, on the historical Ambrosius Aurelius and Enniaun Girt. Obviously, I doubted that Merlin made magic potions, such as that which the romancers say he used to make Uther look like the Duke of Cornwall, or encountered dragons, had swords forged with supernatural powers, fought witches, or obtained chalices that could cure all ills, but during the early Dark Ages, such matters were clearly not beyond belief for people of the time. As a bard, a historical Merlin may well have been endowed with talents that would have appeared magical: knowledge of herbal medicines, military and political foresight based on long experience, and a phenomenal memory. He may even have performed what we would today call hypnosis and administered hallucinogenic substances obtained from plants; both of which he could have utilized to amaze his compatriots and terrify his rivals. Perhaps his contemporaries did imagine they saw dragons, or thought they could shapeshift, with a little help from Merlin's bag of tricks. Merlin's powers aside, there was one thing I was certain about: I had gathered enough evidence to home in on a specific part of the British Isles to best concentrate my search for the historical figure at the very heart of the legend—King Arthur himself. This was the part of what are now England and Wales that had once been the kingdoms of Gwynedd and Powys.

- The original Grail motif, in the form of the head of Bran, seems to have been associated with Dinas Bran in the kingdom of Powys.
- Vortigern has his power base in Powys, and the Pillar of Eliseg recorded him as a Powys king.
- According to Nennius, Ambrosius, seemingly the historical Merlin, first made an appearance as a young boy at Dinas Emrys, on the borders of Powys and the kingdom of Gwynedd.
- Arthur's wife Guinevere (at least one of them) is said to have come from Caer Ogyrfan in Powys.
- Uther Pendragon, if he were indeed based on a historical figure, seems to have been a king of Gwynedd. By the same token, if Merlin was Uther's councilor, then he too would appear to have lived in Gwynedd after his reign as Ambrosius.

All these conclusions I had extrapolated from Dark Age historical sources and Welsh literature that preceded the medieval Arthurian romances by centuries. The authors of the Middle Ages may have decided that Arthur came from the south or southeast of Britain, but the writers of these much earlier works clearly associate the Arthurian events with the kingdoms of Gwynedd and Powys—an area that covers what are now north and east-central Wales and west-central England. It was here that I would now focus my search for a historical King Arthur.

9

A Historical Figure?

Before continuing with our investigation in the area of Britain that once comprised the adjacent kingdoms of Gwynedd and Powys, we need to directly appraise the case for Arthur's existence. In the first chapter I said that even before I began my search for his final resting place, I had compelling reason to believe King Arthur had been a historical figure. It is time to elucidate. I have left it until now, because to appreciate my reasoning requires knowing something about the period in which Arthur is said to have lived; for example, the Roman occupation of Britain, the fall of the Western Empire, and the political and military upheavals in both Europe and the British Isles during the fifth century. We would also need to have examined the Anglo-Saxons and the Celts, the division of Britain into separate kingdoms, where these kingdoms were, who ruled them, and so forth. By the time we got round to considering evidence specifically concerning Arthur himself, we would be halfway through the book. Instead, I have now covered such relevant background material while recounting my search for the man behind the legend, just as it occurred. Furthermore, we have also explored the various themes within the Arthurian saga, discovering how, when, and why they emerged, preparing us to address the principal argument *against* King Arthur as a historical figure. So before presenting the case for him having been a real living person, let's evaluate the case for the opposition.

The way I see it, the essential reason most skeptics refuse to believe

King Arthur could possibly have existed is that the tales about him are just too unbelievable. In which case, they would argue, why bother searching for *any* truth behind the Arthurian legend? Consequently, merely to associate your name with such an investigation is enough to prompt scorn in academic circles, which is why many historians, archaeologists, and literary scholars tend to steer clear of the subject altogether. (Indeed, this is one of the main reasons that the true origins of the legend remained uncovered for so long.) The skepticism is quite understandable. Initially, the story of King Arthur seems completely fictitious. It includes mystical items, such as the Holy Grail, Excalibur, and the sword in the stone, and fabulous themes, such as Avalon, the round table, and Camelot; and there are mythical beings, such as wizards, water nymphs, and dragons. However, one by one, we have seen these seemingly fanciful elements removed as a reasonable argument against Arthur's existence. Often we have found such themes to have derived from genuine Dark Age traditions, characters, and events. For example, the round-table notion might have derived from the Celtic practice of chieftains and their leading warriors sitting in a circle so that feuding over precedence could be avoided; the Isle of Avalon and its nine guardian maidens seem to have arisen from the Celtic practice of sacred lake islands occupied by nine priestesses; and the casting of Excalibur to the Lady of the Lake probably originated with the custom of a votive offering to an ancient water deity. All these traditions existed around AD 500, so it is hardly surprising to find them interpolated into tales of a prominent British leader who lived at that time. The same applies to various characters in the Arthurian saga having Dark Age mythological counterparts: for example, Morgan le Fey and Mórrígan, Guinevere and Gwenhwyfar, and the Grail guardian Bron as the legendary hero Bran. They were all incorporated within mythology as it existed during the period Arthur is said to have lived. And we have also discovered that some of the key players in the saga, such as Merlin, Uther, and Vortigern, were almost certainly based on real people who lived in the right place and at the right time to have been associated with a genuine King Arthur's life.

Even the dragons can no longer be seen as a reason to dismiss Arthur as a historical figure.

The tale of the two dragons Merlin is said to have released from a cave under Vortigern's fort at Dinas Emrys originated with a legend concerning Ambrosius that existed centuries before the medieval romances were composed. In fact, the legend related by Nennius might even have been based on an actual event, not involving real beasts, of course, or even drug-induced hallucinations, but on the discovery of a historical relic. In his narrative Nennius uses the terms *dragons* and *serpents* when referring to the creatures: "The two serpents are two dragons," he says at the end of the anecdote. Today the word *serpent* generally means "snake," but in Nennius's time it also meant a mythical snakelike creature with legs and wings that breathed fire: in other words, a dragon. Dragons came into British mythology from the Romans, who took the concept from the Greeks. (The Greeks had adopted the idea from the Persians, via India, and originally China.) The confusion between the word for snake and dragon came about because the Greek word *drákōn,* from which the Latin and Brythonic words *draconem* and *draig* derived, meant both "dragon" *and* "snake."[1] The Dinas Emrys dragons, described this time as "serpents," appear in an early Welsh tale called *Lludd and Llefelys,* preserved in The Red Book of Hergest.[2] It actually explains how they came to be where they were: the two serpents, the tale relates, were originally hidden in the Dinas Emrys cave by one King Lludd, a legendary character who is said to have ruled Britain before the Romans came. Interestingly, these serpents were not huge fire-breathing dragons as we might imagine, but small enough to be placed in a cauldron, so presumable little more than a couple of feet long. They weren't even living beasts, according to the Welsh triad, *The Three Concealments.*[3] This poem specifically refers to the twin serpents as a sacred relic. The "concealments," we are told, were the head of Bran, the bones of a saint, and "the dragons which Lludd son of Beli buried in Dinas Emrys." All three were said to be talismans to ward off invasion. In other words, the two serpents were some kind of artifacts. They may even have been a single figurine of some kind, depicting intertwined serpents.

In Welsh legend Lludd was the last high king of Britain before the Romans invaded. It's doubtful the Britons had such a supreme leader at the time—the Romans certainly don't refer to one—but during the fifth century the tradition existed that Lludd had been a real king. Judging by Welsh literature, at the time Ambrosius lived this legendary king was considered to have long ago united the country. Presumably, therefore, the young Ambrosius, being the one to find Lludd's twin serpents, implied that the boy was destined to reunite and lead the Britons in their struggle against foreign invasion. The double-serpent motif is found elsewhere in the Arthurian saga with regard to Arthur's sword. Its earliest description is found in a Welsh tale preserved in The Red Book of Hergest, *The Dream of Rhonabwy,* which describes the sword as having "a design of two serpents on the golden hilt."[4] In the medieval romances, Excalibur was Arthur's symbol of authority. Accordingly, something decorated with twin serpents is Arthur's verification as king, just as the two dragons found by the young Ambrosius attest to his future leadership. This suggests that Lludd's talismans may, like the sword, also have been a single item bearing similar ornamentation. But why this particular design? The answer seems to be that the twin-serpent motif had been the emblem of a chief god of the ancient Celts.

According to Julius Caesar in his *Gallic War,* the Celts "worship principally the god Mercury, having many images of him."[5] He goes on to say that the deity was believed to guide them in battle and grant them great influence and acquisitions. As we saw in chapter 5, the Romans usually equated foreign deities with their own, such as Minerva being the name they used for a British water goddess. As such, Caesar is using the god Mercury as the nearest equivalent in the Roman pantheon to this particular Celtic deity, although the Celts would have called him by another name that is now unknown. An apparent depiction of this god survives in the decoration on a silver cauldron found in a peat bog near Gundestrup, Denmark, in 1891. The so-called Gundestrup Cauldron is a bowl thought to have been used for ceremonial purposes. Dating to the first or second century BC, it was made by the Celtic people who migrated to Denmark from

Gaul. A number of mythological images are depicted on the cauldron, but one panel appears to show the chief Celtic god. He is sitting in a kind of half-lotus position with his eyes closed as if meditating; on his head he wears an antler headdress, and in one hand he holds a huge serpent.[6] This representation of the deity makes it clear why Caesar would have associated him with Mercury. In Roman art Mercury was depicted with a winged helmet, similar to the antler headdress of the Celtic god, and he held a serpent wand. Mercury's wand was a short rod with two snakes entwined around it. Known as the *caduceus,* it symbolized, among other things, unity. The motif of two serpents said to have decorated Excalibur's hilt probably had the same meaning as the dragons, or more likely a twin-serpent talisman, said to have been uncovered by Ambrosius. They symbolized British unity: their owner was the fated overlord of the Briton's chieftains and kings.

As seen, the Arthurian legend seems to have had its roots in the area once encompassing Gwynedd and Powys, and there is persuasive, historical evidence that the first of these kingdoms already had the dual serpent as its tribal emblem well before the late fifth century. The *Notitia Dignitatutm* (Register of Dignitaries), a Roman document illustrated with military insignia compiled in the early 400s, includes a picture of a shield bearing the insignia of two crossed serpents.[7] The accompanying text identifies it as the crest of a military "regiment" called the *Segontienses Auxilium Palatinum* or Segontium Imperial Support Unit in English. This unit, consisting of around a thousand men, was comprised of British soldiers enlisted to patrol the area that later became the kingdom of Gwynedd.[8] (The city of Segontium, modern Caernarfon, was the regional capital.) Such auxiliary troops, being made up of local people, often adopted the region's tribal emblem as their unit's insignia. The dual serpent was therefore probably the emblem of the Deceangli tribe, native to northwest Wales. In conclusion, like many of the other Arthurian themes that at first appear purely imaginary concepts, the Dinas Emrys dragons have a firm, historical foundation in the post-Roman era.

Having examined the seemingly fanciful themes contained in the

Arthurian saga, we can now appreciate that contrary to making a case for refuting Arthur as a historical figure, they actually help bolster it. They nearly all seem to have been based on genuine historical or mythological matters contemporary with the period Arthur is said to have lived. Rather than being medieval fables, they have authentic post-Roman counterparts that might easily have surrounded an important British leader who lived around AD 500.

One final issue regarding the case against Arthur as a historical figure concerns the anachronous setting for the events. The Arthurian romances, written between the mid-twelfth and mid-fifteenth centuries, depict Arthur as a medieval king: he fights with a lance and broadsword, is surrounded by knights in shining armor, and lives in a Gothic castle. However, if the action took place around AD 500, as these stories imply, then the entire scenario would have been very different. Arthur's warriors would certainly not have been "knights," as both the term and the institution of such honored fighting men did not exist much before 1100; neither would they have worn the kind of elaborate plate armor we normally associate with the Knights of the Round Table, as it wasn't invented until the period during which these stories were composed. Weapons like the mace, the jousting lance, the longbow, and the broadsword, often seen in romantic Arthurian paintings, movies, and TV shows, weren't developed until the later Middle Ages either. Soldiers of the early Dark Ages would have had late Roman-style clothing and armaments: lighter swords, short-range bows, slow-to-load crossbows, and chainmail and leather for protection—though unlike the earlier Roman army, helmets would have been a rarity, reserved for the elite. Even such reasonably equipped soldiers were few. As Britain was in a state of turmoil and Roman-type civilization had virtually collapsed, steel making and weapon manufacture had been reduced to little more than cottage industries, meaning that most native Britons went into battle with no protection at all, beyond a wooden shield, and armed with a simple spear or farm implements adapted for the purpose. The great castles with thick stone walls, battlements, turrets, moats, and drawbridges were also features of the later Middle Ages. Fortifications in post-Roman Britain would have been wooden stockades, built atop earthen ramparts, surrounded by ditches.[9] Such glaring inaccuracies, skeptics argue, make the entire Arthurian story completely implausible. Not at all: medieval writers simply had limited knowledge of the early Dark Ages.

Although the medieval Arthurian romances were based on earlier Dark Age accounts and traditions, they were set against a background of life, morality, religion, social status, and warfare as it existed at the time of writing during the Middle Ages. Accordingly, warriors were knights, chieftains were kings, bards were wizards, forts were castles, and so forth. Medieval authors had no idea what ancient times were really like. All they had to go on were written and oral accounts concerning the purported actions of Arthur and his contemporaries, with no detail regarding their life and times. It was a good few centuries after the romances were composed before scholars learned what we now know about the Roman and post-Roman eras. Just take a look at any medieval painting of the Crucifixion, for example, and you will see the participants dressed in the clothing contemporary with the period of the artist. Even in the late 1500s, Shakespeare's plays concerning the ancient world are filled with anachronisms: in *Julius Caesar* and *Antony and Cleopatra,* for instance, the stage sets depicted Gothic castles and Tudor mansions, while actors performed the part of Roman dignitaries in the costume of Elizabethan courtiers. Murals, mosaics, and sculptures did survive from the Roman era, but there were few to be found in Britain before the advent of archaeology in the nineteenth century. Even such works of art that survived in plain sight in mainland Europe could not be put into any kind of historical context until after the collapse of the Byzantine Empire in the mid-fifteenth century, when Roman historical records found their way into Western Europe (see chapter 7). And it was not until two centuries later that Western scholars finally began piecing ancient history together.

It was on such grounds that I had already addressed the case for disregarding King Arthur as a historical figure. What reason, however, had

I to believe the legend was based on a real-life individual? To begin with, there was the historical context. Arthur is said to have been a powerful leader who united the Britons against the invading Anglo-Saxons in the late fifth or early sixth centuries. Even if there had never been a man named Arthur, someone who precisely played this role around the year AD 500 did certainly exist.

In chapter 8 we examined how, after the time Ambrosius led the Britons in the 470s, both the archaeological and historical evidence reveals that the Anglo-Saxons were on the offensive again in southern England. The Anglo-Saxon Chronicle records new Saxon invasions in the modern counties of West and East Sussex and in Hampshire.[10] In alliance with the Saxons in the southeast—in today's counties of Kent, Middlesex, and Essex—by the mid-490s they were advancing northwest toward the modern counties of Wiltshire and Somerset. Gildas and Bede give no specific information concerning this period, other than to say that there were successes and failures on both sides. But then everything changed. The Chronicle records no Saxon victories between 495 and 508, except for an isolated skirmish on the south coast in which a British noble was killed. As noted, this in no way means that nothing was going on. The Anglo-Saxon Chronicle celebrated Anglo-Saxon victories and pretty much left out British accomplishments altogether. For example, it makes no mention of Ambrosius or his period of triumph over the invaders. In reality, it seems as though the Anglo-Saxons endured a crushing defeat at this very time. According to Gildas, who wrote within living memory of the events, the Britons achieved a crucial victory at a place called Badon Hill.[11] Even Bede, an Anglo-Saxon, concurs with this.[12] The very similar Baddon (pronounced "Bathon") was the Brythonic name for the city of Bath, leading many historians to conclude that the battle took place somewhere in that area, probably at a fort on Little Solsbury Hill, just outside the town. If this is right, then the battle was of extreme strategic importance. Bath is close to the English west coast, meaning that had the Britons lost, the British forces in central England and Wales would have been completely separated from their compatriots in the south and southwest. Divide and conquer, as the saying goes.

A precise date for the Battle of Badon—as it is usually referred—is difficult to determine. Gildas is the only source for establishing when it occurred. However, when he refers to the event, Gildas's Latin is somewhat confusing. His dating translates as: "And this happened, I know for certain, as the forty-fourth year, with one month now elapsed; it is also the year of my birth."[13] He tells us it occurred the year he was born, that much is clear, but the allusion to forty-four years is rather vague. Some historians consider it to mean that the battle took place forty-four years after the Anglo-Saxons were invited into Britain by Vortigern, something Gildas discusses earlier. Gildas gives no date for this particular event, but the Anglo-Saxon Chronicle records it as 449, which would mean the Battle of Badon occurred in 493. Others, however, interpret Gildas to mean that the battle occurred forty-four years before the time he was writing, which, based on the contemporary events described in his work, was in the mid-540s, dating Badon to AD 500, give or take a year or so. One way or the other, the Battle of Badon had to have been fought somewhere between around 493 and 503. It was certainly a significant turning point in the struggle between the two sides, as both archaeology and the surviving historical sources evince that the Saxons withdrew to the southeast for well over half a century. For example, the kingdom of Sussex, which had initially been so militarily successful, appears to have been completely eradicated by the Britons, as the Chronicle makes no further reference to it or its kings until it was reestablished one and a half centuries later, while archaeology has discovered no evidence of Saxon burials outside the southeast for almost the entire sixth century.[14]

All this implies that sometime during the 490s the Britons had, as during the period of Ambrosius's leadership in the 470s, again united behind a strong leader and successful military commander. The problem is that no inscription or contemporary source still survives to reveal who this was. Whoever this person may have been, he presum-

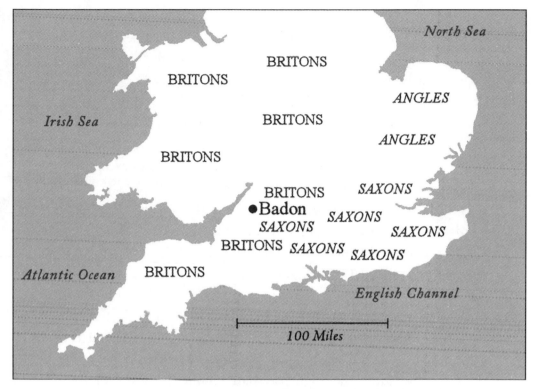

Fig. 9.1. Southern Britain before the Battle of Badon.

ably led the Britons at the Battle of Badon, but frustratingly Gildas fails to name him; neither does Bede. So there is a gaping hole in our historical knowledge concerning the important period around AD 500. The Britons clearly had a powerful, unifying leader who dealt a crushing blow to the Anglo-Saxons at the very time Arthur is said to have been just such a figure. If a man called Arthur did not exist, then someone who did exactly what he is said to have done certainly did. Arthur, however, was the only name linked to this battle during the Dark Ages.

Other than in the works of Gildas and Bede, the oldest surviving reference to the Battle of Badon is found in Nennius's *Historia Brittonum,* written around AD 830. The other two monks may not name the Briton's leader at the battle, but Nennius does—he identifies him as Arthur.[15] Actually, he lists twelve battles Arthur fought against the Anglo-Saxons, Badon being the last. You might think the fact that one of the chief literary Dark Age sources names Arthur in association with the battle would be reason enough for scholars to accept that he was probably a historical figure. However, Nennius's description of the battle, although brief, has been interpreted as legend rather than history. Nennius tells us: "The twelfth battle was on Mount Badon, in which nine hundred and sixty men fell in one day from one attack by Arthur, and no one overthrew them except himself alone."[16] Skeptics infer from this that Nennius was saying that only Arthur, and no other warrior, fought on the British side. In other words, he killed 960 Saxons all by himself. Conversely, the sentence can just as easily be interpreted to mean that Arthur was the only British *leader* involved in the fight: no other regional king or chieftain was involved, and it was Arthur's personal army that beat the Saxons unaided by others. As conflicts are so often described throughout history, the victors' leader is said to have prevailed: Julius Caesar conquered Gaul; George Washington defeated the British; Alexander the Great overthrew the mighty Persian Empire. It's just a figure of speech. None of these people did it all alone; when we write about them today, we are not implying they did. It is simply easier to say "Julius Caesar conquered Gaul" than "Julius Caesar and the Roman legions under his command conquered Gaul." Ancient historical commentators, no matter in what language they wrote, were no different from us. As far as I was concerned, the argument that Nennius's reference to the Battle of Badon was farfetched just did not hold water.

Another Dark Age historical source also mentions the Battle of Badon, again associating it with Arthur. The *Welsh Annals* contains the entry: "The battle of Badon, in which Arthur carried the cross of our Lord Jesus Christ on his shoulders for three days and three nights, and the Britons were victorious."[17] Skeptics have two main objections to this as evidence for Arthur's existence. First, it sounds ridiculous: a British general leading his troops while dragging around a huge wooden cross for three days. However, the phrase "carry the cross" meant, as it still does today, to keep the faith. The scribe was probably implying that it was Arthur's faith in the Lord that allowed him to prevail. The skeptics' argument got me thinking about a line from the nineteenth-century hymn "Keep Thou My Way." The phrase "gladly the cross I'll bear" has been creatively misheard as "gladly the cross-eyed bear." I found myself calling such pedantic arguments "the gladly syndrome." The gladly syndrome aside, the skeptics have another case for rejecting the *Welsh Annals'* Badon reference that requires greater consideration. It lists the battle for the year 518, seemingly much too late to have been the period of the event described by Gildas.

In its surviving form, the *Welsh Annals* was compiled around 954. It does not actually use the AD system of dating, which did not come into standard usage until the later Middle Ages. Instead, it starts with the year Vortigern first invited in the Anglo-Saxon mercenaries, calling this "year 1." It was a significant date, as it marked the so-called Saxon Advent, the beginning of much tribulation for the native Britons (see chapter 7). Bede, who did use the AD dating system, records the Saxon Advent as occurring in 447, so some historians infer this to be the *Annals'* year 1. The Battle of Badon is inserted in what the *Annals* record as year 72, so if the year 1 is 447, the year 72 is 518. However, the Anglo-Saxon Chronicle gives the year of the Saxon Advent as 449, which would mean that year 72 is 520, according to other historians. In fact, modern scholars have obtained additional dates for Vortigern's invitation to the Anglo-Saxons, and so various translations of the *Welsh Annals* provide different dates for the battle, fluctuating by a decade or so either way. Nevertheless, we have seen that, from both the historical and archaeological perspective, the Saxon Advent seems to have occurred around 449, so the *Annals'* year 72 does appear to be sometime in the late second or early third decade of the sixth century. In other words, the dating appears to be historically inaccurate. And if the dating is out by a couple of decades, the reference to the Battle of Badon is dubious, skeptics maintain. However, this does not necessarily follow. The evidently erroneous dating of the Battle of Badon in the *Welsh Annals* may well be due to the different chronology schemes employed during the Dark Ages. Some authors, like Bede, used the AD system, placing the year 1 at the birth of Christ, while others began year 1 at the Crucifixion. This actually resulted in more than just two dating systems, as scribes were uncertain as to when exactly Jesus was born or died. It was only later, after examination of second-century Roman texts, that a standard year for the Nativity was agreed.[18] During the period the *Welsh Annals* was compiled, the texts transcribed to form the work would no doubt have varied wildly regarding specific dating. It is hardly surprising, then, that the surviving *Annals* exhibits confusion regarding some of its chronology. Consequently, the *Welsh Annals* placing Badon too late to fit into a historical context is no reason to dismiss the chronicler's assertion that Arthur was the Briton's leader at the battle.

So where does this leave us? As discussed in chapter 7, the key his-

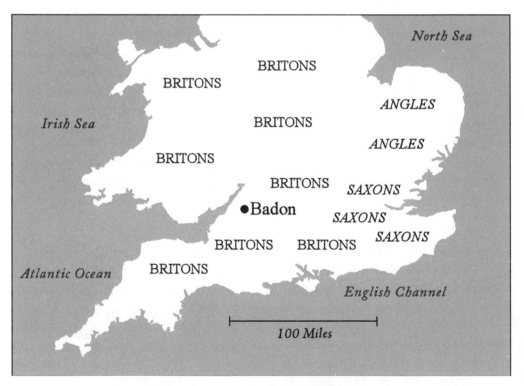

Fig. 9.2. Southern Britain after the Battle of Badon.

torical Dark Age sources covering Britain of the post-Roman period are limited to just five: Gildas, Bede, Nennius, the Anglo-Saxon Chronicle, and the *Welsh Annals*. As four of them reference the Battle of Badon, one of them written within living memory of the conflict, we can be fairly confident that it was a historical event. The only source that fails to mention it is the Anglo-Saxon Chronicle, which excludes almost entirely any success by the Britons. Of the four, two fail to say who led the Britons, while two say it was Arthur. As these historical sources associate no one other than Arthur with British leadership at the Battle of Badon, I decided that, on balance, it was a fair conclusion that he had been a historical figure. Indeed, closer examination of Nennius's work further convinced me that there was a real King Arthur behind the legend.

Skeptics have argued that Nennius should not be trusted as a reliable historian because he includes many purely mythological accounts in his narrative, such as the Britons being descended from the legendary Brutus of Troy (see chapter 2). However, in his history of Britain, Nennius usually includes details that prove remarkably accurate when compared with contemporary Roman accounts; for example, Caesar's attempted invasions of Britain in 55 and 54 BC. Nennius was simply transcribing earlier material he had at his disposal. He tells us this himself at the start of his narrative: "I have heaped together all that I found, from the annals of the Romans, the chronicles of the Holy Fathers . . . the writings of the Irish and the Saxons, and the traditions of our own wise men [the Britons]."[19] He is well aware that some of this material may be unreliable and apologizes: "I ask everyone who reads this book to pardon me for daring to write . . . I yield to whoever may be better acquainted with this skill than I."[20] He admits to be no expert historian, but feels he must preserve what he has compiled before it is lost to future generations. He leaves it to us to decide what is accurate and what is not. Although we should treat Nennius's work with caution, it includes much reliable history. Accordingly, certain of his accounts that cannot be collaborated, when unfettered by myth and elaboration, should not be dismissed out of hand—

such as the account concerning Arthur. Nennius simply, almost matter-of-factly, refers to Arthur as a warrior who led the Britons to victory over the Anglo-Saxons. He records when he lived and lists his battles, and that's it. There is no attempt to elucidate or make Arthur part of a larger or fanciful picture. On the contrary, he tells us frustratingly little: nothing concerning Arthur's origins, the location of his seat of power, or how, where, and when he died. All we really know comes down to a couple of lines.

> In that time the Saxons strengthened in multitude and grew in Britain. On the death of Hengist, Octha his son passed from the northern part of Britain to the kingdom of Kent and from him descend the kings of the Kent [he became Kent's king]. Then Arthur fought against them in those days with the kings of the Britons, but he himself was leader of battles. [21]

There is nothing fanciful about this passage. Quite the opposite: it fits perfectly into a historical context. We know that Hengist was a historical figure who enjoyed considerable success fighting the Britons in 473, just before Ambrosius went on the offensive (see chapter 7). We also know that Kent was a kingdom that remained firmly under Saxon control throughout the era. The Anglo-Saxon Chronicle repeatedly records Hengist as a king of Kent, although the year of his death is unknown. Octha is not mentioned in the Chronicle, but he too appears to have historically existed. He is named in an Anglo-Saxon genealogy contained in a manuscript cataloged as Cotton MS Vespasian B vi in the British Library, dating from around AD 810. Here Octha is recorded as a king of Kent under the Old English *Ocga Hengesting* (Octha, son of Hengist). It seems he was indeed Hengist's son as Nennius states. Nennius's assertion that Arthur began his fight against the Saxons at the time Octha succeeded to the Kentish throne makes perfect sense. Going by the Anglo-Saxon Chronicle and the genealogy in the Cotton Vespasian, this would have to have been in the late 400s, precisely the time Arthur is said to have come to power.

So there you have it. All this may not *prove* that Arthur historically existed, but it gave me, as I stated in chapter 1, good reason to regard him as an enigma worthy of further investigation. And that investigation had led me to the British kingdoms of Gwynedd and Powys.

10

Capital City

During the mid-to-late fifth century, Britain had a succession of influential leaders fitting the sequence of British kings portrayed in the Arthurian saga: Vortigern, followed by Ambrosius, followed by Uther (if he was indeed based on the historical Enniaun as discussed in chapter 8). By the mid-400s Vortigern, the ruler of Powys in central Britain, seems to have established his authority over many of the other British kingdoms, becoming high king, or *tyrannus,* as Gildas calls him in Latin, meaning "absolute ruler." In the 470s Ambrosius succeeded Vortigern in a similar role, uniting the tribal chieftains into some kind of alliance, which seems to have fragmented by the 480s. Britain then appears to have been without an overall commander for around a decade until the early to mid-490s, during which time the regional kings were left to squabble among themselves, allowing Enniaun, the king of Gwynedd, to establish control over much of Wales. Consequently, it would seem that Vortigern established Powys as the largest and most powerful of the post-Roman British kingdoms of the mid-fifth century, and Enniaun made Gwynedd just as influential in the later fifth century: by the last decade of the fifth century, Gwynedd and Powys were the dominant British kingdoms. Nennius describes Arthur as the Britons' "leader of battles" at this time, presumably meaning that he became the new British commander in chief in the 490s. Accordingly, it would make historical sense for Arthur to have originated either in Gwynedd or Powys.

In the medieval romances Arthur is said to rule from an awe-inspiring capital: Camelot, the splendid, most formidable city in the land. As explained in chapter 2, the oldest surviving reference to the name Camelot is found in a poem by Chrétien de Troyes, dating to the 1190s. Although earlier writers, such as Geoffrey of Monmouth, say that Arthur's seat of power was an impregnable fortress at the heart of a magnificent city, not once do they record its name or reveal its location. Chrétien was a creative poet who, although often basing his storylines on historical events, devised many new themes and fictional characters for his works. Consequently, most literary scholars conclude that he invented the name Camelot for the previously unnamed city. Although later authors embraced the name, it is doubtful that any place called Camelot ever existed. Nevertheless, if Arthur was a historical figure, as I have argued, then he must have had a capital somewhere, presumably one that was relatively affluent and well defended. Even if a man called Arthur did not exist, then, as we examined in the previous chapter, *someone* united the Britons to defeat the Anglo-Saxons around AD 500, and whoever this was he must have had some kind of principal stronghold. Find that—whatever its name—and I would have a strong contender for a historical "Camelot." So where was it?

If King Arthur was a historical figure, or was based on the person who led the Britons in the 490s, then the name and location of his capital had been forgotten by the twelfth century. Probably much earlier, as even Dark Age Welsh literature fails to elucidate. My research had eliminated the traditional sites associated with Camelot (see chapter 2) and had led me to the part of Britain that once comprised the Dark Age kingdoms of Gwynedd and Powys as the most probable area for Arthur's origins. From my perspective, if Arthur's capital had been anywhere, then it had to have been in one of these—in central England or northern Wales. When I discussed this idea with various Arthurian enthusiasts, many dismissed it out of hand. Although they agreed with me that many of the customary sites associated with the Arthurian legend were unlikely to have been the historical Camelot, the prevailing theory at the time, and one that is still popular today, is that Arthur had originated in northern Britain. It was a scenario I needed to examine before continuing.

The argument for a northern King Arthur is basically threefold: the Dark Age poems concerning Merlin's demise are set in the kingdom of Rheged in the far northeast; the oldest surviving reference to Arthur is in a poem concerning and composed in the north of England; and one of Arthur's battles listed by Nennius was fought in Scotland. However, my research suggested that this triple contention was rather weak. Regarding Merlin, the Dark Age poems concerning the bard and his demise in the kingdom of Rheged pertain to Merlin Wyllt, or Laleocen, who lived in the late sixth century; they have nothing whatsoever to do with a historical Arthur of AD 500 (see chapter 8). As for the oldest reference to Arthur, this is in a poem titled *Y Gododdin* (The Gododdin), preserved in the National Library of Wales.[1] It concerns the Battle of Catraeth in northeast England, between the Angles and warriors from a southern Scottish kingdom called Gododdin around the year 600. (Most historians believe Catraeth to have been the modern town of Catterick in the county of North Yorkshire.) Thought to have been composed shortly after the battle by a bard from northern Britain, the work refers to Arthur just once, in relation to one of the warriors involved in the battle: "He glutted black ravens on the wall of the fort, although he was no Arthur." In other words, although he fought bravely, feeding the birds with the blood of his enemies, he was no great warrior as Arthur had been. This may well be the oldest reference to King Arthur to still survive, but it is in no way evidence that Arthur came from northern Britain where the battle was fought and the poem composed. It simply tells us that the author considered Arthur to have been a formidable British warrior—who could have come from just about anywhere. Many ancient Roman writers, for example, compared Julius Caesar with Alexander the Great, but they did not mean to imply that Caesar was from Macedonia—which leaves us with the Scottish battle. According to Nennius, Arthur's seventh battle was fought in a place called the Caledonian Wood. As Caledonia was the Roman name for the area north of Hadrian's Wall—modern Scotland and the far north of England—the battle was presumably fought somewhere in this area. But this was only one of Arthur's twelve battles. Here is Nennius's list:

> The first battle was at the mouth of the river Glein. The second, third, fourth and fifth upon another river which is called Dubglas, in the district of Linnuis. The sixth battle was over the river which is called Bassas. The seventh battle was in the Caledonian Wood. . . . The eighth battle was in Fort Guinnion. . . . The ninth battle was waged in the City of the Legion. The tenth battle he fought on the shore of the river called Tribruit. The eleventh battle took place on the mountain called Agned. The twelfth battle was on Mount Badon.[2]

No places bearing these precise names exist today, and apart from Badon, they appear in no additional historical record to survive. Four of the battle sites remain a mystery—the Rivers Bassas and Tribuit, Fort Guinnion, and Mount Agned—but the location of the others can be identified with some degree of confidence. The River Glein could have been either of the modern Rivers Glen, one in Lincolnshire in eastern England, the other in Northumberland in the northeast; Linnuis was almost certainly Linnius, an Angle kingdom in eastern England; as noted, the Caledonian Wood has to have been in or near modern Scotland; the City of the Legion was almost certainly Caerleon in South Wales, as its name derives from "fortress of the legion" in Welsh; and Badon, as we have discussed, was probably around the city of Bath. Only one of these battles can be placed with any certainty in the far north, and another *might* have been fought in the northeast. Using the line of reasoning that because one or two of Arthur's battles were fought in the far north of Britain, he must come from that region is, in my opinion, spurious to say the least. We could use similar logic to argue that he came from Bath, Lincolnshire, or Wales. From this list of probable locations, we can see that Arthur was thought to have fought all over Britain, as indeed would have been the case if he was the Britons' "leader of battles," fighting the Anglo-Saxons in the last decade of the fifth century.[3] Since my original investigation a historical figure has been identified as a possible King Arthur in the far north. He is one Artúr mac Áedáin, a chieftain from the kingdom of Dalriada in southeast Scotland. The name Artúr is indeed similar to Arthur, but there is a big problem. Artúr mac Áedáin lived in the late 500s, a century after the period King Arthur appears to have lived.

Having rejected the idea of a northern Arthur, I began to research what was known concerning the kingdoms of Gwynedd and Powys. In the fifth century both of these kingdoms evolved from earlier Roman

Fig. 10.1. Possible sites for Arthur's battles
according to Nennius.

districts called *civitates* (singular *civitas*). When the Romans conquered Britain, they divided the country into these administrative districts, based on the native tribal regions. During the turmoil of the early fifth century, after the Roman legions departed, central government based in the British capital of Londinium, now London, soon collapsed, leaving the *civitates* to quickly evolve into separate kingdoms. Each was established on old tribal allegiances with its individual chieftain or king. By the 490s, when Arthur seems to have appeared on the scene, what is now Great Britain was divided into numerous kingdoms, a significant number of them held by the Picts and Anglo-Saxons.[4] Scotland, which had not been a part of the Roman Empire, still had its own Celtic kingdoms, such as Gododdin and Dalriada, mentioned above. And during the latter half of the fifth century, the Anglo-Saxons had wiped out the British kingdoms in the east of England, establishing their own. The Angle kingdoms were Bernicia and Deira in the northeast, and Norfolk, Suffolk, and Linnius in the east. The Saxon kingdoms were Essex, Middlesex, and Kent in the southeast, Sussex in the south, and a new kingdom established by the Saxon Gewisse tribe to the east of Bath. The major kingdoms still ruled by the Britons were Rheged and Elmet in the northwest, Dumnonia in the southwest, Gwent, Dyfed, and Gwynedd in Wales, and Powys in central England and Wales. Of these it was the last two that were of particular interested to me. Like other kingdoms still ruled by the Britons, Gwynedd and Powys had evolved from the late-Roman *civitates,* and both had an administrative capital. Accordingly, if Arthur originated in either of these kingdoms, then one of their capitals could have been his seat of power.

I began by examining Gwynedd that covered northern Wales and the Isle of Anglesey. This had been the home of the Deceangli who, like many other such Celtic tribes, had retained their heritage throughout the Roman period. The Romans usually built their major cities on, or close by, the old tribal capitals (the less sophisticated earthen fortifications discussed in chapter 2), and the Roman administrative center for the Deceangli region was at Segontium on the coast of the Menai Straight, separating the mainland from the Isle of Anglesey.

(This was the headquarters of the *Segontienses Auxilium Palatinum* unit mentioned in chapter 9.) Segontium, now the town of Caernarfon, seemed the most likely location for the capital of Gwynedd, once the legions departed.

Various excavations undertaken at Caernarfon throughout the twentieth century uncovered the foundations of many stone buildings dating from Roman times; these included a military garrison, recreational buildings, and what appears to have been the residence of the local governor.[5] The archaeology, however, unearthed no occupation between the end of Roman rule in 410 and the Norman Conquest of 1066. Like so many other Roman towns in Britain, Segontium seems to have been abandoned soon after the legions left. Roman cities did have walls around them, but they were designed to be defended by professional soldiers with proper training and sophisticated weaponry. They were too large and in locations often too exposed to be defended by the native Britons without Roman support. For example, the principal cities in eastern Britain—London, Lincoln, and York—fell easily to the Saxons, Angles, and Picts by the mid-400s. In the west Segontium overlooked the Menai Straight and so afforded easy pickings for Irish raiders, meaning that it was among the first of the Roman towns to be vacated in the fifth century. So where did the inhabitants go? The answer seems to be the stronghold of Caer Ddegannwy (pronounced "Ka-er De-gan-wee"), about halfway along the north coast of Wales.

When I first visited the location, I could immediately see why the people of Gwynedd should have chosen it as the site for their new capital. Almost four hundred feet above the modern village of Deganwy, at the mouth of the River Conwy, Caer Ddegannwy stood on the flat top of a massive outcrop of volcanic rock (see plate 13). It looked like a light-gray version of a mesa, the towering, red sandstone table mountains common to the southwestern United States. Built on the summit, surrounded by almost sheer cliffs, Caer Ddegannwy—Deganwy Castle in English—would have been pretty much invulnerable to attack. Welsh literature depicts this as the Dark Age capital of Gwynedd, and

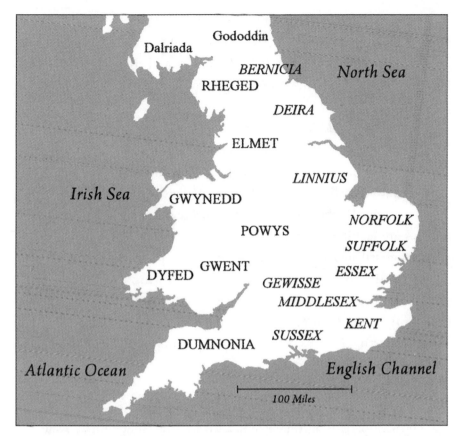

Fig. 10.2. The kingdoms of Britain and southern Scotland in the early 490s: Anglo-Saxon kingdoms in italics, Pict kingdoms in lower case.

archaeology tends to confirm the idea. The stone remains of a medieval castle can now be seen on the plateau, but ditches and mounds of a much earlier fortification are still visible. Excavations in the 1960s not only revealed that extensive timber stockades had been built along the artificial embankments that encircled the site, but that it had been the residence of a series of powerful chieftains. Artifacts such as high-status ceramics indicated that Caer Ddegannwy had been the seat of Gwynedd's royal dynasty from the fifth to ninth centuries.[6] The excavations had been led by archaeologist Leslie Alcock, the same man who excavated the hill fort of Cadbury in Somerset. He had called his book about this Somerset dig *Cadbury/Camelot* (see chapter 2); although I had eliminated that site from my list of probable "Camelots," it now seemed possible that Alcock had unknowingly excavated a more likely location for the fabled stronghold. If Arthur had come from the kingdom of Gwynedd, then Caer Ddegannwy could well have been his capital.

Today, Gwynedd lends its name to a modern county in northwest Wales, but Dark Age Gwynedd encompassed a much larger area and survived as an independent kingdom until the thirteenth century, when it was conquered by the English. Consequently, much concerning its history survived to be transcribed into medieval manuscripts. Although records are lacking regarding the first half of the fifth century, documentation still exists that reveals what took place from around 450. The first allusion we find to Gwynedd following the Roman withdrawal in 410 concerns mercenaries that were invited into the kingdom to help fight the Irish around 450, probably by invitation of the high king Vortigern. Nennius provides the oldest surviving reference to these warriors:

> Cunedda, with his sons, eight in number, came previously from the northern part, from the region called Manaw Gododdin . . . and expelled the Scoti with a very great slaughter from these regions [North Wales].[7]

Manaw Gododdin was the coastal region of the Pict kingdom of Gododdin in southeast Scotland, while *scoti* was a Latin term for "raiders" and was used in post-Roman Britain to refer to the Irish. So Cunedda (pronounced "Cun-e-tha") was evidently a warlord who lent his services to the Britons in order to drive the Irish out of Gwynedd. Although a Pictish kingdom, Gododdin had enjoyed good relations with the Romans during the late period of their occupation of Britain and so presumably were not exactly embraced by other Scottish tribes. This may well have been why they joined forces with the Britons: they were impelled to leave a Scotland that was hostile to them. If it was Vortigern who invited them in, then he probably offered them similar terms to the Anglo-Saxons, including land where they could settle (see chapter 7). Whether or not this included all the kingdom of Gwynedd is unknown, but in the confusion that accompanied the Saxon revolt, and the turmoil that followed Vortigern's demise, Cunedda and his family established themselves as chieftains throughout North Wales. Precisely how many warriors Cunedda and his sons brought with them is not recorded, but we can infer from the Harleian genealogies in the *Welsh Annals* that it was a considerable war band, as they not only managed to decimate the Irish invaders but also established their control over a large area. According to the *Annals:*

> Their territory stretched from the river which is called Dyfrdwy [the modern River Dee], to another river, the Teifi, and they held many districts in the western part of Britain.[8]

This not only included Gwynedd and a small kingdom to its south called Ceredigion but also part of Powys. This made the Cunedda family one of the most powerful in Britain. By the time Gildas was writing in the mid-500s, Cunedda's direct descendant Maelgwn was *the* most powerful ruler among the native Britons. Maelgwn, who is recorded by Gildas, the *Welsh Annals,* and by Nennius, was the king of Gwynedd and is recorded in the Harleian genealogies as the grandson of Cunedda's oldest son Enniaun, the first recorded king of Gwynedd. This is the same Enniaun who seemed to me to be a good contender for a historical Uther Pendragon. As archaeology suggests that Caer Ddegannwy had been the seat of the Gwynedd kings during Enniaun's time, around 480, you can imagine my initial excitement. If Enniaun was Uther Pendragon, then his heir could have been the historical King Arthur. So was Caer Ddegannwy the historical Camelot? Unfortunately, as I had often found during my research, things were not to be that simple. The Harleian genealogies tell us that Enniaun was succeeded by his son Cadwallon, Maelgwn's father.[9] Little is known about him, except that he seems to have spent most of his reign fighting off fresh Irish invasions in the west and was tied up reconquering the

Isle of Anglesey. So whether or not Enniaun was the man behind the legendary Uther Pendragon, his son Cadwallon, although contemporary with a historical King Arthur, does not fit the profile of the person who united the Britons to fight the Anglo-Saxons in the north, south, and east of Britain. As evocative a site as Caer Ddegannwy was, I doubted that it could have been the stronghold for someone who held sway over the other British kings, controlling and coordinating the campaign against an enemy who occupied the south and east of England. In short, Caer Ddegannwy seemed too remote a location to be the capital for a national "leader of battles" around AD 500—and at the time the king of Gwynedd was not called Arthur. I therefore decided that Powys was a more feasible kingdom for Arthur's power base. First, it was a kingdom in the central part of Britain still free from Anglo-Saxon occupation, much better placed to control and coordinate the other British kingdoms. Second, by the 490s when Arthur seems to have lived, it shared borders with the advancing Angles in the east and the Saxons to the south. On balance, a city in Powys seemed more likely than one in Gwynedd to have been the capital of a historical Arthur.

We have seen how many of the sites associated with the early Arthurian tradition are situated in what had been the kingdom of Powys. As noted in chapter 6, one of these was Dinas Bran, the hilltop citadel said to be the castle of the magic cauldron guardian. Historically, this site became the capital of Powys but not until around 650 when the Anglo-Saxons drove the Britons west, conquering the eastern part of the kingdom. It was in east Powys that the original capital had been situated. Just as Gwynedd evolved from the tribal region of the Deceangli, Powys developed in the homeland of the Celtic Cornovii tribe (pronounced "Core-no-vee").[10] During Roman times the area formed the *civitas* of Cornovium; located pretty much in the center of Britain, it was an ideal strategic location from where to organize the war effort of the native Britons of the late fifth century. Its capital had been Viroconium in the modern county of Shropshire. On visiting the site of this old Roman city, I was astonished to find that it stood in quiet countryside just outside the tranquil village of Wroxeter. The remains of most

Roman ruins are situated at the heart of modern cities, much of their ancient secrets buried beneath office blocks, apartment buildings, and busy streets. By contrast, the foundations of Viroconium—including a section of wall around thirty feet high, the largest freestanding Roman ruin in all England—can still been seen today (see plate 14). What now survives above ground is what had been the heart of Viroconium, including a basilica (public court building), a bathhouse, and a recreational hall, together with administrative structures and a public forum.[11] The city had been a thriving metropolis in Roman times, but what about the period when Arthur seems to have led the Britons, some eighty years after the legions departed? Did it still survive, or had it been abandoned like Segontium in Gwynedd? A small museum stood on the site, so I asked the guide. However, she was only knowledgeable concerning the Roman period and suggested I speak to the curator of Rowley's House Museum in the nearby town of Shrewsbury, where most of the archaeological finds from the site were housed. (Today there is a larger museum on the site, containing many of the discoveries.) A few days later I visited the Rowley's House Museum to meet with the curator Mike Stokes, who proved extremely helpful. He explained that as the remains of Viroconium were in open countryside, they provided an excellent opportunity for excavation, and much archaeological work had been conducted there. It not only revealed much about the city during Roman times but also during the post-Roman era.

In the mid-1960s an extensive archaeological excavation was initiated at the Viroconium site. It was to last for well over a decade, bringing to light a series of remarkable discoveries. The dig, led by archaeologist Philip Barker from the University of Birmingham, produced a mass of evidence for the period following the end of Roman rule. The results showed that rather than being abandoned for a more defensive site, like so many other Roman cities, Viroconium not only continued to be occupied but was rebuilt and refortified. From the excavation of post holes, and other telltale signs in the foundations and substructure of the city, the new buildings were found to have been made primarily of timber, not bricks and mortar like the earlier Roman town. When the evidence emerging from the dig was collated, these new buildings were discovered to have been highly sophisticated. From the discovery of the timber remains, it was possible to ascertain that the buildings were large and elaborate constructions of Roman design, with colonnades and orderly facades, many being a number of stories high. It appears, therefore, that shortly after the Romans left, Viroconium assumed a new importance. But the story did not end there. A second stage of rebuilding took place in the mid-fifth century, altogether more grandiose than the first. The excavation in the center of the city showed that the area had been entirely rebuilt. Not only were new buildings erected and streets replanned, but the infrastructure was also repaired. A new drainage system and freshwater supply were installed through an elaborate arrangement of aqueducts. Long stretches of the Roman cobbled roads were also dug up and completely relaid. A new kind of town came into existence. Gone was the leisure complex of the imperial occupation, and in its place arose a dynamic trading center and hive of industry. The central thoroughfare was a covered market or shopping arcade. All the way along this street were newly built dwellings and workshops, surrounded by large storage barns, and a sequence of sturdy industrial buildings containing hearths and furnaces.[12] Far from simply struggling to survive the civil strife afflicting early Dark Age Britain, Viroconium was a thriving industrial complex, the only example of such prosperity from that time discovered anywhere in Britain. Without a doubt it had been the capital of post-Roman Powys right through the fifth century.

When I asked Mike Stokes how such a thing was possible, when other *civitas* capitals had been deserted, the inhabitants making their homes in far less elaborate hill forts, he explained that it was due primarily to two factors. Powys had remained prosperous because it contained some of the most fertile land in Britain, and it was situated well away from the invasions of the Anglo-Saxons, Picts, and Irish that occurred in the mid-fifth century. While many other kingdoms were struggling, suffering famine, and fighting for survival, Powys was free to prosper. There was additional reason for Viroconium's fortune. It stood at a vital strategic location. Not only was it centrally placed,

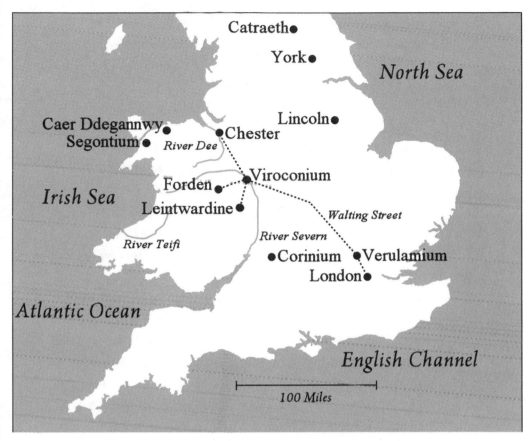

Fig. 10.3. Principle locations and road networks
during the mid-to-late fifth century.

but it also stood at the heart of the arterial trade routes of the period.
At Viroconium, Watling Street, arguably the most important Roman
road in Britain, made contact with the River Severn, one of the country's most significant waterways. Upstream, the Severn penetrates deep
into the heartland of Wales, while downstream it arcs across the west
Midlands, flowing to the sea through the Bristol Channel. Additionally,
the Roman road network linked Viroconium with other important
fortifications in the area, such as Forden to the west, Leintwardine
to the south, and Chester to the north. Much of this network is still
preserved in the pattern of modern roads. Powys and its capital were
in a unique position—quite literally. And someone made good use of

this. The heart of Viroconium was refortified, not with stone walls that needed Roman soldiers to patrol but with timber stockades built on high earthen banks and surrounded by deep ditches, more suitable for repelling less-equipped warriors and hostile Dark Age warlords.

The nerve center of this new Viroconium appears to have been a massive winged building constructed on the site of the old basilica. It seems to have been a Roman-style mansion, accompanied by a complex of adjoining buildings and outhouses, similar to those that had once been the homes of Rome's provincial governors.[13] Archaeologists determined that this must have been the seat of the person who had organized the reconstruction of the city—someone who enjoyed considerable power. Archaeologists seldom speculate, but it was quite clear to me who this person had been. The period of rebuilding in the mid-fifth century corresponded precisely with the reign of Vortigern. Not only did he have the power to make himself overlord of Britain at this time, but he had been a king of Powys, as revealed by the Pillar of Eliseg inscription (see chapter 6). Although the scenario seemed obvious to me, I discovered that archaeologists had not come to this conclusion. In fact, the general consensus was, and still is, that it was the work of a bishop. A bishop! As far as I was concerned, it seemed most unlikely that a bishop could hold a kingdom together at a time when the authority of the Church in Britain was almost nonexistent. Moreover, not one piece of archaeological evidence had been unearthed indicating that a contemporary Christian church had been there, let alone a cathedral that a bishop would warrant. And why decide upon an unnamed, unknown bishop anyway, when the historical sources include the perfect candidate: Vortigern? Mike Stokes told me that he was sure that the idea of Vortigern being the architect *had* occurred to archaeologists, but no one would declare it publicly. Why? Because Vortigern was associated with the Arthurian story, and no self-respecting scholar would link his or her name to that. God only knows what they would have made of what I was thinking. If Viroconium had been the seat of Vortigern, it might well have been the capital of King Arthur himself. In fact, what I was told next made it very possible indeed. Radiocarbon dating on the wooden remains found in the soil, together with ceramic sequencing, suggested that the prosperity of Viroconium lasted until around 520. Even then, the place was not abandoned but gradually declined in importance until around 650 when the Anglo-Saxons moved into the area.[14]

At the time Arthur appears to have assumed power, in the 490s, Viroconium was the most prosperous and well-defended city in the country. At least, as far as anyone knew, or for that matter still knows. During late Roman times it had been the fourth largest city in Britain, but by the late 400s the other three—London, Corinium (modern Cirencester), and Verulamium (modern Saint Albans)—had been overrun by the Anglo-Saxons, leaving it as the principal city in all the country. Arthur is said to have ruled from the most prosperous and well-defended city in Britain at precisely this time. It all fitted into a logical historical scenario. Vortigern had rebuilt Viroconium, Ambrosius could have made it his seat of power after Vortigern's demise, and Arthur had ultimately taken over. I had at last found a feasible contender for a historical Camelot.

11

The Name of the King

My research had led to Viroconium as the most likely seat for a historical King Arthur or, at the very least, whoever it had been who united the Britons at the time Arthur is said to have done just that. As far as I knew, I was the first to suggest that Arthur had been a king of Powys. However, on a visit to Oxford University to further study early British records, I was shocked to discover a passage in an old manuscript implying that someone had already identified Arthur as a Powys king—over thirteen hundred years ago. I came across this fleeting but crucial allusion in the work of a seventh-century bard called Llywarch, its significance apparently completely overlooked by historians for centuries.

In the previous chapter, I briefly discussed the Battle of Catraeth in northeast England, between the Angles and warriors from the Pict kingdom of Gododdin around the year 600. More specifically, it was a major encounter fought for control of northern England between a coalition of the Angle kingdoms of Bernicia and Deira and the British kingdom of Rheged in alliance with Gododdin. The battle was an overwhelming defeat for the Britons, leaving most of northern England under Angle control.[1] Many Britons migrated south, and among them was the young Rheged prince Llywarch, who fled to Powys where he ultimately became a royal bard. As we saw in chapter 5, bards served as advisors to Dark Age kings and were also poets who composed songs, known as "war poems," to record the exploits of their patrons. It is in such surviving works that much regarding Dark Age history has been preserved, and those composed by Llywarch concerned the kingdom of Powys.

It is not known precisely when Llywarch died, but he is commemorated in early Welsh literature as Llywarch Hen, meaning Llywarch the Old, inferring that he survived to a considerable age for someone of his time. He certainly lived for another half century after the Battle of Catraeth, as he wrote a series of poems titled *Canu Llywarch Hen* (Songs of Llywarch the Old) recording the struggle of Powys to maintain its eastern territories in the 650s.[2] The fight was ultimately lost, the Britons of the kingdom being forced west into what is now central Wales, abandoning their royal court, referred to by Llywarch as Llys Pengwern (Court of Pengwern). Its location is not revealed, but we can hazard a guess as to where it was. In Welsh, *pen* means "head," either referring to the body part, or a principal person, place, or thing (just as in modern English), while *gwern* is the word for the alder tree. This court of the kings of Powys could perhaps have been anywhere in the eastern part of the kingdom, but a probable location was in the city Viroconium, as archaeology has revealed that it was finally abandoned by the Britons at this time (see chapter 10). Pengwern—or the court of Alderhead in English—may have been the name of the royal residence at the heart of Viroconium, mentioned in the previous chapter.

Along with surviving members of the Powys court, Llywarch was forced to flee for a second time in his life; on this occasion into central Wales, where he settled in a small monastic community at the northern end of Lake Bala, around forty miles west of Viroconium (see plate 15). According to legend, while sitting on the lake's northeastern shore, he composed the *Marwnad Cynddylan*—the "Elegy of Cynddylan." This was a war poem concerning his patron, King Cynddylan of Powys, who died valiantly attempting to defend the eastern half of his kingdom from Anglo-Saxon invasion. The work now survives at Oxford University, in the Bodleian Library, where it is preserved, alongside other Dark Age Welsh literature, in The Red Book of Hergest. From linguistic analysis the poem seems to have been committed to writing in its present form around the year 850. However, as many of the events, people, and skirmishes portrayed in the work are attested to and confirmed in Bede's *Ecclesiastical History of the English People,* the *Welsh Annals,* and the Anglo-Saxon Chronicle and also fit with modern archaeological discoveries, historians generally consider it to have been composed much closer to the events described. In other words, the poem as it now survives is likely to be an accurate rendition of Llywarch's original.

Before discussing Llywarch's reference to King Arthur, I need to explain a little concerning the state of Britain in the early seventh century. By the year 600 the Angle kingdoms of Norfolk and Suffolk had united into the new kingdom of East Anglia—the East Angles—and had pushed west into central England, where the new Angle kingdom of Mercia was founded (the name coming from the Anglo-Saxon *mierce,* meaning "border people"), absorbing many smaller British kingdoms to ultimately share borders with Powys. After the Angle victories in the north, the kingdoms of Bernicia and Deira united as the powerful kingdom of Northumbria, which, over the following half century, expanded south through the British kingdom of Elmet, threatening not only Powys but also their fellow Angle kingdom of Mercia. For the first time in two centuries, the Britons and their Germanic enemies formed a military alliance: Powys and Mercia united in an attempt to defeat Northumbria.[3] Initially, the pact between Cynddylan of Powys and the Mercian king Penda was a success. The *Welsh Annals* refers to the Battle of Cogwy in 644, between the Mercians and Northumbrians, where the Northumbrian king Oswald was killed.[4] Bede also mentions the battle and Oswald's death,[5] as does the Anglo-Saxon Chronicle,[6] although they both give its date as 642. In his *Elegy of Cynddylan,* Llywarch refers to this battle, where the British king and his army join the Mercians to save the day: "I saw the armies at Maes Cogwy [Cogwy Field], and the cry of men hard pressed until Cynddylan brought them aid."[7]

The Powys-Mercian alliance kept the enemy at bay for around a decade, achieving their last victory over the Northumbrians at a site Llywarch calls Caer Luitcoet, generally favored as being the old Roman fortification of Letocetum on Watling Street, some forty miles east of Viroconium. Shortly after, however, the tides turned, and the Britons and Mercians were in full retreat. The *Welsh Annals* records that Penda was killed in 657,[8] while Bede and the Anglo-Saxon Chronicle give the year as 655,[9] elucidating that in a decisive battle not only Mercia's own army but also those of their allies were decimated. Bede says that the conflict occurred near a river called the Vinwed, its location now uncertain.[10] Wherever the battle was fought, the Northumbrian king Oswy, Oswald's son, continued to advance. According to the *Welsh Annals,* the following year "Oswy came and took plunder,"[11] suggesting that this was when eastern Powys was occupied by the Northumbrians and its native Britons driven into Wales. According to Llywarch's poem, the Powys king Cynddylan died at this time, fighting with his back against a river called the Tren, possibly the River Tern where it meets the Severn just outside Viroconium.

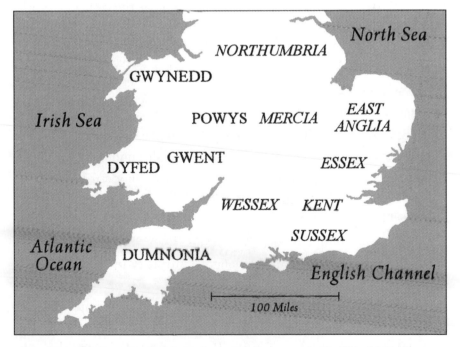

Fig. 11.1. The kingdoms of southern Britain around AD 650: Anglo-Saxon kingdoms in italics.

■ ■ ■

It was in Llywarch's description of Cynddylan's last successful battle at Caer Luitcoet that I found his reference to Arthur. In an English translation of the *Elegy of Cynddylan,* made in the 1970s by the respected British historian John Morris, senior lecturer in ancient history at University College London, Cynddylan and his brothers were referred to as Arthur's heirs.[12] If this was correct, then Llywarch was evidently saying that the king of Powys in the mid-600s was a direct descendant of King Arthur, implying that Arthur had been a king of Powys himself—or, at the very least, that he was believed to have once been a king of Powys at the time. If the poem dated from the mid-seventh century as experts believed, then this was the second oldest known reference to King Arthur still in existence, the only earlier one being in *The Goddodin* poem discussed in the previous chapter. In fact, as *The Goddodin* reference fails to say where Arthur was thought to have originated, the *Elegy of Cynddylan* would be the oldest surviving work to place Arthur in a geographical setting. Not in the south or southwest of England, or in South Wales, or even northern England, as other Arthurian researchers had suggested, but in the central kingdom of Powys, precisely where my investigation had led. I had to see the original poem for myself.

Having obtained a photocopy of the relevant page in The Red Book of Hergest from the Bodleian Library, I read the original text, which was written in Old Welsh: this was the British language into which Brythonic was developing by the seventh century; modern Welsh came about by the 1300s. In the poem, Cynddylan and his brothers were described by the words *canawon artir.* The first person to translate the *Elegy of Cynddylan* into modern Welsh was Ifor Williams—professor of Welsh language and literature at Bangor University in North Wales—in 1935.[13] In his work he transcribed the word *canawon* as the modern Welsh *cenawon,* meaning "whelps." This is a word for a puppy dog, or a young animal or cub, but Williams's research indicated that in Old Welsh it was often used to refer to offspring generally, particularly ill-fated human descendants. John Morris had clearly followed the same reasoning, which is why he had interpreted *canawon* to mean "heirs" in English. The word that both Williams and Morris took to be Arthur was *artir;* so, if correct, this would mean that the most accurate modern English translation of *canawon artir* would be "the ill-fated heirs of Arthur."

But why should Arthur have been written as *artir*? Arthur is the spelling of the name pronounced "Ar-ther" in modern English, but there was no consistency of spelling until the first widely accepted English dictionary published by Samuel Johnson in 1755. In the medieval romances Arthur's name is spelled in many ways, such as Arther, Artur, Ardure, Ardur, Ardir, and Arddyr. During the Middle Ages the *th* sound, as in "teeth" for example, was seldom written with a combination of the letters T and H.[14] The same is true for Welsh, which followed the English example and only adopted a common spelling in the eighteenth century. In modern Welsh, the *th* sound can be written as a TH but is more usually written as a double D, such as in the name of the kingdom of Gwynedd—pronounced "Gwyneth."[15] In Old Welsh works, and in earlier Brythonic, the *th* sound was spelled variously in Roman letters with a double or single D, with a T and H, or with a simple T. Likewise, the *ur* sound could be written with a UR, a YR, an ER, or an IR. So *artir* could indeed have been pronounced "Arthur," just as Williams and Morris transcribed it.

However, since my book on King Arthur was published in 1992, which alluded to this reference, various scholars who had never questioned the translations of the *Elegy of Cynddylan* made by Williams and Morris began to query its mention of Arthur. *Artir,* they protested, had to mean something else. First, there were those who said that as the word did not begin with a capital A, then it could not have been a personal name. In fact, the capitalization of the first letter of proper nouns did not become consistent in written English or Welsh until the late Middle Ages. (None of these people seemed to have noted that Nennius also wrote Arthur with a lowercase A.) Then there were those who decided to break the word apart. The word *artir* does not exist in Welsh, nor is it found in any ancient Brythonic text, implying that it was in fact a personal name. So some scholars came up with the notion that it might have been two separate words, *ar* and *tir,* which would indeed mean something in Welsh: "on land." Accordingly, they interpreted the phrase as *canawon ar tir,* the "ill-fated heirs on [the] land," leading others to jump one step further and translate it as "heirs *of* the land." However, the original text clearly has *artir* as one word. Elsewhere, the poet employs the word *ar* (on) and *tir* (land) without ever joining them with other words. It was clear to me that some historians and literary scholars would go to any lengths to prevent Arthur from becoming more acceptable as a historical figure. I wondered if these same people would have questioned Shakespeare's historical existence because his name appears in pre-nineteenth-century documents under various spellings, such as Shackspeare, Shaxsper, Shakspere, and Shakfer.

Some academics even resorted to complete irrelevancies in an attempt to dismiss the reference to Arthur in the *Elegy of Cynddylan.* I remember once being on a British radio show with a literary authority, invited on to dispute my King Arthur theory, who was reduced to questioning the *authorship* of the poem. There is a reasonable historical issue concerning Llywarch's existence: he may possibly have been a legendary bard whose name was only later linked with the poems. The works now collectively called the *Songs of Llywarch the Old* might have been written by someone else. I personally doubted this but fair enough. The expert brought this up, saying that Llywarch may not have existed. The young academic stared at me with a glint of triumph in his eyes. Apparently, he was convinced he had blown my case out of the water. All I could do was shake my head and utter the single word "And?" The man was simply being pedantic. Whatever his or her name, *someone* had written the poem that seems to have been composed close to the time in question. The scholar quickly changed the subject.

Nevertheless, the big question still remained: Who *had* ruled Powys at the time Arthur is said to have lived? Putting a name to that enigmatic figure, however, was easier said than done. Records concerning the kingdom of Powys during the relevant period are almost nonexistent;

it was going to take some doing to identify its king around the year 500. The Pillar of Eliseg had been inscribed with a list of the kingdom's rulers, from which we know that Vortigern was king of Powys in the mid-400s (see chapter 6). However, it was of no help at the current phase of my quest. The inscription was severely weathered, even when Edward Lhuyd copied it in 1696, and a period covering over two and a half centuries was missing. In his *History of the Britons,* Nennius tells us that Vortigern had three legitimate sons: Vortimer, Categrin, and Pascent, and the Pillar of Eliseg revealed that the third of these eventually secured his father's throne, although Nennius explains that Pascent only ruled in the region of western Powys by permission of the high king Ambrosius.[16] Between Pascent's name and those of his later successors, the pillar's surface had crumbled, leaving a gap in the list of kings from Pascent's time, around 480, until the mid-eighth century. All that could be discerned from the inscription concerning this illusive period by Edward Lhuyd was a partial reference to the Powys king Concenn, the man who erected the stone around the year 850. The visible section recommenced with one Guoillauc, Concenn's great-great-grandfather, in the mid-700s. Examining the Harleian genealogies in the *Welsh Annals* in the hope of filling the gap proved confusing to say the least.

One roll of Powys kings in the *Welsh Annals* chronicles Guoillauc as a distant successor to Pascent but records Pascent as the son of someone called Cattegir, not Vortigern, while a second list of Powys kings in the same manuscript makes Pascent himself Concenn's great-great-grandfather.[17] If the latter is right, then Pascent lived around 750, meaning Vortigern must have existed three centuries after he clearly did, while the former fails to name Vortigern at all—a man whose existence is attested to by nearly all the historical sources. I realize family relationships, great-grandparents and all that, can be rather bewildering—it certainly is to me—but the bottom line is that no contemporary, or even near contemporary record, inscription, or genealogy revealed exactly who ruled Powys from around 480 to the early 600s, when one Cyndrwyn (Cynddylan's son) came to the throne, as described in the *Songs of Llywarch the Old.* The *Welsh Annals* provides only one list of

kings for the other British kingdoms included in the Harleian genealogies, but it has *three* for Powys, which all differ considerably in the
names, number, and order of rulers. From this we can safely infer that
whatever was going on in Powys during the late fifth and the sixth centuries, it had become a garbled memory by the time the king lists were
committed to writing in the 900s (when the surviving *Welsh Annals*
was transcribed); the reason most likely being that Powys was invaded
and plundered by the Northumbrians in the seventh century.

I decided to concentrate further on the archaeological work at
Viroconium. As none of the finds unearthed from the ruins of the
ancient capital of Powys contained in the Rowley's House Museum
in Shrewsbury seemed to further my theory that it might have been
the historical Camelot, its curator Mike Stokes suggested I visit the
University of Birmingham, from where the excavations at Viroconium
had been initiated and organized. I hoped that its archaeologists may
have uncovered evidence to support my idea, its implications perhaps unwittingly disregarded. After all, no one, as far as I was aware,
had previously suggested Viroconium to have associations with the
Arthurian legend. I decided to keep any mention of King Arthur out of
my inquiries, merely expressing an interest in Viroconium as a possible
post-Roman capital of Britain. Birmingham, in the center of England,
is Britain's second largest city, and its department of Classics, Ancient
History, and Archaeology is respected throughout the world. They had
done exemplary work over two decades, piecing together the history of
Viroconium, and one of the first things I learned about the city's post-
Roman era implied something of which I had been completely unaware.
I already knew that part of western Powys had been annexed by the
Cunedda family of Gwynedd by the late 400s (see chapter 10), but one
particular archaeological discovery suggested that they may have taken
over the kingdom entirely.

We examined in chapter 8 how important Celtic individuals often
assumed animal names as epithets, sometimes passed on from generation to generation, and the Cunedda family was no exception. Cunedda
and many of his successors bore the *cun* element in their names, which

in Brythonic was pronounced "qune" and meant "hound": such as Cunnan, Cuncar, Cunuit, Cunhil, Cunis, and many more. They are found in the Harleian genealogies and other Dark Age family trees, spread throughout the areas annexed by Gwynedd in north and central Wales during the late fifth and early sixth centuries. It is no hard and fast rule, but if you find the *cun* affix in the name of high-status Britons from the early Dark Ages, then it probably means that their ancestors originated in Gwynedd. And the grave of one such person was found in the ruins of Viroconium. During excavations in 1967 a tombstone was discovered just outside the city ramparts, bearing the inscription *Cunorix macus Maquicoline*—"Cunorix, son of Maquicoline" (now in the onsite museum at Viroconium). Archaeologists who found the stone believed that it had once stood in a more prominent position within the city, having been dragged to its eventual location by farmers at some point over the last few centuries.[18] Whoever Cunorix was, he seems to have been an important individual, as the name suffix *rix* was a Celtic derivation of the Latin word *rex,* meaning "king." The true name of the individual the tombstone was inscribed to commemorate appears therefore to have been King Cuno. The use of the word *macus,* a latinized version of the Gaelic *mac,* for "son of," rather than the Brythonic *map,* additionally indicates that he was of Irish descent. This was not unusual for important figures in late fifth century Gwynedd; once they secured power in Gwynedd and drove out the Irish raiders, the Cunedda family enlisted the help of more friendly Irish settlers to bolster their numbers, partly explaining their successful military expansion. Consequently, the inscription implies that Cunorix was of mixed Irish British parentage and had become chieftain of some region occupied by the Cunedda family. From its style of writing, the stone was dated to about 480, around the time that Ambrosius seems to have relinquished power, and Enniaun was expanding the influence of Gwynedd into much of northern Wales and eastern Powys (see chapter 10). Although none of the archaeologists I spoke to appeared to have considered the idea, it occurred to me that the burial of a likely high-status member of the Cunedda line in Viroconium implied that Gwynedd's influence had stretched much further into Powys than merely its western borders. Perhaps they had occupied the capital itself.

It's doubtful that Cunorix would have been the actual king of Powys—his tombstone was not elaborate enough for that. Probably he was a visitor from another region who happened to die at Viroconium. But whoever he was, the trademark *cun* affix of the Cunedda dynasty got me thinking. It was while I was talking to the Birmingham team about the Cunorix stone that I was told something else I had previously not known. In the early post-Roman period, the Brythonic word for "hound" was, in Roman lettering, spelled *cun,* but from around AD 600 it began to appear on inscriptions as *cyn,* which is also how it was then written in various manuscripts. The reason being that in Brythonic the vowel in the word was somewhere between U and Y and, in modern Welsh, is pronounced more like the letter I, as in "chin." (Accordingly, some genealogies also spell *cun* as *cin.*) The first king of Powys we know of with any degree of certainty after Vortigern's son Pascent was Cyndrwyn, named in the *Songs of Llywarch the Old* as the ruler of Powys in the early 600s, who, the poet tells us, was succeeded by his son Cynddylan. Both of these kings bore the *cyn* affix in their names, which would earlier have been written as *cun.* So these seventh-century rulers of Powys were almost certainly descended from the Cunedda line, which, together with the presence of a King Cuno in Viroconium around 480, would suggest that from the late 400s until the final abandonment of Viroconium by Cynddylan (whose name I now knew would have been pronounced "Qune-th-lan") in the mid-650s, Powys had probably been annexed by the kingdom of Gwynedd. Accordingly, during the period Arthur seems to have assumed his role as high king of the Britons in the 490s, whoever ruled from Viroconium—the most likely seat of Arthur, if my theory was correct—had been a prominent member of the Cunedda family.

Whoever this was, he was probably closely related to Enniaun, the Gwynedd king who expanded his influence throughout much of Wales and into Powys in the 480s. In the last chapter we discussed how Enniaun's son Cadwallon had been the king of Gwynedd during the 490s and discounted the likelihood of him having been the person who united the Britons to successfully push back the Anglo-Saxons at the time, spending much of his reign repelling fresh Irish invasions and retaking the island of Anglesey. So who might have taken charge in Viroconium? As the Pillar of Eliseg inscription and the various Dark Age genealogies provided no answer, I decided to examine what the monk Gildas had to say about the state of Britain during the time he wrote in the mid-540s. As this was only a generation or so after the period in question, perhaps there were clues as to who had ruled Powys around the year 500 in his *On the Ruin and Conquest of Britain.* I had to search for clues in his work because, frustratingly, Gildas fails to name anyone who ruled anywhere at that time.

As implied by its title, Gildas's work was basically a tirade against his fellow Britons for fighting among themselves to allow the Anglo-Saxons supremacy. According to the Anglo-Saxon Chronicle, in 514 a new wave of Saxons landed on the southern shores of Britain, forcing the Britons to retreat north, and within a few years they had established the new kingdom of Wessex (West Saxons) throughout the modern counties of Hampshire and Wiltshire.[19] Bede reveals the reason for the Britons' renewed misfortunes, saying that it was due to the civil wars fought between the various British kingdoms. He even cites Gildas as reprimanding the Britons for their stupidity.[20] It was not too late for the Britons, however, as there is no literary or archaeological indication that the Saxons in the southeast or the Angles in the north and east of England had recovered from their defeats around the turn of the century. In his tirade Gildas urges the British kings to forgo their "wickedness" and unite once more to repel the invaders. He personally addresses the kings of the largest and most powerful British kingdoms by name. He reproaches Constantine of Dumnonia in southwestern England,[21] and a king called Vortipor,[22] whom he calls the tyrant of the Demetarum—the Demetea tribe who had established the kingdom of Dyfed in southwestern Wales—both of whose names have been found inscribed on contemporary monuments. And there is Maglocunus,[23]

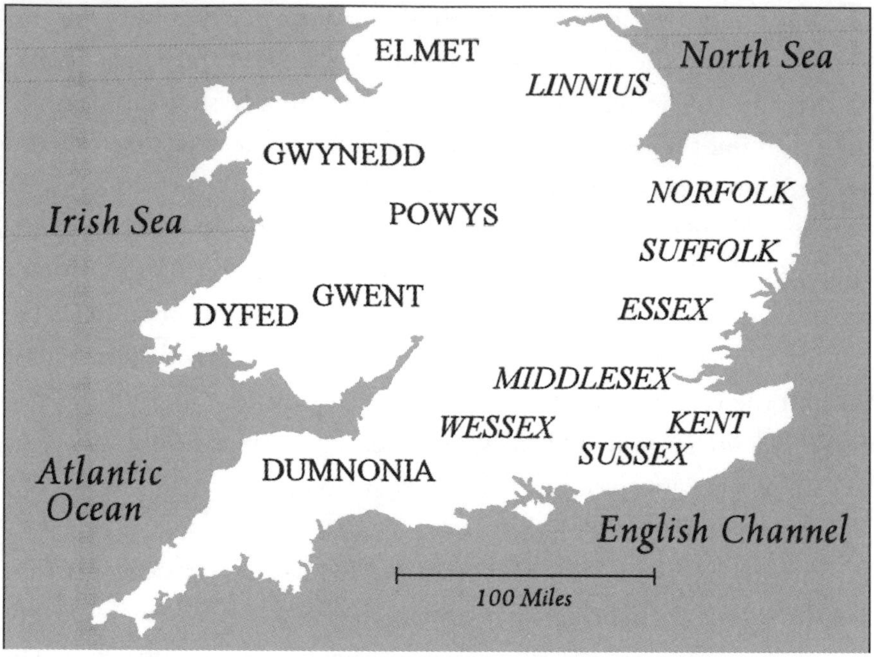

Fig. 11.2. The kingdoms of southern Britain around AD 545:
Anglo-Saxon kingdoms in italics.

the original Latin name of the king of Gwynedd recorded in the *Welsh Annals* and in various Dark Age accounts under the later Welsh rendering as Maelgwn (see chapter 10). Gildas addresses two other contemporary kings, Aurelius Conanus (possibly a descendant of Ambrosius, going by the name),[24] and Cuneglasus[25] but fails to reveal which kingdoms they ruled. As we have already seen, the largest native British kingdoms around AD 500 where Rheged, Elmet, Gwynedd, Powys, Dyfed, Gwent, and Dumnonia, which still survived intact by Gildas's time, as the Saxons had established their new kingdom of Wessex in the area previously divided between less powerful British chieftains in the south. Gildas identifies the kings of three of these: Dyfed, Dumnonia, and Gwynedd. Aurelius could have been from any of the other four, but where Cuneglasus ruled seemed fairly obvious to me. Judging by the *cun* affix in his name, Cuneglasus must have come from a territory previously annexed by Gwynedd. As there is no reliable evidence that Gwynedd extended its influence into South Wales (where Gwent was situated) or northern England (the regions of Elmet and Rheged) until after Gildas's death, then the most probable kingdom over which Cuneglasus ruled was the only one left on the list: Powys.

I had managed to identify a viable king of Powys who reigned at the time Gildas wrote, around the year 545. So what was known about Cuneglasus? Sadly, very little! Gildas considered him a heretic, a butcher, and an adulterer and implied that, other than Maglocunus, he was the most powerful king in the land. Gildas speaks of him as the "ruler of many" and of waging war against his fellow countrymen with "special weapons," presumably meaning that he had a formidable army.[26] If Arthur had been actively engaged fighting the Anglo-Saxons in the 490s, as the various historical sources imply, then we can guess that he would have been, say, thirty-five or forty years old at the turn of the century. He might still have been alive around 520 but probably not much later for someone of the time. It is not known exactly how old Cuneglasus was in the mid-440s, but he was no spring chicken. Gildas chastises him for wasting his youth and early years, squandering his riches, and engaging in small-minded squabbles. Presumably, we can infer that he was at least middle aged, perhaps in his forties in 445. The person who ruled Powys around the year 500 could well, therefore, have been his immediate predecessor. The $64,000 question: Who had that been?

The *Welsh Annals* genealogies make mention of Cuneglasus, under the later Welsh spelling as Cinglas.[27] He appears in the family tree of one Iguel map Caratauc. This was the Old Welsh spelling of Hywel map Caradog, the ruler of a small kingdom called Rhos around the year 800. By this time, the Anglo-Saxons had driven the Britons pretty much out of all that is now England and into what is now Wales. Powys had been reduced to a small region in west-central Wales, while Gwynedd had broken up into a number of smaller kingdoms, one being Rhos, a tiny area on the coast of northwest Wales still ruled by Cunedda's descendants. Because Hywel (pronounced "Hugh-el") had been a king of Rhos around the year 800, in no way means that his remote ancestor Cuneglasus ruled in that same area two and a half centuries before.

Nonetheless, even today, many authors and websites refer to Cuneglasus as the king of Rhos, based solely on the evidence that his descendants had later ruled that kingdom. Contrary to what seems to be popular opinion in some circles, the kingdom of Rhos simply did not exist at the time Gildas was writing. Gildas himself tells us that Gwynedd was the mightiest of the British kingdoms; it was not to break up until well after his time. He even says that its king Maglocunus was triumphant, defeating and plundering other kingdoms.[28] This hardly sounds like a man whose kingdom was falling apart. Remember, this is one of the very few contemporary accounts to survive from post-Roman Briton: Gildas is actually writing about someone alive at the time. Gwynedd was strong and intact and showing no signs of breaking up into smaller kingdoms, such as Rhos, when Gildas wrote. It is not known precisely when the kingdom of Rhos came into existence, but it was certainly not as early as Cuneglasus's time. I really seemed to have upset some people in that region of north Wales by questioning their supposed history. I remember once, well after my King Arthur book was published, receiving a phone call from a disgruntled local who insisted that Cuneglasus had been a king of Rhos, based on his name appearing in the genealogies of that kingdom. I made my counterargument, and the phone call finished with—what I assumed—was us agreeing to disagree. However, a few weeks later the same individual called someone who had just published a piece concerning my work, incensed that I continued to propound that Cuneglasus was a Powys king—even though he had told me I was wrong. Some people! I could only retort with what I have since had to repeat on many occasions. To say that Cuneglasus had been king of the tiny kingdom of Rhos, just because his descendant had been, would be like saying that George Washington had been president of England, not the United States, because his great-grandfather had come from here.

There could be little doubt in my mind that Cuneglasus had been a king of Powys. What further supported this conjecture was that the Harleian genealogies list Cuneglasus and Maglocunus as cousins: both were the paternal grandchildren of Enniaun, the powerful king of

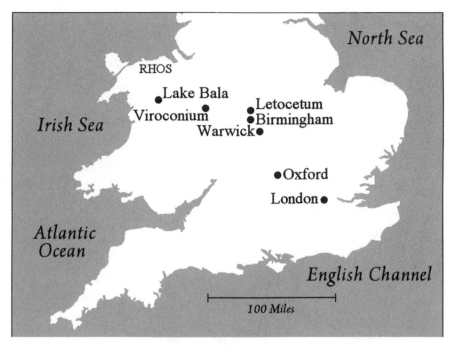

Fig. 11.3. Southern Britain, showing the location of
the eighth century kingdom of Rhos.

Gwynedd, who seems to have annexed Powys by the 480s.[29] His son
Cadwallon had succeeded him in the 490s (see chapter 10), followed
by *his* son Maglocunus. Cuneglasus is listed as the son of Cadwallon's
brother. The implications are that after Enniaun's death, his lands had
been divided between his two sons, Cadwallon inheriting Gwynedd,
and his brother Powys. Alternatively, Cadwallon might have been overall king of the two regions, and when he became tied up dealing with
fresh invasions from Ireland, his sibling declared independence. One
way or the other, their respective sons Maglocunus and Cuneglasus
both ruled separate kingdoms by the time Gildas was writing a generation later. However, the *Welsh Annals* genealogies were not only sup-
portive evidence that Cuneglasus was indeed a king of Powys, but they
also revealed the name of the most likely person to have been ruling the
kingdom at the time Arthur seems to have lived: he was Cadwallon's
brother and Cuneglasus's father. His name was Owain Ddantgwyn
(pronounced "Owen Than-gwin"), Ddantgwyn meaning "white tooth."

He presumably was so named because he had particularly good teeth for someone of his time.[30] This was certainly a big kick in the teeth for me. I had finally put a name to the most likely figure to have ruled from Viroconium around AD 500. But the person who seemed closest to being the historical figure behind the King Arthur legend—having lived in the right place and at the right time—was not called Arthur. My entire investigation collapsed to nothing, just when thought I was so close to solving one of the world's great mysteries.

It took some time for me to recover from this revelation and to appreciate that all was not lost: far from it. His name might not have been Arthur, but I was convinced I had identified the man around whom the Arthurian legends eventually formed. An examination of the surviving historical sources, alongside the archaeological evidence, clearly revealed that, following a period of defeat in the 480s, something dramatically changed for the Britons: they went on the offensive during the 490s, ultimately achieving a decisive victory over the Anglo-Saxons at the Battle of Badon around AD 500. And someone—a strong and influential British leader—had to have been behind it. No contemporary or even *near* contemporary work, record, or inscription reveals who this person was or where he or she had come from. If it did, then there would be no mystery to solve. Nevertheless, *someone* had to have united the various British kingdoms into a formidable force during the 490s, just as Ambrosius had done in the 470s. The oldest surviving work to identify this leader is Nennius's *History of the Britons,* dating to around 830, that records his name as Arthur. (Although the older works, *The Gododdin* and, seemingly, the *Elegy of Cynddylan* poems, make reference to Arthur, they are fleeting allusions in which he is not specifically identified as the British leader around the year 500.) After this time the various accounts, stories, and legends concerning this Arthur were committed to writing, establishing the basis for the later Arthurian romances of the Middle Ages. In all likelihood they already existed in some form or other, as Nennius seems to have considered Arthur to have been a well-known figure. If he had not been, then it's reasonable to assume that the author would have told us more about him, such as where he came from or how he had assumed power. Instead, he merely tells us: "Then Arthur fought against them in those days with the kings of the Britons."[31] We can surely infer from this terse introduction that Nennius expected his readers to know exactly who Arthur was. Historically, the most likely kingdom from which this leader came was Powys, and its capital of Viroconium was by far the most sophisticated city in Britain during this period, a period when most Roman towns had been long abandoned and many Britons had reverted to living in elevated armed settlements or hill forts. As far as I was concerned, the person who initiated the British campaign that severely damaged the Anglo-Saxon cause for decades and led the Britons to victory at Badon had his or her seat of power in Viroconium. This surely had to have been the same person who Nennius later referred to as Arthur. I may not have found an individual called Arthur, but I had almost certainly identified the man later referred as such—namely, Owain Ddantgwyn.

How, then, did the name Arthur originate? Maybe it was a later invention, applied to the man who led the Britons around the year 500, as his true name had been forgotten. Just like his capital eventually became known by the fictitious name Camelot. Alternatively, Owain's name may have morphed into Arthur during the period separating his life from the time Nennius wrote, similar to Ambrosius becoming Emrys in later Welsh literature (see chapter 6). Some Arthurian researchers had suggested the name evolved from the Latin Artorius. The idea was popularized when the Arthurian poem *Artorius* was published by the English poet John Heath-Stubbs in 1973, followed by the King Arthur novel *Artorius Rex* by fantasy author John Gloag in 1977. Historically, there were a couple of Roman soldiers recorded with that name in Britain: Lucius Artorius Castus during the late second century and Artorius Justus in the third. Nevertheless, I found nothing to back up the notion that Artorius was the original version of the name Arthur. Certainly, no one by the name Artorius is known to have had links with Britain anywhere around AD 500. What I did find interesting is that the name Arthur did not seem to have been used in any context until after the time King Arthur is said to have lived.

The name Arthur (in whatever spelling) does not appear on record anywhere until the late sixth century. Around this time, no less than six British genealogies include children named Arthur. All of these people were born too late to have been the fabled king around the year 500, but it does suggest that the name had suddenly become popular. The given name Gordon was in vogue in the late nineteenth and during the twentieth century, beginning with Victorian parents christening their sons with that name after the British general Charles Gordon became a national hero, dying at Khartoum in the Sudan in 1885. Before this time Gordon had only been a surname. Perhaps something similar had occurred during the sixth century: people began to name their sons after a recent national hero. It occurred to me that this not only indicated that a famous figure called Arthur might have lived in the early 500s, but that, as the name did not appear earlier, whoever this figure was he might well have been the first to have that name. Was it coined especially for him? There are plenty of examples from world history where titles first bestowed on a particular warrior later became adopted as given names, for example, the Mongolian warlord Genghis Khan, whose name was actually his personal title, meaning "Universal Ruler." The name Genghis (Universal) was afterward given to many Mongolian children. Something similar might have happened with Arthur. So, like Genghis Khan, did his name have some original meaning?

Arth, the first syllable in the name Arthur, is the Welsh word for "bear," just as it had been in earlier Brythonic. Could the name Arthur, I began to wonder, have derived from a title—the Bear? As we have seen, it was common practice for Britons at the time to adopt or be designated by the names of real or imagined creatures to denote their prowess or some specific trait. Maglocunus, for example, is specifically referred to by Gildas as the Dragon,[32] the title he seems to have inherited from his grandfather Enniaun. The significance of this had not occurred to me before. My investigation abruptly assumed an entirely new complexion. Maybe Arthur had actually been the *title* of the historical figure later remembered by that name. It would not be the first time famous historical figures had gone down in history under their epithets. Other than Genghis Khan, whose real name was Temujin, there were the Roman emperors Caligula, a term meaning "little boots" (a nickname he acquired as child as he enjoyed dressing as a soldier), whose true name was Caius, and Augustus, a title meaning "majestic," whose real name was Octavian. In these cases we happen to know their real names as records have survived. But what if our fabled king of the Britons had only been remembered under his title, his real name having been either forgotten or simply superseded by his more familiar epithet? If so, then Owain Ddantgwyn could well have been King Arthur after all.

Just as the name Ambrosius has been shortened to Ambrose and rendered in Welsh as Emrys in a very short time (see chapter 6), the title Arth could just as easily—in fact, far more readily—have become Arthur. I could envisage a number of ways it might have occurred. For example, those who spoke Latin might have called him by their word for bear, ursus. Perhaps he was known by Brythonic speakers as Arth, and Latin speakers as Ursus, the two eventually being joined to form Arthursus, later shortened to Arthur, as Marcus is shortened to Mark and Antonius to Antony. Another possibility: in Welsh "the bear" is written as *yr arth* (pronounced "ur arth"), which might simply have developed into the more lyrical Arthur. One way or the other, the name Arthur almost certainly originated with a title derived from the word for bear, just as many members of the Cunedda dynasty had the Brythonic word for hound in their names. Accordingly, Owain was not only an excellent candidate for a historical Arthur, he may even have been called by that appellation. Perhaps, after assuming power, his birth name was discarded; like Genghis Khan and Augustus Caesar, he was only referred to by his title, particularly since Owain was a common name at the time.

Other than his name appearing in the genealogies, nothing whatsoever was known about Owain Ddantgwyn. (At the time of writing, I see that some websites still refer to Owain Ddantgwyn as a king of Rhos. The same argument regarding Cuneglasus applies: there is no evidence whatsoever that Owain was a king of Rhos.) I decided, therefore, to return to the work of Gildas to see if I could learn more about his son Cuneglasus. Immediately, I was staggered to see something that I had previously read over without taking much notice. While chastising Cuneglasus concerning his behavior, Gildas refers to him as the Bear:

> Why have you been rolling in the filth of your past wickedness since your youth, you bear, ruler of many, driver and rider of the chariot which is the bear's receptacle?[33]

This is a fairly literal translation of Gildas's original Latin, but it imparts far more than may first seem apparent. For a start Gildas is not implying that Cuneglasus is tearing along in an actual chariot, literally playing around in his own excrement. That much might be obvious, but the author is employing a further metaphor. The term he uses, *receptaculi ursi* (bear's receptacle), would not mean literally the "bear's cup" but was denoting something of importance that had once belonged to the bear. In Latin the word *receptaculum* does mean a vessel meant to contain something, but Roman writers often used it metaphorically to refer to a cherished object, place, or concept: something that held significance. And his words *sessor auriga que currus* (meaning "driver and rider of the chariot") were also used to imply domineering control or despotism. The Latin term for charioteer was also used to refer to the leader of an army. So what Gildas is really saying is that Cuneglasus is in command of something significant that had once been the bear's. Some academics translate this line into English as "commander of the bear's stronghold," inferring his kingdom, and others as "commander of the bear's army." But there's a mystery. Gildas specifically refers to Cuneglasus as the bear. So how can he be the bear himself but also apparently the commander of the bear's kingdom or army? We can only infer that he is saying that Cuneglasus, known as the Bear, was *now* in charge of either the forces or kingdom that had once been the powerbase of someone *previously* called the Bear. This passage seemed to have puzzled historians, but from what I had pieced together, it all made perfect sense. These animal name epithets were often passed on to successors, such as the dragon kings of Gwynedd. It appeared, then, that not only had

Cuneglasus been given the sobriquet or title, the Bear, but had inherited it from his predecessor. As this had been his father, then it would seem that in Gildas's *On the Ruin and Conquest of Britain*—written within living memory of the Battle of Badon—I had found confirmation that Owain Ddantgwyn had indeed been known as the Bear, or Arth in Brythonic. Evidently, not only was Owain the historical figure upon whom the legends of Arthur were later based, but he could indeed have been known as Arthur.

Nonetheless, some historians I spoke to suggested that Gildas's use of the word *bear,* when referring to Cuneglasus, might *also* have been metaphorical. There is a passage in the Bible, in the Book of Revelation, where the Great Beast—the antichrist—is described:

> And the beast which I saw was like unto a leopard, and his feet were as the feet of a bear, and his mouth as the mouth of a lion: and the dragon [the Devil] gave him his power, and his seat, and great authority. [34]

Gildas addresses five of his contemporary British kings: Cuneglasus and Maglocunus, whom he calls respectively the Bear and the Dragon, and likens the other three to two of the other creatures mentioned in this biblical verse. Concerning Vortipor of Dyfed, he says he is dangerously cunning "like a spotted leopard,"[35] while he insults Constantine and Aurelius by insinuating that they are bound to the whims of their mothers, as are "lion whelps."[36] I agreed that Gildas may indeed have been inspired by the quotation from the Book of Revelation, but he probably got the idea to associate his nation's rulers with the antichrist as two of these figures already bore the titles of two of the creatures associated with the Great Beast. He addresses Cuneglasus and Maglocunus directly as the Bear and the Dragon,[37] while clearly only *comparing* the other three to the animals in question. We have already seen that Maglocunus was undoubtedly known as the Dragon. This was certainly not as a term of denigration, as demonstrated by the fact that the epithet was passed on to later generations. Indeed, when Gwynedd again rose to prominence in later centuries and assumed control over much of Wales, the insignia of its leader—the dragon—was adopted as the symbol of all Wales and is still on the national flag. (Try telling the Welsh that their country's emblem was inspired by a reference to the antichrist.) On further investigation I found that exactly the same applied to Cuneglasus's descendants.

Approximate Dates	Kings of Gwynedd	Kings of Powys
480 - 490	Enniaun	*Unknown*
490 - 520	Cadwallon (son of Enniaun)	Owain (son of Enniaun)
520 - 550	Maglocunus (son of Cadwallon)	Cuneglasus (son of Owain)
550 - 600		*Unknown*
600 - 630		Cyndrwyn
630 - 660		Cynddylan (son of Cyndrwyn)

Fig. 11.4. Rulers of Gwynedd and Powys from
the late fifth to mid-seventh centuries.

We discussed above how Penda and Cynddylan formed an alliance in the mid-600s. In his *Ecclesiastical History of the English People,* Bede provides evidence that this alliance was cemented by an interdynastic marriage between the ruling families of the Angle kingdom of Mercia and the British kingdom of Powys. He names Penda's wife—Mercia's queen—as Cynwise.[38] Not only is this a British name, as opposed to an Anglo-Saxon one, but it also has bears the affix *cyn*, of Cynddylan's dynasty. Bede also refers to Cynwise and Penda's daughter as Cyneherga, a half Brythonic, half Anglo-Saxon name.[39] There can be little doubt that some leading member of the Powys royal family, perhaps Cynddylan's sister or daughter, was married to Penda in order to seal the treaty, as was common practice in the ancient, post-Roman, and medieval world. And their descendants continued the line as rulers of Mercia. Following the death of Penda around 655, the Mercians came under Northumbrian domination, but a few years later they revolted, and Penda's son Atheldred defeated the Northumbrians at the Battle of Trent in 679. By the mid-700s Mercia had become the most powerful kingdom in England, but a century later it was superseded by the Saxon kingdom of Wessex, which eventually conquered the entire country, founding the united kingdom of England under King Athelstan in the early 900s.[40] Athelstan and his successors allowed many of the former Anglo-Saxon kingdoms a certain degree of autonomy, though relegating them to what were called earldoms, and their rulers were known as earls (from the Saxon word for chieftain). There were therefore the earls of Northumbria, Kent, Sussex, and so forth, who now functioned as regional barons. The former dynasty of the kingdom of Mercia became the earls of Mercia. Over time these earldoms became further divided into what we would now call counties, which is why many modern British counties (including those in Wales, which was annexed by the English during the Middle Ages) carry the names of the old kingdoms, such as Essex, Middlesex, Gwynedd, and Powys. By the medieval period Mercia was divided into a number of such regions, one of which was the county of Warwick (see plate 16), whose earls were directly descended from the ancient kings of Mercia. (Today it is called Warwickshire, and its capital, or county town, is what had been the seat of the medieval earls, the town of Warwick). Significantly, during the Middle Ages, the heraldic crest of the Warwick earls was the image of a bear holding a staff. Just like the Welsh Dragon, the Warwick banner seems to have originated with the earls' ancestors, the rulers of Mercia, who had used the bear as *their* emblem.

According to the John Rous, an English historian writing around 1450, the earls of Warwick were descended from an ancient warrior called Arthgallus, who had lived at the time of Arthur and whose emblem had been a bear. (Rous's work, commonly known as the *Rous Roll,* is preserved in the British Library, London, where it is cataloged as

Add. MS 48976.) Astonishingly, Rous says the reason why Arthgallus had used this image is because "the first syllable of his name, in Welsh, means bear." Nothing else is known concerning this Arthgallus. However, John Rous only went halfway translating the name. The second syllable, *gallus,* is a Gaelic word of original Celtic origin meaning "bold," still used in common speech in parts of Scotland today. So the name Arthgallus actually means "Bold Bear." I could not help but wonder whether this Bold Bear, who was thought to have lived at the time of Arthur, was none other than Arthur himself. One way or the other, the Mercians had adopted the bear as their kingdom's emblem, just as Gwynedd had adopted the dragon. So the notion that Gildas is calling Cuneglasus the "bear" merely to insult him is quite clearly wrong.

It was only at this point that I realized something else—something extremely significant—about Owain Ddantgwyn that fitted with the Arthurian saga. Geoffrey of Monmouth and the subsequent romancers portrayed Arthur as the son of Uther Pendragon. I had previously identified Enniaun of Gwynedd as the most likely historical figure upon whom Uther was based, the words *Uthr Pen Dragon* in Welsh, meaning "Terrible Head Dragon" (see chapter 8). Owain Ddantgwyn was Enniaun's son! Remarkably, not only was Owain the most likely historical figure behind the King Arthur story—a man who seems to have borne the title Arth—his father may have been known as Uther Pendragon. I now had no doubt that I had finally identified the man at the heart of the Arthurian legend.

12

Camlann

Although I had identified a historical King Arthur, my quest was far from over. The ultimate aim was to discover his final resting place—and that was going to be anything but easy. Almost nothing was known concerning the life of Owain Ddantgwyn, let alone where he was buried. I at least knew *how* he died. In his *On the Ruin and Conquest of Britain,* Gildas reveals that Owain was slain in battle.[1] We shall return to this reference shortly, but let's take things one step at a time. During the Dark Ages when important figures died in action, unless they were relatively close to their family burial site, they would generally be buried nearby (so long as there was anyone left to bury them). If I were to discover where Owain was laid to rest, I first needed to determine where he fell. As Gildas unfortunately neglects to reveal this essential information, I returned my attention to the Arthurian legend. Where was Arthur thought to have died? The quick answer, as we saw in chapter 3, was at a place called Camlann. However, precisely where this was originally thought to have been was far more difficult to answer.

The popular story of Arthur's death is that he was killed during a civil conflict, fighting his rebellious nephew Modred. In a single battle Modred is slain by Arthur, but not before he inflicts a fatal wound on his uncle, and the action ends in stalemate. This is the account made popular by Thomas Malory during the fifteenth century in his *Le Morte d'Arthur.*[2] Malory did not invent the themes in his narrative, however. Although he certainly added elaborations, he transcribed and retold accounts that had already developed throughout the Middle Ages. Malory sets the ill-fated battle between Modred and Arthur near the town of Salisbury in southern England, although he apparently did this to fit with his locating Camelot at nearby Winchester—which is a purely fictional interpolation, as we determined in chapter 2. Earlier authors tended to place the Battle of Camlann in Cornwall, inspired by Geoffrey of Monmouth's *History of the Kings of Britain* of 1136.[3] We also saw how Geoffrey's reliability is suspect when it comes to his Cornish Arthurian connections, as he appears to have been pandering to his patron's brother, the Earl of Cornwall. Nevertheless, neither Geoffrey nor any other medieval author invented the Battle of Camlann; it is listed in the *Welsh Annals* that record "the strife of Camlann, in which Arthur and Medraut perished."[4] So we know for certain that in the 900s, when the *Welsh Annals* was compiled in its present form, Arthur was believed to have died at Camlann along with someone called Medraut. Although Medraut was the Old Welsh rendering of the name Modred, the *Welsh Annals* fails to say who he was, or indeed whether he fought on the same or opposite side to Arthur. Nevertheless, this does additionally indicate that the notion of Arthur dying alongside his nephew Modred was not invented by Geoffrey of Monmouth or any other medieval author.

As with so many Arthurian sites, my attempt to locate Camlann was not helped by the medieval romances. Although Camlann was named as the site of Arthur's last battle, other than the spurious locations near Salisbury and in Cornwall, none seemed to reveal where it was fought. Even the earlier Welsh Arthurian tales appeared to be of no use. Nonetheless, even if the battle was merely a legend, there had presumably been a place called Camlann where the story was set. Sadly, like Badon, Camlann no longer survives on the modern map. British place names have often changed considerably since the post-Roman era; sometimes completely—after the invading Anglo-Saxons, Vikings, and Normans renamed a location—and sometimes due to the evolution of language. (We don't speak the same today at we did in Shakespeare's time, and Shakespeare didn't speak much like someone from the Middle

Ages.) Add to this the inconsistency of spelling in earlier times, and it is often the case that locations cited in Dark Age works can no longer be identified. Unfortunately, the name Camlann itself was of little help. In Welsh *cam* means "crooked," as in bent or winding, found for example in the name of the London district of Camden, meaning "Crooked Valley." And *lan* most directly translates as "shore" but can be applied to any waterside, such as the sea, a lake, or a stream. It is particularly associated with rivers, such as the town of Rhuddlan, meaning "Red Bank," beside the River Clwyd in northwest Wales. Camlann, therefore, probably meant "Crooked Bank," but this was of little help in locating where the battle was fought. The Crooked Bank in question could have been just about anywhere in the country.

Some scholars have speculated that the word *Camlann* inspired Camelot as the name for Arthur's court. We discussed in chapter 2 how the name Camelot appears to have been the invention of the twelfth-century French poet Chrétien de Troyes. He might indeed have been so inspired. Nevertheless, there is no suggestion in any of the Arthurian romances that Arthur's final battle was fought at his capital. There are many locations throughout the British Isles that Arthurian researchers have identified as Camelot (see chapter 2), but strangely the same is not true for Camlann. Usually, authors tend to go along with the romance writers, locating the battle either near Salisbury or in Cornwall. There is one notable exception. Those who subscribe to the theory of a northern King Arthur favor Camlann to have been the Roman fort of Camboglanna that stood toward the western end of Hadrian Wall. This fort, close to Carlisle in northwest England, is recorded in the early fifth-century Roman military document, the *Notitia Dignitatum* (discussed in chapter 9), its name thought to be derived from the Brythonic Cambo Glanna, meaning "Crooked Glen," Certainly *cam* meant "crooked," and *glan* was a Gaelic word for "glen," so this was quite possibly the original name of the district in which the fort stood. However, unless you happened to agree with the northern King Arthur theory, which I personally doubted (see chapter 10), then there seemed no particular reason to favor it over many other places in Britain, such as Camden, Camberley, and Camelsdale, all of which meant Winding Valley (*den, ley,* and *dale* are all old words for a valley).

Having reached something of a dead end trying to identify a place once called Camlann, I turned my attention to the enigmatic Modred, Arthur's opponent at the battle. Who exactly was he? Malory depicted him as both Arthur's nephew *and* his son, conceived during an incestuous affair with his sister Morgause. In later adaptations Morgan le Fey became Modred's mother, being portrayed as Arthur's half-sister, who transformed into a malicious sorceress when she failed to inherit the throne. However, in the original romances Modred was the son of Arthur's sister Anna and her husband, a man named Lot. Early Welsh literature also referred to Modred as Arthur's nephew but without elaborating on his parentage. Significantly, though, the Welsh triads (see chapter 6) portrayed Modred in a somewhat different light to the popular Arthurian saga. The Battle of Camlann was mentioned a number of times in the triads, where, as in the medieval romances, it was said to be the result of internal British strife between Arthur and Modred. The triads differed, however, in depicting the battle as a victory for Modred. The triad, *The Three Unfortunate Councils,* for example, blamed Arthur for dividing his forces at Camlann, affording Modred the advantage.[5] Although Arthur was said to have died at the battle, nothing was disclosed concerning Modred's death. What was made clear, however, was that after the battle the country returned to a state of feuding between its native British kingdoms. The big problem I faced, once again, was that the triads failed to reveal *where* the Battle of Camlann was fought.

Something I did find particularly interesting was the parallel between the story of Arthur's demise and the death of Owain Ddantgwyn. Like King Arthur, Owain appeared to have been killed by his nephew. Gildas tells us that Maglocunus overthrew his uncle in battle: "Did you not, in the first years of your youth, bitterly crush with sword, spear, and fire, your uncle the king and his courageous soldiers?"[6] Although Gildas typically failed to name this king, there is only one person it could be: Owain Ddantgwyn, the only uncle we know of who was actually a king. Although the medieval Arthurian romances had

Arthur and Modred dying together, whereas Maglocunus certainly did not die fighting *his* uncle, Owain's fate did fit with the Welsh triads portraying Modred as the victor at Camlann. The triad authors seemed to have drawn upon reliable information concerning the state of Britain immediately after the time Arthur was thought to have lived. The triad *The Three Frivolous Causes,* for example, referred to the Battle of Camlann as a direct cause of the eventual loss of England to the Anglo-Saxons:

> The third [frivolous cause of the Britons' woes] was the battle of Camlann, between Arthur and Modred, where Arthur and 100,000 of the best British warriors were killed. Because of these three foolish battles, the Saxons took the country of Lloegria [England] from the Cymry [Britons], for there were too few left to oppose them.[7]

As seen in chapter 11, the Saxons did renew their advance in the early sixth century, ultimately conquering all England. As these triads, evidently summarizing earlier Dark Age war poems (see chapter 6), appeared to demonstrate an accurate grasp of post-Roman British history, it was reasonable to suppose that the original accounts the authors adapted had portrayed Modred as both the victor at Camlann and as a survivor of the conflict. There was, however, a big difference between all the accounts—medieval and Old Welsh—concerning Arthur's death at the hands of his nephew and Owain being killed by *his* nephew. The usurpers have different names: Modred and Maglocunus. Was the name Modred, I wondered, a later rendition of the name Maglocunus?

Maglocunus's name certainly did change over time. It is thought to derive from the Latin *magnus* (great) and the *cun* element (hound) that so often appears in the Cunedda lineage. Later Welsh works refer to him as Maelgwn. The first syllable, *mael,* in Gaelic means "chief," while the second, *gwn,* is thought to have been a localized spelling of the Brythonic *cun.* So the Latin Maglocunus and the Old Welsh Maelgwn mean basically the same thing: "Great Hound." It must have been rather confusing to later generations that no longer employed creature names as titles: a man born Maglocunus, the Great Hound, became known as Maelgwn, but also bore the title the dragon. No wonder there is so often ambiguity in early Welsh and medieval literature about exactly who did what and to whom. The name Modred also appears in various renderings, such as Medrawd, Medrod, and Medraut. It was only after Geoffrey of Monmouth in the twelfth century that the name Modred was settled upon, but even then the inconsistency of spelling still resulted in variations, such as Mordred, Moddred, and Medred. The origin of the name Medraut, as it is found in the earliest work to include him, the *Welsh Annals,* is a mystery. It doesn't readily break down into anything in Welsh or Brythonic. However, the nearest meaningful term, *mudrwg,* from the Welsh *mud* (silent) and *drwg* (evil) refers to a sleeping or undetected enemy. This, therefore, could have been a name coined by the Britons for the traitor who destroyed British unity and handed the initiative to the common enemy. Perhaps confusion concerning the man's two names, Maglocunus and Maelgwn, together with his tile, the dragon, was made all the more problematic after he was further dubbed with a term for traitor. This might well have resulted in a single person being later recorded as two separate figures.

Alternatively, it's possible that accounts of Arthur being killed by his nephew were misconstrued by early Welsh authors. Noting references that someone called Medraut died with Arthur, they wrongly assume he was the nephew in question. Certainly by the time the *Welsh Annals* was compiled in the 900s, Modred and Maglocunus were regarded as different people, as Medraut is said to have died at Camlann, while Maelgwn died of plague a few decades later.[8] However, this Medraut may have had nothing to do with Arthur's death. Welsh authors might deliberately have ignored reference to Maglocunus being Arthur's treacherous nephew, as he became something of a national hero, or "founding father," to the Welsh when Gwynedd's influence spread throughout much of the country in the seventh century. Once Maglocunus's name was effectively expunged from the Arthurian saga, later writers seized upon the Medraut who fell at Camlann—someone about whom nothing else was known—as the most likely villain of the plot. Nonetheless, whether or not Modred and Maglocunus were one and the same was not the salient issue I needed to resolve. Owain Ddantgwyn was the figure I had identified as the historical Arthur, and he *was* killed by his nephew. The big question was still "where?"

The major problem I faced was Gildas's failure to reveal the location of the battle where Maglocunus defeated his uncle. It certainly seemed to have taken place around the most likely period in which Arthur's last battle was fought. The only historical source to date the Battle of Camlann is the *Welsh Annals*, which lists it as year 93. As we saw in chapter 9, the *Welsh Annals* does not use the AD system of dating. Instead it starts with the Saxon advent as its year 1, which according to the Anglo-Saxon Chronicle occurred in AD 449. Accordingly, year 93 would be 541. Bede, conversely, dates the Saxon advent as 447,[9] which would mean that the *Annals'* year 93 is 539. (Various scholars derive different dates, a couple of years either way.) However, we also saw that the *Welsh Annals* is sometimes out by a decade or so regarding the dating of early events. One thing that we can be sure of, though, is the number of years the *Annals* separates the battles of Badon and Camlann. It lists the Battle of Badon as year 72, which means that, according to the compiler, twenty-one years divided the two events. We derived a reliable dating of Badon to around AD 500, give or take a couple of years, from Gildas's work, and this tallies with what we deduced from Nennius's account, which, on analysis, places Arthur's period as British leader as beginning in the 490s (see chapter 9). Nennius does not mention the Battle of Camlann, however, as his writing concerned only Arthur's earlier victories.[10] If the *Welsh Annals'* separation of the two battles by twenty-one years is right, then Camlann would have occurred sometime around the year 520, which fits with the Anglo-Saxon Chronicle recording that in 519 the Saxons renewed their advance into British territory, defeating the Britons and establishing their kingdom of Wessex.[11]

The tide of warfare had clearly turned against the Britons around 520 and continued thereafter in favor of the Anglo-Saxons. This would appear to be the period Gildas laments, blaming Maglocunus for overthrowing his uncle, an act that divided the country and resulted in the onslaught of the pagan enemy. Gildas specifically relates how this occurred in the early years of Maglocunus's reign, as he describes him as a youth at the time.[12] Like his cousin Cuneglasus, Maglocunus appears to have been middle aged around 545 when Gildas wrote, which would indeed make him a young man a quarter of a century earlier. (Interestingly, this is another correlation with the Arthurian story, in which Modred is depicted as a youth when he rebels against King Arthur.) So I had a date for both Owain's demise and for Camlann coinciding around AD 520. And this certainly did help to narrow down the location of the battle.

I had deduced that Owain Ddantgwyn was king of Powys. If he was Arthur, then this would not contradict with him also being the overall British leader. Nennius relates that Arthur had fought "with the kings of the Britons, but he himself was leader of battles," implying that although he was supreme commander, the various British kingdoms remained intact and autonomous.[13] Arthur could indeed have been king of one such kingdom. I had also reasoned that when Gildas wrote, around 545, unity had collapsed, and Owain's son Cuneglasus retained power only in Powys, while Maglocunus ruled Gwynedd. Gildas blames Maglocunus almost entirely for destroying British unity, ranting on for three whole chapters about his wicked deeds after killing his uncle.[14] As the uncle in question was Owain Ddantgwyn, a king of Powys, then this would suggest that Maglocunus attempted to take over that kingdom. However, he must ultimately have failed, as by the period Gildas wrote, Cuneglasus seems to have ruled Powys. So the most likely scenario would appear to be that, after Badon, the alliance of British kings remained intact for a couple of decades while Owain was alive, but as he grew older and his hold on power lessened, Maglocunus saw the opportunity to attack his uncle and attempt to seize his kingdom. This meant that the site of the battle between Owain and his nephew would have to be somewhere in either Gwynedd or Powys.

There is actually a valley called Camlan, spelled with one *n,* some five miles to the east of the Welsh town of Dolgellau, and another, ten miles farther east, near the village of Mallwyd, both being in the east-ern region of Gwynedd as it existed in the early 500s. However, neither was a likely site for a major battle fought between Gwynedd and Powys at the time. The Gwynedd capital had been at Caer Ddegannwy on the north coast of Wales, around fifty miles to the north of either Camlan, while the Powys capital of Viroconium was some fifty miles to the east of even the closest of the two locations. They both seemed completely out of the way for any strategic engagement between the primary forces of the two kingdoms.

I decided to contact a group that specialized in the reenactment of Dark Age battles and ask their opinion. From Gildas's narrative it seemed that Maglocunus was the aggressor, so it was more probable that he was marching against Viroconium rather than Owain marching on Caer

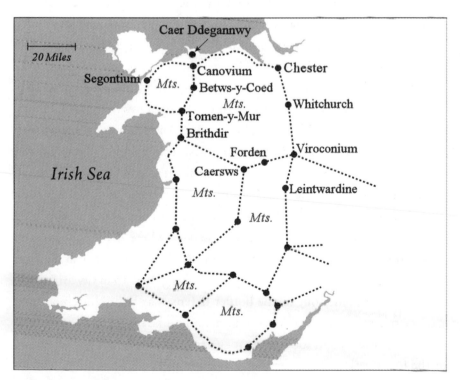

Fig. 12.1. Wales and west-central England: the principal Roman road network still in use in the early sixth century.

Ddegannwy. What strategy, I asked, would Owain have adopted had he learned of an army advancing from Gwynedd? Would he be advised to stay put in the capital, or move his forces out to meet them? The experts unanimously agreed that it would be far better to encounter the opposition in the field, rather than risk a siege. They concurred with my assessment that the two Camlans were too distant: it would have been crazy for Owain to march out so far from Viroconium when there were far better places to make a stand against Maglocunus's army nearer to home. He would most likely have engaged the enemy at one of the defensive sites established where the old Roman roads crossed the border between the two kingdoms.

The Roman road network still survived pretty much intact and was by far the best, if not the only, way to maneuver armies in the early sixth century. The alternative was a long and treacherous haul over the mountainous regions circumvented by the roads. During the period there were only two logical routes to move a sizable armed force between Caer Ddegannwy and Viroconium. Two important Roman roads met at the fortification of Canovium, just to the south of Caer Ddegannwy. One followed the northern coast from Segontium to Chester, and then south to Viroconium, passing through the Roman town of Mediolanum, modern Whitchurch. The other, known as Sarn Helen, meaning Helen's Causeway (named after a Roman empress), followed the River Conwy down to modern Betws-y-Coed, where it turned southwest through mountain passes to the old Roman fortifications at Tomen-y-Mur, and then south to Brithdir near the estuary of the River Mawddach. From here another road ran east to Caersws where it met the road to Viroconium, which passed through the Roman settlement at Forden. In the case of the first route, the experts suggested that Owain would be advised to march out to the border defenses at Whitchurch, around twenty-five miles north of Viroconium, and make his stand there; and in the case of the second route, they suggested that he should make a stand at the fortifications at Forden, some twenty miles to the southwest of his capital. It was while investigating the area around Forden that I came across a place name that seemed strangely familiar.

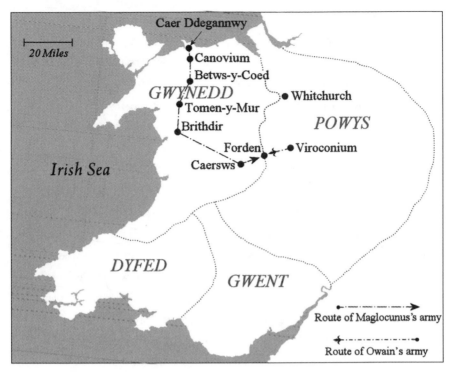

Fig. 12.2. Wales and west-central England: the likely
kingdom boundaries and routes taken by Maglocunus's and
Owain's armies to their battle at Forden.

The Roman road at Forden runs beside the ninth-century Anglo-Saxon defensive embankment of Offa's Dyke. According to the experts' reasoning, Owain's forces would have established their position just beside this road, on high ground now marked by a later Norman earthwork known as a Motte and Baily, a series of defensive embankments and ditches surrounding an artificial hillock. Driving around this area, I came across a farm called Rhyd-y-Groes. I could not think where, but I was sure I had seen this name before somewhere during my investigations into the King Arthur mystery. I stopped to ask if anyone knew of any Arthurian associations with the area. No one immediately recalled anything, but I did learn that the meadow to the immediate south of the farmhouse had been called Rhyd-y-Groes for centuries. In English, the Welsh Rhyd-y-Groes meant "Ford of the Cross" and was originally the name of a ford crossing a minor river that wound through the land. A stone cross was thought to have once stood there, but now a bridge, called Shiregrove Bridge, takes the modern A490 road over the river at the location where the ford once crossed. On returning home I finally discovered where I had seen reference to Rhyd-y-Groes before. It was a passing mention in one of the Welsh Arthurian tales called *The Dream of Rhonabwy,* the same story that included the oldest description of Arthur's sword (see chapter 9).

The Dream of Rhonabwy, now preserved in The Red Book of Hergest, is generally considered to have been composed in Powys around 1150 to address Madog ap Maredudd, a historical figure who ruled the kingdom in the mid-twelfth century. In 1149 Madog recaptured part of the county of Shropshire from the English, but while his army was away, the king of Gwynedd seized the opportunity to invade northern Powys. The story seems to have been written between that date and Madog's death around 1159, as a cautionary tale likening his rash campaigning with King Arthur's ill-fated demise at the battle of Camlann centuries before. I had virtually discarded *The Dream of Rhonabwy* as being of any help in my search for a historical King Arthur as it seemed to be largely allegorical in context. On reading it again I was shocked by its implications. Apart from Geoffrey of Monmouth, who unreliably places Arthur's final battle in Cornwall, and Wace, who followed his lead (see chapter 3), it was the oldest surviving narrative to provide an actual location for the battle of Camlann—and a very precise one at that. I could not believe that I had not appreciated its relevance earlier. But then again, as far as I could tell, no other Arthurian researcher had either.

The tale concerns a dream experienced by its central character, Rhonabwy, one of Madog's servants, in which he goes back to the time of King Arthur. At the start of the vision, Rhonabwy meets a messenger from Camlann who miraculously transports him to Arthur's camp immediately before the battle.[15] Soon after the hero meets King Arthur, the story becomes a symbolic tale concerning good and evil, right and wrong, and the power of the church versus the power of kings. Although the later part of the tale involves a mixed dreamscape concerning various episodes in Arthur's life, such as him receiving his sword, the Battle of Badon, and the formation of his court, all jumbled with complex symbolism, the location of the battle of Camlann is quite specific. The tale ends before the commencement of the battle itself and provides no details concerning the actual engagement. However, Arthur's encampment in the run up to the battle, where he is joined by various troops of horsemen, is said to be at a ford, specifically named as Rhyd-y-Groes, which crossed a river in the Havren Valley, a mile from his main forces.[16] The area I visited around Forden exactly matched this description. The Havren, now spelled Hafren, is the Welsh name for the River Severn, and the ford of Rhyd-y-Groes that I had found was not only in the Severn Valley but exactly a mile to the southeast of the fortification at Forden where the experts on warfare of the period had suggested Owain's main army would have been.

Astonishingly, I had been led to this area as one of the most likely locations for the battle fought between Owain and his nephew Maglocunus, quite independently of anything in any Arthurian narrative. Yet it was precisely here that *The Dream of Rhonabwy* author located the Battle of Camlann between Arthur and his nephew Modred. I was certain that I had identified both the site of Owain and Arthur's final battle. Surely, it was far beyond coincidence that they were fought in the same place, especially as I had already reasoned that the two men were one and the same. We have seen how many of the early Welsh Arthurian writers had drawn upon earlier material as background to their narratives. It was therefore a reasonable assumption that either *The Dream of Rhonabwy* author had based his location for the battle on an earlier Dark Age war poem, or that during the twelfth century, in the kingdom of Powys where the story was composed, it was commonly believed that Rhyd-y-Groes was where Arthur's final battle was fought. One way or the other, it seemed that this location had long been overlooked by Arthurian researchers because everyone was focusing on either the south or far north of England. Powys had been completely ignored.

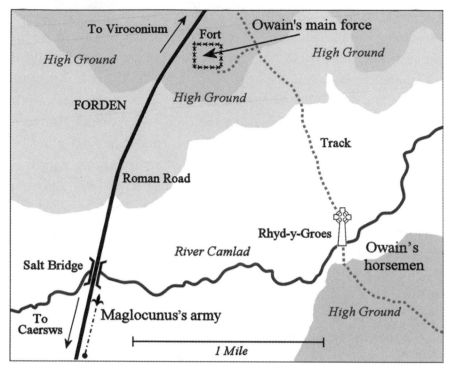

Fig. 12.3. The probable military scenario immediately before Owain's final battle.

When I returned to survey the area in more detail, I could easily picture what may have occurred. The narrative places Arthur and his horsemen at the ford, a mile away from his main forces. Historically, the likely place for Owain's army to have established its position was about a mile to the northwest of Shiregrove Bridge, on high ground overlooking the site. Through Forden the modern B4388 road follows the course of the old Roman road exactly, and to reach the fortification any advancing army would have to cross the river downstream from Rhyd-y-Groes where the road crosses it at a location now called Salt Bridge. Between the Shiregrove and Salt Bridges, the river winds its way across a smooth plane, but at the site of the original ford, it bends slightly around a spur of land rising sharply to the south. This meant that a considerable force of mounted warriors could remain there, hidden from anyone traveling along the Roman road from where it begins at today's village of

Caersws, fifteen miles to the southwest. It was the perfect place for an ambush by the Powys cavalry. If this was indeed where Owain fought his last battle, then I could imagine his horsemen charging across the valley to engage the enemy around Salt Bridge. The plan may have been for the troops in the Forden fort to come out to join them, catching the enemy in a pincer movement. Something, however, must have gone drastically wrong. Perhaps Gwynedd scouts had spotted Owain and his contingent at Rhyd-y-Groes, and Maglocunus attacked them instead. If so, with the element of surprise lost, the outcome would almost certainly have been Owain's defeat. If this was how the Battle of Camlann was played out, it would certainly explain why the triads depicted it as a catastrophe caused by Arthur dividing his forces.

I was certain that somewhere along the winding river at Rhyd-y-Groes, the man behind the legend of King Arthur had finally met his fate. It was not just the fact that the tightly meandering river matched with a place called Camlann (Crooked Bank) that finally persuaded me beyond reasonable doubt that this was the site of the battle, but the name of the river itself. As far back as records went, this tributary of the nearby River Severn was—and still is—called the Camlad (see plate 17).

13

The Once
and Future King

I was convinced that I had finally indentified the historical King
Arthur: the British chieftain whose original name had been Owain
Ddantgwyn. Not only was Owain known by the title Arth, but his
father seems to have been called Uther Pendragon. Furthermore, just
like Arthur, Owain was toppled by his rebellious nephew. Owain was
a king of Powys, and the oldest reference to place Arthur's origins in a
geographical setting puts him in precisely that kingdom. He ruled from
the most sophisticated city in the country during the specific period
Arthur's court was said to have been at just such a capital. His final
battle was fought around AD 520, the very time Arthur seems to have
fought *his* final battle, and the most likely location for this conflict was
right where the oldest reference to provide an exact location for Arthur's
last battle was set. Owain was doing the same things as Arthur, at the
same time, and in the same place! Who else could he be but the King
Arthur of legend? Now that I had discovered where this historical King
Arthur ultimately fell, I was ready to tackle the crucial question. Where
was he laid to rest?

In the Arthurian tradition the battle of Camlann ended in a kind
of stalemate that weakened the entire nation to the advantage of the
Anglo-Saxons. Historically, exactly the same occurred following the
demise of Owain Ddantgwyn at the winding River Camlad, a name

that could easily have derived from Camlann, "Crooked Bank." If his final battle had been fought in some remote location, then Owain could have been buried anywhere nearby. But it wasn't. It occurred in his own kingdom, just a few miles from his capital. If the battle resulted in an outright victory for his enemy, and they accordingly conquered his realm, then his body might either have been left to rot or interred by survivors as quickly as possible somewhere in the immediate vicinity. But it wasn't. The forces on both sides were critically diminished during the encounter; Maglocunus retreated to Gwynedd, while Owain's son Cuneglasus succeeded to the throne of Powys and his kingdom remained intact. Accordingly, Owain would almost certainly have been laid to rest at the customary burial site for the Powys royal family. But where was that?

There was no doubt where the kings of Powys were interred a century and a half later. After the defeat of Powys at the hands of the Northumbrian king Oswy in the mid-600s, the Britons of the region where impelled to retreat into the western part of their kingdom, to the safety of the Welsh mountains. Their new capital was at Dinas Bran in Llangollen (see chapter 6), and the Powys kings were buried at the royal mausoleum in what is now Saint Tysilio's Church at Meifod in the Vyrnwy Valley, twenty miles to the south. When I was researching in the 1990s, the whereabouts of their original burial site was still a mystery. Owain, I guessed, might have been buried at Viroconium, but this seemed unlikely. Following an original Roman custom, the Britons of the period considered it inappropriate to bury their honored dead within town walls. In fact, in Britain the Celtic people tended to bury the privileged classes at remote, sacred locations, some distance from major settlements. The later mausoleum at Meifod, for instance, was in an isolated vale, some twenty miles from the contemporary capital. The Powys dynasty of 150 years earlier was probably buried where the chieftains of the region had been interred for centuries. Find that, and it would be odds-on that I had found the last resting place of the man who was Arthur. However, it was not only problematic that nothing from the Roman or post-Roman era specifically recorded its location, but the grave of no British ruler from the late fifth and early sixth century had ever been discovered. So I faced yet another big challenge.

To start with I needed to determine the British funerary practices of the early 500s. By the end of the seventh century, Catholicism was reasserting its influence in Britain, but during the period around AD 500, the religion of the native Britons was a kind of hybrid pagan-Christianity. At best, there was a somewhat blurred dividing line between Christianity and paganism (see chapter 4). Although many people were nominally Christian—believing in Christ and the Bible—religious convention still involved what we might today consider pagan customs. The old sacred sites were still revered, although churches and chapels were erected over earlier shrines; funerary rites still involved such things as votive offerings; and people were buried with their belongings, known as grave goods. Astonishingly, many pagan traditions can still be found interpolated in modern Christianity: holly, ivy, and Christmas trees were all druidic adornments for the midwinter solstice, and painted eggs at Easter were sacred to the goddess Eostre—indeed the festival is actually named after her. During the post-Roman era pagan deities and demigods continued to be venerated but were usually transmogrified into biblical figures or characters from early Christian mythology. For example, Bran became Saint Bron, Jesus's uncle; Macha became Saint Mary, Jesus's mother; and Anann became Saint Anne, Jesus's grandmother. As noted in chapter 5, the type of burial site from the period that I hoped to find was in all probability an island in a sacred lake—perhaps an island that had once had a Celtic church or more than one church upon it, such as the two chapels on Station Island and the Isle of Maree (see chapter 4). The problem was that there were a number of such potential lake islands in ancient Powys.

There did, however, survive a Dark Age war poem that might help narrow down the search. Remarkably, two people who had been members of the royal court at Viroconium during the mid-seventh century had endured to write about its final days. One of them was Llywarch, whom we met in chapter 11, and the other was the sister of King Cynddylan, whom we also met briefly in chapter 5. Princess Heledd (pronounced "Helleth") fled eastern Powys when the kingdom was plundered by the Angle king Oswy in 658 and finally settled in the kingdom of Gwent, in what is now the village of Llanhilleth, named after her, four miles to the west of Pontypool in southeast Wales. Llanhilleth, meaning Saint Heledd, was so named because the princess was canonized after her death for founding a priory at the site where she was said to be buried. A church dedicated to Saint Illtyd now marks the spot (see plate 18). Not only a princess and a saint, Heledd also became a bard, and a number of poems were attributed to her. Heledd features in The Red Book of Hergest (see chapter 11) where she is referred to by the epithet *hwyedic,* Old Welsh for "hawk."[1] It would seem then that Hawk may have been her bardic title, as Merlin was the Eagle (see chapter 8). A particularly fascinating reference to the princess is found in the Welsh triad, the *Three Unrestricted Guests of Arthur's Court.*[2] Both Heledd and her contemporary bard Llywarch are named as two of these privileged guests. These historical figures lived a century and a half too late to have really been associated with King Arthur, but if Arthur was Owain Ddantgwyn, then the court at Viroconium—by Heledd's time, the seat of her brother Cynddylan—would indeed have been what was once Arthur's court. Perhaps this is what the triad implied.

One of the poems attributed to Heledd still survives in The Red Book of Hergest. Called the *Canu Heledd* (Song of Heledd) in its present form, it dates from the ninth century, but many linguists consider it to have been copied from an original dating to the mid-to-late 600s.[3] Written in the first person, it concerns Heledd grieving the death of her brother the king and most of her family, the destruction of the court, and the devastation of her homeland by the Anglo-Saxons. As the *Song of Heledd* recounts the death of King Cynddylan and his brothers, I decided to visit the Bodleian Library and read through an English translation in the hope of finding some mention of the burial site of the Powys royal family. (At the time there were no published English versions readily available.) I was completely astonished to find that the poem not only referred to the burial site but actually named it. I realized that it was most unlikely that any scholar would have read the

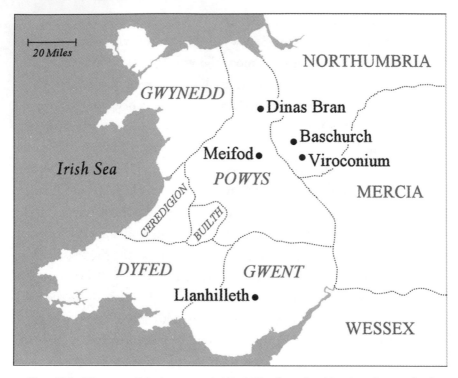

Fig. 13.1. Western Britain around AD 660, after the Northumbrians had invaded eastern Powys.

poem in an attempt to discover King Arthur's grave, but was shocked that no one seemed to have appreciated that it provided the location of such an important Dark Age cemetery. If they had, then nothing was done about it.

As we saw in chapter 11, according to the *Welsh Annals* the Powys king Cynddylan died in 657, but it was not until the following year that "Oswy came and took plunder."[4] It was after this assault on eastern Powys that the *Song of Heledd* was set. Mourning the loss of Cynddylan and other members of her family, Heledd recounted how the capital and its court, the Hall of Cynddylan, were deserted, and other settlements lay in ruins. After describing the desolation, she talked about a desecrated compound called Eglwyseu Bassa,[5] which seemed to have been a particularly sacred location as it was described by the Old Welsh *breint,*[6] which in modern Welsh is *fraint,* meaning "a person, place, or thing of special status or privilege." Eglwyseu Bassa, the poet explained, was where the king lay buried. In Old Welsh the poem described Eglwyseu Bassa as Cynddylan's *orffowys,*[7] now the modern Welsh *gorffwys,* meaning "resting place," and went on to call it his *diwed ymgynnwys.*[8] In modern Welsh *diwedd* means "final" and *ymgynnwys* means "place of containment." In other words, Eglwyseu Bassa was the site of Cynddylan's final resting place and his grave. I could be left with little doubt regarding this translation, as the location is also described as being *tir mablan Cynddylan wyn,*[9] Old Welsh meaning literally "place of the little land of fair Cynddylan." *Mablan* (little land) was the term used for a "grave plot." The poem also related that the king's siblings were buried there: *Eglwysau Bassa ynt yng heno, etivedd Cyndrwyn* ("Eglwysau Bassa affords space tonight to the progeny [children] of Cyndrwyn [Cynddylan's father]").[10]

It would seem, therefore, that the family burial site of the Powys dynasty was originally at Eglwysau Bassa. But where exactly was that? The word *bassa,* I learned, was unknown in Brythonic, Old Welsh, or modern Welsh, so the experts I spoke to at Oxford University thought that it was probably a personal name. In Old Welsh *eglwyseu* meant "churches"—plural—and as Bassa seemed to have been someone's name, Eglwyseu Bassa must have meant "Bassa's Churches" or "Churches of Bassa." So it was evidently a place with more than one church, but exactly who was Bassa?

There are around a dozen places in Britain now bearing the prefix *bas;* most of them are listed by the *Oxford Dictionary of British Place Names* as being named after someone called Bassa.[11] The authors of most books, and today's websites, usually suppose this Bassa to have been an Anglo-Saxon chieftain. Quite where this idea originated is far from clear. Personally, I have failed to find contemporary reference to any Anglo-Saxon with that name. There are only two with some similarity. The Anglo-Saxon Chronicle records a priest called Bass who built a church in the village of Reculver in Kent in the year 669,[12] while Bede records a soldier called Bassus in the army of King Edwin of Northumbria in 633;[13] neither of them were of any great significance. The town of Basingstoke and the nearby village of Old Basing in the southern county of Hampshire go further than the other "Bas" locations in boasting their founder to have been a specific Bassa: a Saxon leader who settled the area around AD 700. In fact, it is claimed that his tribe, the Basingas, were named after him. However, both these assertions are highly suspect. Although the Anglo-Saxon Chronicle does mention a battle at Basing (probably Old Basing) in 871, there is no historical reference as to how the place got its name and nothing whatsoever about a tribe called the Basingas—let alone a man called Bassa. All references I uncovered regarding this tribe and its supposed founder can be traced back to an entry in *The Concise Oxford Dictionary of English Place Names* by the Swedish author Eilert Ekwall, published in 1940.[14] My conclusion: If the *bas* prefix in British place names did originate with someone called Bassa, then whomever this was he was clearly not an Anglo-Saxon important enough to have been recorded. The name Bassa did exist, however. It was actually a Roman name—and a female one at that. Bassus was a relatively common man's name, and Bassa was the feminine equivalent, like Julius and Julia. Famous Roman women bearing the name include Rubellia Bassa, a member of the imperial family in the first century; Julia Quadratilla Bassa, the daughter of Julius Quadratus Bassus, a consul in the second century; and a wealthy aristocratic lady known simply as Bassa, who became a leading Christian in Jerusalem in the mid-fifth century.

The British places bearing the prefix *bas* are found all over the country: for example, Baslow (Bassa's Mound) in the county of Derbyshire, Bassingbourn (Bassa's Stream) in Cambridgeshire, Bassingfield (Bassa's Field) in Nottinghamshire, and Bassingham (Bassa's Village) in Lincolnshire. These locations, which were all occupied during the Roman and post-Roman eras, are distributed right across Britain, so they were clearly not named after some local hero. More likely, they were named in honor of a woman of *national* importance. It seemed to me that, as no historical figures were known to have borne that name in post-Roman Britain, the character in question was probably a goddess.

Interestingly, Nennius includes a location called Bassas as the site of one of Arthur's battles. His Latin, *Sextum bellum super flumen quod vocatur Bassas,* translates directly as: "The sixth battle was over the river which is called Bassas."[15] Today there is no river bearing this name, and the battle site remains unidentified, but it does show that when Nennius wrote during the early 800s, there was a river that seems to have been sacred to a goddess, or a revered woman, called Bassa. (As apostrophes were not used until the sixteenth century, Bassas means Bassa's—as in, belonging to Bassa.)

We examined in chapter 5 how the Brythonic language formed from a combination of Celtic and Latin, and that many Roman designations were adopted for native British deities, such as Minerva. Bassa, therefore, may well have been the name assumed for a goddess, later a saint, of the Britons. The place name suffixes such as *ham* and *bourn,* mentioned above, were indeed Anglo-Saxon words for "village" and "stream," but as the Anglo-Saxons became Christians in the seventh century, and if Bassa was considered a saint, there would be no need for them to erase her name from the locations they renamed. They simply changed the Welsh words for village and stream—*pentref* and *nant*—for the Old English equivalents, but kept the name of the saint. Accordingly, Eglwyseu Bassa probably meant "Churches of the Goddess Bassa," or by Christian times, as there were churches at the site and gods often became saints, the "Churches of *Saint* Bassa."

No place in Britain is still called Eglwyseu Bassa or the Churches of Bassa today, but was there anywhere in what had been the kingdom of Powys that might once have borne that name? Indeed there was: a village called Baschurch, around twelve miles northwest of Viroconium. Now in the English county of Shropshire, it stands in scenic countryside and has a population of around fifteen hundred. It has been called Baschurch as far back as surviving records go, which is almost a thousand years. When I first visited the place in the 1990s, local historians did consider it to have been the location mentioned in the *Song of Heledd;* specifically, that the original Eglwyseu Bassa was an ancient earthwork on the edge of the modern village. Standing on a plain of marshy land, it was comprised of a small hill covering some four and a half acres, surrounded by two artificial circular embankments, together with an oval area of raised ground, around an acre in size, 130 yards to the northeast, also surrounded by a man-made earthen rampart. The two earthworks were connected by a linear causeway, and a further 260-yard causeway linked the hill to rising ground to the south. Today much of the low-lying area around the complex has been drained for farming, but in earlier times, when water levels were considerably higher, the two enclosures were islands surrounded entirely by water. The causeways therefore linked the islands together and the larger island to the surrounding land. Today the hillock is called Berth Hill, and the oval acre is known locally as the Enclosure; both features, together with the causeways, are collectively called The Berth (see plate 19). So during the Dark Ages, The Berth consisted of a pair of connected islands in the middle of a lake about half a mile long and wide. Part of this original lake, now called Berth Pool, still survives to the immediate south of the hill, much of the rest is pastureland used for the grazing of livestock. The word *berth* comes from the Anglo-Saxon word *burh,* meaning "fort," which would appear to have been the name applied to it by the Angle Mercians who used it as a fortification in the later Dark Ages. Its original name is unrecorded, so it is reliably considered to have been the site that the *Song of Heledd* refers to as Eglwyseu Bassa—the Churches of Bassa. (Today Baschurch is the name for the village and its surrounding district, which includes The Berth.) Although local historians did regard The Berth as the site of Eglwyseu Bassa named in the *Song of Heledd,* no one I interviewed seemed to have realized the significance of the poem concerning the location's status as the burial site of the kings of Powys.

I returned to the Rowley's House Museum in nearby Shrewsbury to again question its curator Mike Stokes. What *was* known about the site? The earliest official survey of The Berth was conducted by the Shropshire Archaeological Society in 1937, which concluded that because of its low-lying position it was unlikely to have been constructed as a primary fortification, although its ramparts did suggest a limited defensive purpose. It was certainly no hill fort and was too small to have been a fortified settlement. The expert's conclusion, Stokes explained, was that it served as some form of ceremonial compound. The only archaeological excavations of the site were carried out in 1962 to 1963 by archaeologist Peter Gelling of Birmingham University. They were, however, severely limited due to a lack of funding. Basically just a trial dig, it did unearth evidence, such as pottery fragments, to determine that the earthworks had been constructed in pre-Roman times but that the complex was still in use, or certainly being reused, during the post-Roman era. The general consensus was that the embankments circling each of the islands would have supported timber stockades, surrounding buildings constructed for religious purposes. So it did indeed seem to have been a ritual center where high-status figures might well have been buried, just as the *Song of Heledd* implied.

So my research had led me to the following conclusions: the historical Arthur was Owain Ddantgwyn; Owain was a king of Powys; and the kings of Powys seem to have been buried at The Berth. From the dating of occupation, this site would almost certainly have been where the kingdom's royal family had been interred as far back as the early sixth century, if not earlier. I had found a viable last resting place for King Arthur. But this left me with a seemingly insurmountable dilemma. The Berth might contain dozens of burials! How on earth would it be possible to identify which of them was the grave of Owain Ddantgwyn?

Before continuing I needed to further collate what I had learned about early Dark Age funerary practices. Until the late twentieth century, historians tended to assume that during the post-Roman period pagan burials included grave goods, such as jewelry, weapons, and pottery, whereas Christian burials did not. These days, archaeology has proved such assumptions to be far too simplistic. There was in fact a considerable overlap from late Roman times, right through until the eighth century.[16] The Christian prohibition of grave goods did not become widespread until the later Dark Ages. In fact, as we have seen in Britain of the fifth and sixth centuries, the dividing line between

Christian and pagan was anything but clearly defined. High-status individuals tended to be interred, rather than cremated, and were usually buried in a circular pit, dug to a depth of around six feet. Some had personal belongings buried with them, which, in the case of warriors, would often include weapons.[17] As noted in chapter 4, the warrior's sword would often be cast into a river, lake, or pool, either as a votive tribute to a water deity if he were pagan or an offering to an equivalent saint. Consequently, another weapon might be buried with him, such as his shield. So at least I knew what to look for, but once again, this was of no help in specifically locating Owain's grave.

I decided that the next thing was to archaeologically verify that The Berth really had been used as the burial site of the Powys kings. The land was privately owned, in fact, by three separate farms, but it was also a listed monument. That meant that for any archaeological work to be approved, I would not only need the permission from the landowners but from English Heritage. English Heritage is an executive department of the British government whose purpose is to protect and preserve structures and sites of historical interest. The Berth was known to have been an ancient site worthy of preservation. So to prevent it from being damaged by digging, building, or other invasive activity, English Heritage had instituted a preservation order. This meant that it was illegal, even for the landowners, to excavate the area without government permission. In order to secure such agreement, those involved in any such work would have to be professional archaeologists. Even then, there would need to be extensive evidence to justify an excavation. Luckily, by this time there was a way to survey The Berth without disturbing the site: a scientific procedure called geophysics that employs sophisticated electronic equipment to determine what lies beneath the earth without the need for intrusive digging. However, geophysics surveys don't come cheap. Apart from the fact that much of Berth Hill was covered with trees, thick brambles, and undergrowth that would need to be cleared, to survey the entire complex would take weeks. Way beyond any budget that I could hope to raise. If I was to get any esteemed archaeologists involved, I would have to come up with a practicable and precise area of The Berth to be surveyed. And an idea occurred to me.

I might have no way of knowing specifically where Owain was buried, but there *was* evidence for the location of Cynddylan's grave. The *Song of Heledd* had revealed that Cynddylan was buried at the Churches of Bassa, though not exactly where. But another poem did. This was in Llywarch's *Marwnad Cynddylan* (Elegy of Cynddylan), the same work that referred to Cynddylan and his brothers as Arthur's heirs (see chapter 11). Although the *Elegy of Cynddylan* is attributed to the court bard Llywarch, the poem concerns Princess Heledd mourning the death of Cynddylan as she attends his grave. In Llywarch's transcription of what was evidently her funerary dirge, many verses begin with a line that translates as "I shall lament [the death of Cynddylan] until I lie [in my grave]."[18] Heledd expects to eventually lie at peace with her brother, but, as we have seen, this never came to pass as she was forced to flee into Wales and was ultimately laid to rest in Llanhilleth. The poet describes how Heledd hopes to be buried in the same place and in the same manner as the dead king; she will lament for Cynddylan until she too is interred in a fashion Llywarch describes with the Old Welsh words *derwin* and *fedd*.[19] The first word, *derwin,* in modern Welsh is *derwen,* meaning "oak," and the second word, *fedd,* is rendered *bedd* (pronounced "beth"), in modern Welsh, which means "grave." This, in the English version I consulted at the Bodleian Library, had been translated as "oak coffin," but most Welsh historians I consulted disagreed. In modern Welsh the word for coffin is *arch,* or would have been written *erch* or *eirch* in Old Welsh. The author, they told me, is specifically saying that the term is an *oaken grave,* and there's a big difference. Archaeology has revealed that during the seventh century, the dead were usually interred in a circular pit, its earthen walls lined with wooden planks; in the case of high-status figures, they would often be made of oak. Heledd is saying that, like her brother, she too expects to be buried in a timber-lined pit, befitting her status.

The poet provides a further description of the grave as being in *erw trafael,*[20] which had been translated as a "humble grave plot." But, once again, this seemed to be wrong. The word *trafael* is a mystery, leading the translator to divide it into two words approximating the modern Welsh *tra gwael,* meaning literally "while poor," hence the English translation as "humble." *Trafael,* however, in the original text is a single word, leading other translators, such as Williams and Morris (see chapter 11), to interpret it as a proper noun—the name of a specific place. This would tally with the other term *erw.* It does not mean "grave plot" at all; in both Old and contemporary Welsh, it is the word for an acre of land (in modern terms, around the size of an American football field). Accordingly, *erw trafael* actually translates as "Trafael's Acre," probably named after a real or mythical figure once associated with the site. There was only one particular location at the Berth matching the description, the oval field—approximately an acre in size—now called the Enclosure. This smaller of the two islands readily lent itself to a geophysical survey. Within its ramparts the ground was dry and flat; it was a grassy pasture, free from trees, bushes, and complicating vegetation, and it was small enough to be surveyed within a reasonable time scale. It was a practical and hopefully affordable site for a geophysics team to examine.

In 1995 I finally managed to initiate the first archeological work undertaken at The Berth in over thirty years. Permission was obtained from the relevant landowners, and a team of specialists from Geophysical Surveys of Bradford were retained to conduct the work. These geophysicists were the world's first group to use such technology to specialize exclusively in archaeology. The project was overseen by the eminent archaeologist Dr. Roger White of Birmingham University and was financed by a British production company that wanted to film the enterprise. I must stress that these experts had no particular stance concerning my theories about King Arthur, nor did they regard him as having any association with The Berth. What interested them was that this was a site of considerable historical interest, and they were keen to learn more about it. With a limited budget the geophysics was to last for just one day, but fortunately this was enough time to fully survey

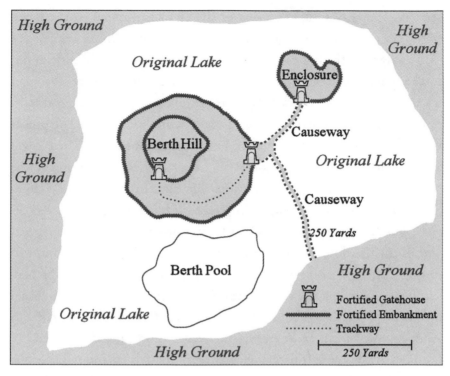

Fig. 13.2. The Berth at Baschurch in Shropshire, showing the original lake and basic fortifications of the post-Roman era.

the so-called Enclosure. The geophysics team used three types of equipment: first, a proton magnetometer that measured any magnetic anomalies beneath the surface, revealing the presence of objects made of iron; second, a resistivity meter—a double-pronged device that sent an electric current through the ground to measure changes in resistance—that could detect different types of materials beneath the surface, such as stones, bricks, and foundation walls; and finally, a ground-penetrating radar scanner that could produce a computer-generated image of what lay deep below the ground.

The results were certainly fascinating. It seems that two wooden buildings had once stood on the site, plus a larger stone structure. Their precise date and purpose were impossible to determine with certainty without digging, but the wooden buildings were probably earlier constructions, while the stone structure might have been a later ecclesiastical shrine: perhaps one of the chapels implied in the name of the site, the Churches of Bassa. The most significant discovery was located right in the middle of the Enclosure. It was a single circular pit, some six feet deep, consistent with a burial ditch of the post-Roman era. Although the technical restraints of the equipment made it impossible to reveal the presence of aged and fragile bones at that depth, it was able to detect metal, and right in the center of the ditch, there was a diamond-shaped piece of metal about six inches wide, possibly the central boss of an ancient shield. This was both exhilarating and unexpected. If this was an ancient burial, then—if I had interpreted the *Elegy of Cynddylan* correctly—it had to be the grave of Cynddylan; it was within this Enclosure that he had evidently been laid to rest. But, surprisingly, there was no evidence of any other graves from the comprehensive survey of this entire compound. Where were the graves of the other members of the Powys royal family mentioned in the *Song of Heledd*? And more importantly, where was the grave of Owain Ddantgwyn?

Perhaps, because The Berth was being hastily abandoned by the Britons retreating from the Anglo-Saxons, Cynddylan, the last Powys king to rule the region, was laid to rest in a part of the site previously used for purposes other than burials. The other members of the royal family, and hopefully his ancestors, must have been buried on the larger of the two islands, now Berth Hill. Nonetheless, the survey certainly seemed to have proved the accuracy of the *Song of Heledd* and the *Elegy of Cynddylan*. Not only myself but members of the archaeological team were optimistic about a further survey being conducted on the larger of the two islands. However, the sheer amount of work that would be necessary to clear the area was financially prohibitive. It was to be sixteen years before I got another shot at finding the grave of the man I believed to have been King Arthur.

In 2011 I was approached by a production company working for the National Geographic Channel. They were interested in making a documentary involving my search for King Arthur and, astonished that no further archaeological work had been done at The Berth since the mid-1990s, offered to finance another geophysics survey. If further evidence justified it, then they would consider paying for a proper excavation. It might seem strange that, despite the fact that there was already evidence for a burial in the Enclosure, and the possibility that it was the grave of a Dark Age king, no dig had been conducted. The problem was that funds for archaeological excavations are extremely limited, and there are many sites and many archaeologists competing for what little there is. Those who controlled the purse strings, for whatever reason, evidently did not consider The Berth worthy of consideration. But now there was an offer of such finance. Dr. Roger White, who had overseen the original survey, was contacted and was again keen to be involved. Regardless of his personal views concerning King Arthur or the original function of The Berth, he was enthusiastic to see a professional investigation conducted at a site of historic interest.

I wanted the survey to concentrate on the larger of the islands, on and around Berth Hill, but once again, due to limited time for the investigation to be completed, this was impractical. It was decided that there should be another geophysics survey of the Enclosure. Sixteen years had meant significant advances in technology, so although the equipment now to be used was basically the same as the first survey, it was far more sophisticated. Giant leaps had also been made in computer power, meaning that processing would produce far superior results and researchers would be able to indentify features undetectable in the mid-1990s. The results confirmed the initial scans. Near the middle of the Enclosure, there was the circular ditch, which White was certain had not been a house or any other similar structure and was likely to have been a burial. As the geophysics confirmed that there were no other similar readings on the plot, it would appear to be an isolated grave, and therefore probably someone of importance. The iron object was again detected at the center of the ditch, which White suggested might be an axe, a sword, or a shield. It was to some extent disappointing that no further graves were discovered, but on the positive side the anomaly—the geophysics term for something different from what is around it—warranted a limited archaeological dig of that specific location. If it proved to be the grave of a high-status individual dating from Cynddylan's time, then it would justify a further geophysics survey of Berth Hill itself and hopefully a wider excavation of the ancient complex.

Sadly, at the time of writing, nothing more has been done. Another archaeologist who subsequently examined the results from the survey thought that the ditch might in fact have been a furnace, and this probably gave those with the financial clout to organize further exploration the excuse to hang on to such resources in times of severe fiscal restraint. However, as far as I was concerned, this was a pretty weak argument. Smelting iron results in a significant amount of slag—lumps of stony, waste matter separated from the ore during the smelting process. The ground-penetrating radar was sensitive enough to detect such deposits of slag in the pit or surrounding area—and evidence of none whatsoever was found. Nevertheless, a second and more ambitious project was funded by the National Geographic Channel to examine Berth Pool.

In chapter 4 we saw how prized possessions were thrown into lakes by the Britons as offerings to a water goddess and that the custom continued during the post-Roman era—even by Christians—though in their case as tributes to an equivalent female saint. The theme of Excalibur being cast to the Lady of the Lake might well have originated with this tradition, possibly as part of a funeral rite. Maybe, I suggested, the historical Arthur's sword could have been thrown into the lake surrounding The Berth complex. As part of this lake still survived as Berth Pool, an elaborate exploration was initiated to examine the lake floor. The team, led by forensic marine archaeologist Ruth McDonald from Liverpool University, included both surface technicians with specialist equipment in a boat and underwater divers. One of the first questions McDonald asked me was what precisely she was looking for, and I was able to show her what we were hoping to find. I had asked one of Britain's leading authorities on armaments of the early Dark Ages, British post-Roman military expert Dan Shadrake, to make an illustration of a chieftain's sword of around AD 500. It turned out that they were not the long medieval swords as Excalibur is usually depicted but two-foot, Roman-style cavalry swords with stunted cross-guards. As *The Dream of Rhonabwy* had actually described Arthur's sword as having the design of two serpents on its golden hilt (see chapter 9), Shadrake incorporated a double-serpent motif in the style of the period on the sword's hilt in his drawing. Based on Shadrake's artist's impression, a replica was made by the company that still forged ceremonial swords for the British military. They crafted a stunning recreation of a historical "Excalibur" in gold and shining steel. Although perhaps in nowhere near as good condition, it was possible that the mud of the lake bed would have preserved such an artifact. McDonald began by crisscrossing the lake in a boat outfitted with an impressive array of scientific equipment. Sonar was used, so was radar, while a deep-penetrating magnetometer scanned for metal well beneath the layer of lake-bottom sediment. Although the results revealed that there were dozens of metal objects down there, many of which could have been ancient swords or other votive offerings, it was hardly helpful. Which anomalies were the underwater team to investigate? The divers were deployed and spent an entire day searching the locations where the most promising objects were located, but it all ended in frustration. Underwater archaeology is difficult in the best of conditions, but the water of Berth Pool was prohibitively murky, and a four-foot layer of glutinous sediment lay on top of the harder bed mud below. It was out of the question to even consider an excavation.

All may not be lost in a search for a historical King Arthur's sword, however. Far from it! Berth Pool was only a fraction the size of the original lake. The sword—and many other ancient votive offerings—might lie in the excavatable, now dry land surrounding the Berth. Indeed, just such an artifact was discovered there in 1906 by a workman cutting turf at the edge of a stream close to the causeway that once joined the larger island to the mainland. It was a bronze cauldron, around eighteen inches high and twelve inches wide. Dating from the Roman period, it is now in the British Museum where it is believed to have been cast into the lake as a votive offering during the first century AD. This had been a chance discovery, but a proper geophysics survey could well reveal many such artifacts in the area of the original lake that has never been excavated.

Someone once said that extraordinary claims required extraordinary evidence, and claiming to have discovered a real King Arthur was certainly an extraordinary claim. Nevertheless, I had extensive evidence that Owain Ddantgwyn was the historical King Arthur, and I also had significant evidence for The Berth being Owain's burial site. What I didn't have was a *precise* location for his grave. Like the Avalon of legend, The Berth was an ancient island sanctuary; a sacred site used by the Celtic Britons for centuries. Isolated, silent, and eerie, often rising above early morning mist, it could hardly be a more appropriate setting for the last resting place of the man who was Arthur. But where on The Berth was he actually buried? Perhaps I could find clues as to where King Arthur was thought to have been laid to rest in the various medieval and earlier Welsh Arthurian traditions.

The initiator of the medieval Arthurian romances, Geoffrey of Monmouth in the 1130s, failed to say exactly where Arthur was buried. In his *History of the Kings of Britain,* he wrote that "King Arthur himself received a deadly wound, and was borne unto the island of Avalon for the healing of his injuries."[21] Geoffrey said absolutely nothing of his death or burial. In his *Life of Merlin,* written around the same time, he added a little more detail, saying that after the battle of Camlann, the wounded Arthur was taken to Avalon, "where Morgan received him with honor, and placed him in her chamber . . . and with her own hand she uncovered his wound. . . . At length, she said that his health might be restored by her healing art if she stayed with him a long time."[22] Once more, we are not told whether Morgan successfully healed Arthur or if he died, let alone where he was buried. The Jersey author Wace, writing about twenty years later in his *Romance of Brutus,* claimed, like Geoffrey, that he took his information from an earlier British chronicle. It was presumably a different chronicle, as Wace suggests that Arthur actually died on the battlefield—"wounded in his body to the death"—and was taken to Avalon in the hope of resurrection. The Britons (i.e., the Welsh), he adds, believed that he still lies there, awaiting the day of his rebirth.[23] Although Geoffrey was the author to popularize the Arthurian story to a medieval readership, he was by no means the first to write about the fabled king. A decade before Geoffrey's works, the respected historian William of Malmesbury, in his *Deeds of the English Kings* of 1125, stated that he believed Arthur to have been a historical figure, although the whereabouts of his tomb was unknown. He too talks about the legend that Arthur would one day live again, possibly the notion that one of his descendants would eventually retake the British throne.[24] Most of the earliest surviving works that refer to Arthur's grave either state directly or imply it to have been on the Isle of Avalon, but the location of that island seems to have been lost in the mists of time. Even as early as the ninth century, it would appear that the whereabouts of Avalon and Arthur's last resting place had been forgotten. An Old Welsh poem, *Englynion y Beddau* (The Stanzas of the Graves)—now preserved in The Black Book of Carmarthen (see chapter 8) and on linguistic grounds thought to date from the 800s— said that the location of Arthur's grave was a mystery to all.[25]

The oldest work I could discover to provide any specific details concerning Arthur's last resting place was in one of the Vulgate stories (see chapter 3), titled *La Mort le Roi Artu* (The Death of King Arthur), dating from around 1230.[26] Its anonymous author also claims to have consulted an ancient British source that maintained Arthur died in Avalon and was buried there, specifically, "within the black chapel." If the historical Avalon was The Berth and, of course, if the Vulgate author is right, then Arthur might have been buried in a chapel that was one of the original Churches of Bassa. The work even describes the burial site as a tomb rather than a simple grave: "On the marvelous and rich tomb there was writing, saying: 'Here lies King Arthur, who by his valor subjugated twelve kingdoms.'" Presumably the epitaph referred to the kingdoms of the Anglo-Saxons and might relate to the twelve decisive battles recorded by Nennius. The same theme was later taken up by Thomas Malory, writing in the mid-1400s, who also refers to Arthur's tomb in a chapel, although, due to the popularity of Arthur's supposed grave at Glastonbury, he suggests the site to be somewhere in that vicinity.[27] Malory's *The Death of Arthur* is an amalgamation of earlier Arthurian works, so the chapel reference probably came from the

Vulgate tale, but he evidently employed a further, now lost source as he includes a different epitaph written in Latin:

HIC IACET ARTHURUS REX QUONDAM REX QUE FUTURES

[Here Lies King Arthur, the Once and Future King]

Just how seriously we can take the claims that Arthur was buried in a chapel on Avalon and that there was some kind of decorative sepulcher with an inscription is open to question. These are late references, but it's all there is to go on. There almost certainly were chapels at the Churches of Bassa, or The Berth would not have been called by that name in the seventh century. What may have been the foundation stones of one of these churches seems to have been detected during the geophysics scan in 1995. As the place name included the plural "churches," we can assume that there had to be at least one other, and as both geophysics surveys revealed no second stone structure on the smaller island at The Berth, then there was probably a further church on the larger island, now Berth Hill. As dwellings, fortifications, and other practical structures were generally built from wood during the post-Roman period, stonework was reserved almost exclusively for churches. So, if the Vulgate author really did employ some earlier, Welsh source—possibly a war poem similar to the *Song of Heledd*—in composing *La Mort le Roi Artu,* then my suggestion for a further geophysics survey would be to scan for a stone structure on Berth Hill. If one is found and there is also evidence of a burial there, then perhaps I will finally have found the historical King Arthur. Surely that would persuade English Heritage to permit an excavation! And if such a dig is initiated, then there might, just possibly (and I sincerely hope), be an inscription to fully validate my theory.

However, as I said earlier, Berth Hill would be a difficult place for geophysics. It is partly wooded and covered with undergrowth. If the opportunity does arise for a further survey, then I would have to suggest a specific part of the hill to scan. Fortunately, I discovered one possible location suggested to me by Mike Stokes of the Shrewsbury museum. He directed me to an observation made by an archaeologist in 1925, when there was far less vegetation obscuring the land. Examining the area, Lily Chitty, at the time the local secretary for the Royal Archaeological Society in Shropshire, noticed a raised plot of land on the hill that, she learned from a local schoolteacher, was said to be the burial site of a royal warrior who had been interred there after a fatal battle. This was obviously just a local legend that still existed at the time, but folklore can sometimes lead to real archaeological discoveries. For instance, on Cornwall's Bodmin Moor there is an ancient mound called Rillaton Barrow, where local tradition long held that a druid once lived there who possessed a miraculous golden goblet that never ran dry. When the mound was excavated in the nineteenth century, a stone-lined vault was unearthed, containing a human skeleton buried with a ceremonial cup made from pure gold. Now in the British Museum, the artifact has been dated to around 1500 BC. Another example concerns folklore regarding a mound known as Bryn-yr-Ellyllon (Goblin's Hill) near the town of Mold in North Wales. Legend told of a small figure wearing a golden coat that was said to haunt the location, hence its name. When the site was excavated in 1833, a stone burial chamber was discovered containing a skeleton buried in a solid gold half-tunic. Now known as the Mold Cape, the item is thought to have been worn around the shoulders, chest, and upper arms of someone of authority during religious rites—presumably the person who was buried there. Made from 23-carat gold, and weighing over two pounds, it is around four thousand years old and is considered one of the finest Bronze Age artifacts in the world. These are just two of many similar instances where local folklore appears to have retained the ancient memory of a real, historical burial of an important individual. Perhaps the same is true of the legend Lily Chitty recounted concerning The Berth.

From Mike Stokes, I learned the precise location of this area of land but have deliberately withheld that information to avoid any irresponsible attempts to dig there. Besides which, any burial would be far too deep for amateur equipment, such as metal detectors. Only a professional geophysics survey, conducted by experts, would have any success in discovering what lies beneath that spot. All of The Berth is on private land, so even a visit to the location requires permission from the relevant landowners. There are stringent laws about metal detecting or digging on private land in the UK. Both are illegal without prior permission from the owner. Concerning The Berth, as it is a scheduled archaeological site, metal detecting or excavation of any kind is entirely forbidden under all circumstances without consent from the Secretary of State for Culture, Media, and Sport. Under British law, illegal digging on a scheduled ancient monument carries a penalty of two years' imprisonment or an unlimited fine.

At the start of this book, I said that I had set out to discover the whereabouts of King Arthur's grave, and I believe I have succeeded in doing just that. In my opinion he is buried at The Berth in the country of Shropshire, in pretty much the center of Britain. I have a good idea about the precise spot and earnestly hope that a new geophysics survey will soon be conducted there; and after that, if all goes well, there will be an archaeological excavation. Perhaps then, Arthur may not return from the dead as the Dark Age Britons once believed, but he will finally be accepted by scholars throughout the world as an authentic British king.

APPENDIX

Chronology

ROMAN PERIOD (AD 43–410)

43   Britain invaded by Romans

POST-ROMAN (410–660)
DARK AGES (410–1066)

410   Roman legions leave Britain
446   Quintus Aurelius, Roman consul
449   Saxon Advent
450   Cunedda and his mercenaries invited into north Wales
451   Attila the Hun defeated at the Battle of Châlons
455   Saxon Revolt
465   Death of Vortigern
473   Anglo-Saxons advance westward
475   Ambrosius becomes high king of Britain
476   End of Roman Empire in the West
477   Ambrosius leads the Britons to push back Anglo-Saxons
479   Anglo-Saxons confined to east and southeast England
480   Enniaun Girt becomes king of Gwynedd
485   Renewed Anglo-Saxon advance in the southeast

490   Anglo-Saxons pushing west all across Britain

495   Owain Ddantgwyn becomes king of Powys

500   Battle of Badon

519   Battle of Camlann: Anglo-Saxons renew advances into British territory

520   Maglocunus, king of Gwynedd; Cuneglasus, king of Powys

545   Gildas writes *On the Ruin and Conquest of Britain*

573   Battle of Arfderydd

610   *The Gododdin* composed

644   Battle of Cogwy and the death of the Northumbrian king Oswald

657   Death of Penda; Mercia defeated by Northumbria

658   Northumbria invades Powys; Death of Cynddylan; Abandonment of Viroconium

659   Dinas Bran becomes new capital of Powys

END OF POST-ROMAN PERIOD (AD 660)

670   Llywarch composes *Elegy of Cynddylan*

675   Heledd composes *Song of Heledd*

700   Saxons conquer most of England

731   Bede completes *The Ecclesiastical History of the English People*

890   Anglo-Saxon Chronicle compiled

830   Nennius writes *The History of the Britons*

850   Pillar of Eliseg erected

900   *The Spoils of Annwn* composed

927   Unified kingdom of England established

954   *Welsh Annals* compiled in its present form

END OF DARK AGES (AD 1066)

MEDIEVAL OR MIDDLE AGES (1066–1485)

1066   Norman invasion of England

1125   William of Malmesbury writes the *Deeds of the English Kings*

1130   William of Malmesbury writes the *Ecclesiastical History of Glastonbury*

1136 Geoffrey of Monmouth completes his *History of the Kings of Britain*

1150 Geoffrey of Monmouth writes the *Life of Merlin*

1155 Wace composes the *Romance of Brutus*

1170 Chrétien de Troyes writes *Erec and Enide*

1171 England begins invasion of Wales

1180 *Lancelot* composed by the French poet Chrétien de Troyes

1184 Glastonbury Abbey fire

1190 Chrétien de Troyes writes *The Story of the Grail*

1191 "Arthur's grave" discovered at Glastonbury

1195 Robert de Boron's *Joseph of Arimathea* written

1200 Robert de Boron's *Merlin* written. Layamon writes *Brut*

1230 The Vulgate *Death of Arthur* written

1230 The Vulgate *Merlin* written

1250 *Fouke le Fitz Waryn* romance composed

1282 Wales conquered by the English

1453 Fall of Constantinople and final collapse of the Byzantine Empire

TUDOR PERIOD (1485–1603)

1485 Thomas Malory's *Le Morte d'Arthur* published

1539 Glastonbury Abbey dissolved by King Henry VIII

1540 Henry VIII's chief antiquarian John Leland examines the Galstonbury lead cross

1566 Mary Queen of Scots commissions the making of an "Arthurian Round Table"

1567 *The Triads of Britain* published by William Salesbury

1603 Death of the last Tudor monarch, Elizabeth I

Notes

CHAPTER 1. HERE LIES KING ARTHUR

1. Gerald of Wales, *On the Instruction of Princes.*
2. Ibid.
3. Scott-Stokes, *Glastonbury Abbey during the Crusades.*
4. Radford, *Arthurian Sites in the West.*
5. Camden, *Britannia.*
6. Geoffrey of Monmouth, *History of the Kings of Britain.*
7. William of Malmesbury, *Antiquities of Glastonbury.*
8. William of Malmesbury, *The History of the English Kings.*
9. Robert de Boron, *Joseph of Arimathea.*
10. Adam of Damerham, *Historia de Rebus Gestis Glastoniensibus.*
11. Phillips and Keatman, *King Arthur: The True Story.*

CHAPTER 2. CAMELOT

1. Malory, *Le Morte D'Arthur.*
2. Harding, *Chronicle of England.*
3. Wace, *Wace's Roman de Brut.*
4. Einhard, *The Life of Charlemagne.*
5. Lacy, *The New Arthurian Encyclopedia,* 391.
6. Ibid.
7. Munby, Barber, and Brown, *Edward III's Round Table at Windsor.*
8. Warnicke, *Mary Queen of Scots,* 133.
9. Biddle, *King Arthur's Round Table.*
10. Chrétien de Troyes, *Lancelot or the Knight of the Cart,* verses 31–32.
11. Ibid.
12. Geoffrey of Monmouth, *History of the Kings of Britain.*
13. Alcock, *Cadbury/Camelot.*
14. Leland, *John Leland's Itinerary: Travels in Tudor England.*

CHAPTER 3. SWORDS OF POWER

1. Farmer, *Oxford Dictionary of Saints.*
2. Loomis, *Arthurian Literature in the Middle Ages,* chap. 19.
3. Malory, *Le Morte D'Arthur,* book 1, chap. 5.
4. Ibid., chaps. 2–3.
5. Ibid., chap. 5.
6. Ibid.
7. Schofield, *St. Paul's Cathedral Before Wren.*
8. Translated from surviving fragment of Robert de Boron's *Merlin,* in Nitze, *Le Roman de l'Estoire dou Graal,* 126–30.
9. Marsden, "The Excavation of a Roman Palace Site in London, 1961–1972," 63–64.
10. Geoffrey of Monmouth, *History of the Kings of Britain.*
11. Topsfield, *Chrétien de Troyes.*
12. Gantz, *The Mabinogion.*
13. Russell and Cohn, *Preiddeu Annwfn.*
14. Lacy, *Lancelot-Grail.*
15. Bromwich, *Trioedd Ynys Prydein: The Triads of the Island of Britain.*
16. Lacy, *Lancelot-Grail.*
17. Nennius, *British History and the Welsh Annals.*
18. Carew, *The Survey of Cornwall.*
19. Borlase, *Observations on the Antiquities, Historical and Monumental, of the County of Cornwall.*

CHAPTER 4. AVALON

1. Geoffrey of Monmouth, *History of the Kings of Britain,* book 9, chap. 4; book 11, chap. 2.
2. Geoffrey of Monmouth, *Life of Merlin: Vita Merlini.*
3. Ibid., verse 38.
4. Ibid.
5. Wace, *Wace's Roman de Brut: A History of the British.*
6. Ibid., final verse, 34.
7. Topsfield, *Chrétien de Troyes: A Study of the Arthurian Romances.*
8. Chrétien de Troyes, *Erec and Enide,* verse 1919.
9. Everett, *Layamon and the Earliest Middle English Alliterative Verse.*
10. Robert de Boron, *Joseph of Arimathea: A Romance of the Grail.*
11. Lacy, *Lancelot-Grail: The Old French Arthurian Vulgate and Post-Vulgate in Translation.*
12. Malory, *Le Morte D'Arthur.*
13. Gantz, *The Mabinogion.*
14. Evans, *Poems from the Book of Taliesin.*
15. Gantz, "Branwen Daughter of Llyr" in *The Mabinogion,* 67–82.
16. Ibid.

17. Robert de Boron, *Joseph of Arimathea: A Romance of the Grail.*
18. Gantz, "Branwen Daughter of Llyr" in *The Mabinogion,* 67–82.
19. Bromwich, *Trioedd Ynys Prydein: The Triads of the Island of Britain,* 16.
20. Gantz, "Peredur" in *The Mabinogion,* 218–57.
21. Chrétien de Troyes, *Perceval: The Story of the Grail.*
22. Translated from Chrétien de Troye, *Perceval, le Conte du Graal,* in MS f. fr. 794.
23. Translated from *Peredur,* in The Red Book of Hergest.
24. Harleian MS 3859.
25. Geoffrey of Monmouth, *History of the Kings of Britain,* preface.
26. Wace, *Wace's Roman de Brut: A History of the British.*
27. William of Malmesbury, *The History of the English Kings.*
28. William of Malmesbury, *Antiquities of Glastonbury.*
29. Translated from William of Malmesbury, *De Antiquitate Glastoniensis Ecclesiae,* in Gale, *Historiae Anglicanae Scriptores.*
30. Cunliffe, *Iron Age Communities in Britain: An Account of England, Scotland and Wales from the Seventh Century BC.*
31. Barnes, *Tertullian: A Historical and Literary Study.*
32. Hilary of Poitiers and John of Damascus, *Nicene and Post-Nicene Fathers,* second series, vol. 9.
33. Osborne, "Hoards, Votives, Offerings," 1–10.
34. Gilley, *A History of Religion in Britain.*
35. Steele, *Llyn Cerrig Bach.*
36. Tacitus, *The Annals: The Reigns of Tiberius, Claudius, and Nero.*
37. James and Rigby, *Britain and the Celtic Iron Age.*
38. Piggott, *The Druids.*
39. McNeill, *The Celtic Churches.*
40. Laing, *The Archaeology of Celtic Britain and Ireland.*
41. Thompson, *Saint Germanus of Auxerre and the End of Roman Britain.*
42. Mayr-Harting, *The Coming of Christianity to Anglo-Saxon England.*
43. Laing, *The Archaeology of Celtic Britain and Ireland.*
44. Redknap and Lane, "The Early Medieval crannog at Llangorse, Powys: An interim statement on the 1989–1993 seasons," 189–205.
45. Dark, *Britain and the End of the Roman Empire.*
46. Strabo, *Geography: Books 3–5,* book 4, chap. 4, verse 6.
47. Berry, *Geography/De Situ Orbis A.D. 43.*
48. Mela, *De Situ Orbis,* book 3, verse 47.

CHAPTER 5. MORGAN AND HER SISTERS

1. Briggs, *An Encyclopedia of Fairies.*
2. Flower, *The Seer in Ancient Greece.*
3. Knott, *Togail Bruidne dá Derga.*
4. Macalister, *Lebor Gabála Érenn.*

5. Ellis, *The Mammoth Book of Celtic Myths and Legends,* 28.

6. Malory, *Le Morte d'Arthur,* book 21, chap. 5.

7. Nutt, *The Voyage of Bran.*

8. Lynn, *Navan Fort: Archaeology and Myth.*

9. Laing, *The Archaeology of Celtic Britain and Ireland.*

10. Ibid.

11. Bord and Bord, *Sacred Waters.*

12. Malory, *Le Morte d'Arthur,* book 21, chap. 6.

13. Wilhelm, *The Romance of Arthur,* 343.

14. Coyne, *An Upland Archaeological Study on Mount Brandon and The Paps,* 21–22.

15. Cronin, *In the Shadow of the Paps,* 38–50.

16. Edwards, *Local Saints and Local Churches in the Early Medieval West,* 234.

17. See Brooks, *The Early History of the Church in Canterbury,* 17, 21; Maxfield, *The Saxon Shore: A Handbook,* 145; Esmonde-Cleary, *The Ending of Roman Britain,* 178–79.

18. Henig, *Religion in Roman Britain.*

19. Allason-Jones and McKay, *Coventina's Well.*

20. Graves, *The White Goddess.*

21. Murray, *The Witch-Cult in Western Europe.*

22. Booth, *A Magick Life.*

23. Collingwood and Wright, *The Roman Inscriptions of Britain.*

24. Bird and Cunliffe, *The Essential Roman Baths.*

CHAPTER 6. THE WHITE LAND

1. Kightly, *Castell Dinas Brân.*

2. Wright, *The History of Fulk Fitz Warine.*

3. Gantz, *The Mabinogion,* 66–82.

4. Evans, *Valle Crucis Abbey.*

5. Gantz, *The Mabinogion.*

6. Bromwich, *Trioedd Ynys Prydein: The Triads of the Island of Britain.*

7. Hughes, "Old Oswestry Hillfort: Excavations by WJ Varley 1939–40."

8. Gantz, *The Mabinogion.*

9. Bromwich, *Trioedd Ynys Prydein: The Triads of the Island of Britain,* 18.

10. See, for example, "Culhwch and Olwen" in Gantz, *The Mabinogion,* 148.

11. Martin, *The Historical Ecology of Old Oswestry.*

12. Bromwich, *Trioedd Ynys Prydein: The Triads of the Island of Britain.*

13. Toghill, *Geology of Shropshire.*

14. Wright, *The History of Fulk Fitz Warine.*

15. Ibid.

16. Ibid.

17. Ibid.

18. Skeels, *Didot Perceval or The Romance of Perceval in Prose.*

19. Phillips, *The Chalice of Magdalene.*

20. Wright, *The History of Fulk Fitz Warine.*
21. Geoffrey of Monmouth, *History of the Kings of Britain,* chaps. 17–19.
22. Mathew and Harrison, *Oxford Dictionary of National Biography.*
23. Nennius, *British History and the Welsh Annals.*
24. Ibid., chaps. 40–42.
25. Remfry, *Castell Dinas Emrys.*
26. Nennius, *British History and the Welsh Annals.*
27. Garmonsway, *The Anglo-Saxon Chronicle.*
28. Gildas, *De Excidio Britanniae.*
29. Lhuyd, *Archaeologia Britannica: Texts and Translations.*

CHAPTER 7. LAST OF THE ROMANS

1. Thompson, *Saint Germanus of Auxerre and the End of Roman Britain.*
2. Gildas, *De Excidio Britanniae.*
3. Nennius, *British History and the Welsh Annals.*
4. Bede, *The Ecclesiastical History of the English Nation.*
5. Garmonsway, *The Anglo-Saxon Chronicle.*
6. Nennius, *British History and the Welsh Annals.*
7. Kennett, *Anglo-Saxon Pottery.*
8. Jolliffe, *Pre-Feudal England: The Jutes.*
9. Owen-Crocker, *Rites and Religions of the Anglo-Saxons.*
10. Gildas, *De Excidio Britanniae,* chaps. 23–24.
11. Bede, *The Ecclesiastical History of the English Nation,* book 1, chap. 15.
12. Yorke, *Kings and Kingdoms of Early Anglo-Saxon England.*
13. Nennius, *British History and the Welsh Annals,* chap. 47.
14. Bede, *The Ecclesiastical History of the English Nation,* book 1, chap. 16.
15. Gildas, *De Excidio Britanniae,* chap. 25.
16. Ibid.
17. Bede, *The Ecclesiastical History of the English Nation,* book 1, chap. 16.
18. Nennius, *British History and the Welsh Annals,* chap. 42.
19. Jones, Martindale, and Morris, *The Prosopography of the Later Roman Empire.*
20. Bland and Johns, *The Hoxne Treasure: An Illustrated Handbook.*
21. Nennius, *British History and the Welsh Annals,* chap. 47.
22. Gildas, *De Excidio Britanniae,* chap. 25.
23. Bede, *The Ecclesiastical History of the English Nation,* book 1, chap. 16.
24. Hamerow, Hinton, and Crawford, *The Oxford Handbook of Anglo-Saxon Archaeology.*
25. See Kennett, *Anglo-Saxon Pottery;* Lucy, *The Anglo-Saxon Way of Death: Burial Rites in Early England.*
26. Jacobsen, *A History of the Vandals.*
27. Ward-Perkins, *The Fall of Rome: And the End of Civilization.*
28. Jordanes, *De Origine Actibusque Getarum: The Origin and Deeds of the Goths,* chap. 45.
29. Chadwick Hawkes, *Soldiers and Settlers in Britain: Fourth to Fifth Century.*

CHAPTER 8. MERLIN THE BARD

1. Nennius, *British History and the Welsh Annals,* chap. 42.
2. Bromwich, *Trioedd Ynys Prydein: The Triads of the Island of Britain.*
3. Pennar, *The Black Book of Carmarthen.*
4. Evans, *The Poetry in the Red Book of Hergest.*
5. Joceline and Ailred, *Two Celtic Saints.*
6. Evans, *The Poetry in the Red Book of Hergest.*
7. Stephenson, *Political Power in Medieval Gwynedd.*
8. Gildas, *De Excidio Britanniae,* chap. 26.
9. Bede, *The Ecclesiastical History of the English Nation,* book 1, chap. 16.
10. Yorke, *Kings and Kingdoms of Early Anglo-Saxon England.*
11. Nennius, *British History and the Welsh Annals.*
12. Gildas, *De Excidio Britanniae in History,* chap. 33.
13. Bury, *A History of the Later Roman Empire.*
14. Stewart, Williamson, and Down, *Celtic Bards, Celtic Druids.*
15. Edwards and Salter, *The Bibliotheca Historica of Diodorus Siculus,* book 5, chap. 31.
16. Strabo, *Geography: Volume 5,* book 5, chap. 4.
17. Caesar, *Caesar: Gallic War Books VI and VII,* book 6, chap. 13.
18. Ibid.
19. Ibid., book 6, chap. 14.
20. Wardle, *Cicero on Divination: Book 1,* chap. 40.

CHAPTER 9. A HISTORICAL FIGURE?

1. Watts, *The Oxford Greek Dictionary.*
2. Gantz, *The Mabinogion,* 128–13.
3. Bromwich, *Trioedd Ynys Prydein: The Triads of the Island of Britain.*
4. Gantz, *The Mabinogion,* 184.
5. Caesar, *Caesar: Gallic War Books VI and VII,* book 6, chap. 17.
6. Taylor, "The Gundestrup Cauldron."
7. Silvius, *Notitia Dignitatum: Primary Source Edition,* chap. 5.
8. Casey, Davies, and Evans, *Excavations at Segontium (Caernarfon) Roman Fort, 1975–79.*
9. Laycock, *Warlords: The Struggle for Power in Post-Roman Britain.*
10. Garmonsway, *The Anglo-Saxon Chronicle.*
11. Gildas, *De Excidio Britanniae,* chap. 26.
12. Bede, *The Ecclesiastical History of the English Nation,* book 1, chap. 16.
13. Gildas, *De Excidio Britanniae in History,* chap. 26.
14. Meaney, *Gazetteer of Early Anglo-Saxon Burial Sites.*
15. Nennius, *British History and the Welsh Annals,* chap. 50.
16. Ibid.
17. Nennius, *British History and the Welsh Annals,* chapter 6.
18. Blackburn and Holford-Strevens, *The Oxford Companion to the Year: An Exploration of Calendar Customs and Time-Reckoning.*
19. Nennius, *British History and the Welsh Annals,* chap. 3.

20. Ibid.
21. Ibid., chap. 50.

CHAPTER 10. CAPITAL CITY

1. Jarman, *Aneirin-Y Gododdin.*
2. Nennius, *British History and the Welsh Annals,* chap. 50.
3. Ibid.
4. Morris, *The Age of Arthur: A History of the British Isles from 350 to 650.*
5. Casey, Davies, and Evans, *Excavations at Segontium (Caernarfon) Roman Fort, 1975–79.*
6. Alcock, "Excavations at Degannwy Castle, Caernarfonshire."
7. Nennius, *British History and the Welsh Annals,* chap. 62.
8. Nennius, *British History and the Welsh Annals.*
9. Ibid.
10. Dark, *Civitas to Kingdom: British Political Continuity 300–800.*
11. Webster, *Viroconium, Wroxeter Roman City, Shropshire.*
12. Barker, *Wroxeter Roman City: Excavations 1966–80.*
13. Ibid.
14. Barker, *From Roman Viroconium to Medieval Wroxeter: Recent Work on the Site of the Roman City of Wroxeter.*

CHAPTER 11. THE NAME OF THE KING

1. Higham, *The Kingdom of Northumbria, A.D. 350–1100.*
2. Williams, *Canu Llywarch Hen.*
3. Zaluckyj, *Mercia: The Anglo-Saxon Kingdom of Central England.*
4. Nennius, *British History and the Welsh Annals.*
5. Bede, *The Ecclesiastical History of the English Nation,* book 3, chap. 9.
6. Garmonsway, *The Anglo-Saxon Chronicle.*
7. Williams, *Elegy of Cynddylan* in *Canu Llywarch Hen.*
8. Nennius, *British History and the Welsh Annals.*
9. Garmonsway, *The Anglo-Saxon Chronicle.*
10. Bede, *The Ecclesiastical History of the English Nation,* book 3, chap. 24.
11. Nennius, *British History and the Welsh Annals.*
12. Morris, *The Age of Arthur.*
13. Williams, *Elegy of Cynddylan* in *Canu Llywarch Hen.*
14. Upward and Davidson, *The History of English Spelling.*
15. Davies, *The Welsh Language: A History.*
16. Nennius, *British History and the Welsh Annals,* chap. 47.
17. Nennius, *British History and the Welsh Annals.*
18. Barker, *Wroxeter Roman City: Excavations 1966–80.*
19. Garmonsway, *The Anglo-Saxon Chronicle.*
20. Bede, *The Ecclesiastical History of the English Nation,* book 1, chap. 22.

21. Gildas, *De Excidio Britanniae,* chap. 28.
22. Ibid., chap. 31.
23. Ibid., chap. 33.
24. Ibid., chap. 30.
25. Ibid., chap. 32.
26. Ibid.
27. Nennius, *British History and the Welsh Annals.*
28. Gildas, *De Excidio Britanniae,* chaps. 33–35.
29. Nennius, *British History and the Welsh Annals.*
30. Ibid.
31. Ibid., chap. 50.
32. Gildas, *De Excidio Britanniae,* chap. 33.
33. Ibid., chap. 32.
34. King James Bible, Book of Revelation, chap. 13, verse 2.
35. Gildas, *De Excidio Britanniae,* chap. 31.
36. Ibid., chaps. 28, 30.
37. Ibid., chaps. 32–33.
38. Bede, *The Ecclesiastical History of the English Nation,* book 3, chap. 24.
39. Ibid., book 3, chap. 21.
40. Burnett, *Ancient Kingdom of Wessex.*

CHAPTER 12. CAMLANN

1. Gildas, *De Excidio Britanniae,* chap. 33.
2. Malory, *Le Morte D'Arthur.*
3. Geoffrey of Monmouth, *History of the Kings of Britain,* book 11, chap. 2.
4. Nennius, *British History and the Welsh Annals.*
5. Bromwich, *Trioedd Ynys Prydein: The Triads of the Island of Britain.*
6. Gildas, *De Excidio Britanniae* in *History,* chap. 33.
7. Bromwich, *Trioedd Ynys Prydein: The Triads of the Island of Britain.*
8. Nennius, *British History and the Welsh Annals.*
9. Bede, *The Ecclesiastical History of the English Nation,* book 1, chap. 15.
10. Nennius, *British History and the Welsh Annals,* chap. 50.
11. Garmonsway, *The Anglo-Saxon Chronicle.*
12. Gildas, *De Excidio Britanniae* in *History,* chap. 33.
13. Nennius, *British History and the Welsh Annals,* chap. 50.
14. Gildas, *De Excidio Britanniae* in *History,* chaps. 33–35.
15. Gantz, "The Dream of Rhonabwy" in *The Mabinogion,* 180–81.
16. Ibid., 181.

CHAPTER 13. THE ONCE AND FUTURE KING

1. Heledd, *Canu Heledd,* lines 234, 237.
2. Bromwich, *Trioedd Ynys Prydein: The Triads of the Island of Britain.*

3. Heledd, *Canu Heledd.*

4. Nennius, *British History and the Welsh Annals.*

5. Heledd, *Canu Heledd,* lines 133–53.

6. Ibid., line 145.

7. Ibid., line 133.

8. Ibid., line 134.

9. Ibid., line 141.

10. Ibid., lines 139–40.

11. Mills, *Oxford Dictionary of British Place Names.*

12. Garmonsway, *The Anglo-Saxon Chronicle.*

13. Bede, *The Ecclesiastical History of the English Nation,* book 2, chap. 22.

14. Ekwall, *The Concise Oxford Dictionary of English Place Names.*

15. Nennius, *British History and the Welsh Annals,* chap. 50.

16. Geake, *The Use of Grave-Goods in Conversion-Period England, c. 600–c. 850.*

17. Petts, *Burial in Western Britain AD 400–800.*

18. Williams, "Marwnad Cynddylan" in *Canu Llywarch Hen,* 50–52.

19. Ibid., 50, line 4.

20. Ibid., 52, line 62.

21. Geoffrey of Monmouth, *History of the Kings of Britain,* book 11, chap. 2.

22. Geoffrey of Monmouth, *Life of Merlin: Vita Merlini,* verse 39.

23. Wace, *Wace's Roman de Brut: A History of the British.*

24. William of Malmesbury, *The History of the English Kings.*

25. Blake and Lloyd, *The Stanzas of the Graves: In Search of the Graves of Arthur and the Warriors of Britain.*

26. Lacy, *Lancelot-Grail: The Old French Arthurian Vulgate and Post-Vulgate in Translation.*

27. Malory, *Le Morte D'Arthur,* book 21, chap. 7.

Bibliography

Adam of Damerham. *Historia de Rebus Gestis Glastoniensibus.* Edited by William Adam. Whitefish, Mont.: Kessinger Publishing, 2010.

Alcock, Leslie. *Cadbury/Camelot.* London: British Academy Publishing, 1984.

———. "Excavations at Degannwy Castle, Caernarfonshire." *The Archaeological Journal* 124, no. 1 (1967).

Allason-Jones, Lindsay, and Bruce McKay. *Coventina's Well.* Oxford, UK: Oxbow Books, 1985.

Barker, Philip. *Wroxeter Roman City: Excavations 1966–80.* London: Department of the Environment Publications, 1980.

———, ed. *From Roman Viroconium to Medieval Wroxeter: Recent Work on the Site of the Roman City of Wroxeter.* Pershore, UK: West Mercian Archaeological Consultants, 1990.

Barnes, Timothy David. *Tertullian: A Historical and Literary Study.* Oxford, UK: Clarendon Press, 1985.

Bede. *The Ecclesiastical History of the English Nation.* Translated by J. A. Giles. London: Everyman's Library, 1970.

Berry, Paul, trans. *Geography/De Situ Orbis A.D. 43.* Lewiston, N.Y.: Edwin Mellen Press, 1997.

Biddle, Martin. *King Arthur's Round Table: An Archaeological Investigation.* Woodbridge, UK: Boydell Press, 2000.

Bird, Stephen, and Barry Cunliffe. *The Essential Roman Baths.* London: Scala, 2006.

Blackburn, Bonnie, and Leofranc Holford-Strevens. *The Oxford Companion to the Year: An Exploration of Calendar Customs and Time-Reckoning.* Oxford, UK: Oxford University Press, 1999.

Blake, Steve, and Scott Lloyd. *The Stanzas of the Graves: In Search of the Graves of Arthur and the Warriors of Britain.* Cardiff, UK: Welsh Academic Press, 2005.

Bland, Roger, and Catherine Johns. *The Hoxne Treasure: An Illustrated Handbook.* London: British Museum Press, 1995.

Booth, Martin. *A Magick Life: A Biography of Aleister Crowley.* London: Hodder & Stoughton, 2000.

Bord, Janet, and Colin Bord. *Sacred Waters.* London: Granada, 1985.

Borlase, William. *Observations on the Antiquities, Historical and Monumental, of the County of Cornwall.* Farmington Hills, Mich.: Gale Ecco, 2010.

Briggs, Katharine. *An Encyclopedia of Fairies.* New York: Pantheon Books, 1976.

Bromwich, Rachel, ed., *Trioedd Ynys Prydein: The Triads of the Island of Britain.* Cardiff, UK: University of Wales Press, 2006.

Brooks, Nicholas P. *The Early History of the Church in Canterbury.* Leicester, UK: Leicester University Press, 1984.

Burnett, John, J. *Ancient Kingdom of Wessex.* Hove, UK: Book Guild Publishing, 1984.

Bury, John, B. *A History of the Later Roman Empire.* Port Chester, N.Y.: Adegi Graphics, 1999.

Caesar, Julius. *Caesar: Gallic War Books VI and VII.* Edited and translated by C. Du Pontet. London: William Blackwood and Sons, 1901.

Camden, William. *Britannia.* Farmington Hills, Mich.: Gale Ecco, 2010.

Carew, Richard. *The Survey of Cornwall.* Memphis, Tenn.: Rare Books Club, 2012.

Casey, P. J., and J. L. Davies. *Excavations at Segontium (Caernarfon) Roman Fort, 1975–1979.* With J. Evans. CBA Research Report 90. London: Council for British Archaeology, 1993.

Chadwick Hawkes, Sonia. *Soldiers and Settlers in Britain: Fourth to Fifth Century.* Oxford, UK: Oxford University Press, 1961.

Chrétien de Troyes. *Erec and Enide.* Translated by Burton Raffel. New Haven: Yale University Press, 1997.

———. *Lancelot or the Knight of the Cart.* Translated by C. R. Hardwood. Athens: University of Georgia Press, 1990.

———. *Perceval: The Story of the Grail.* Translated by Burton Raffel. New Haven, Conn.: Yale University Press, 1999.

Collingwood, Robin George, and Richard Pearson Wright. *The Roman Inscriptions of Britain.* Oxford, UK: Clarendon Press, 1965.

Coyne, Frank. *An Upland Archaeological Study on Mount Brandon and The Paps, County Kerry.* Limerick, Ireland: Aegis Archaeology, 2006.

Cronin, Dan. *In the Shadow of the Paps.* Killarney, Ireland: Crede, Sliabh Luachra Heritage Group, 2001.

Cunliffe, Barry. *Iron Age Communities in Britain: An Account of England, Scotland and Wales from the Seventh Century BC until the Roman Conquest.* 4th ed. Abingdon, UK: Routledge, 2005.

Dark, Kenneth. *Britain and the End of the Roman Empire.* Stroud, UK: The History Press, 2002.

———. *Civitas to Kingdom: British Political Continuity 300–800.* London: Continuum International Publishing, 1994.

Davies, Janet. *The Welsh Language: A History.* Cardiff, UK: University of Wales Press, 2014.

Edwards, Frederick Millet, and H. L. R. Salter, eds. *The Bibliotheca Historica of Diodorus Siculus.* Translated by John Skelton. Oxford, UK: Early English Text Society, 2002.

Edwards, Nancy. *Local Saints and Local Churches in the Early Medieval West.* Oxford, UK: Oxford University Press, 2002.

Einhard. *The Life of Charlemagne.* Oxford, UK: Acheron Press, 2012.

Ekwall, Eilert. *The Concise Oxford Dictionary of English Place Names.* Oxford, UK: Oxford University Press, 1940.

Ellis, Peter, ed. *The Mammoth Book of Celtic Myths and Legends.* London: Robinson Publishing, 2003.

Esmonde-Cleary, Simon. *The Ending of Roman Britain.* London: Batsford, 1989.

Evans, Derek Haydn. *Valle Crucis Abbey.* Cardiff, UK: Cadw Welsh Historic Monuments, 2008.

Evans, J. Gwenogvryn, ed. *Poems from the Book of Taliesin.* Charleston, S.C.: Nabu Press, 2001.

Evans, J. Gwenogvryn. *The Poetry in the Red Book of Hergest.* Llanbedrog, UK: Gwenogvryn Evans Press, 1911.

Everett, Dorothy. *Layamon and the Earliest Middle English Alliterative Verse.* Westport, Conn.: Greenwood Press, 1978.

Farmer, David. *Oxford Dictionary of Saints.* Oxford, UK: Oxford University Press, 1997.

Flower, Michael. *The Seer in Ancient Greece.* Berkeley: University of California Press, 2008.

Gale, Thomas. *Historiae Anglicanae Scriptores.* Vol. 15. Oxford, UK: Thomas Gale, 1691.

Gantz, Jeffrey, trans. *The Mabinogion.* Harmondsworth, UK: Penguin, 1976.

Garmonsway, George Norman, trans. *The Anglo-Saxon Chronicle.* London: Everyman's Library, 1967.

Geake, Helen. *The Use of Grave-Goods in Conversion-Period England, c. 600–c. 850.* British Archaeological Reports 261. Oxford, UK: Archaeopress, 1997.

Geoffrey of Monmouth. *Life of Merlin: Vita Merlini.* Translated by Basil Clarke. Cardiff, UK: University of Wales Press, 1973.

———. *History of the Kings of Britain.* Translated by Lewis Thorpe. London: Penguin, 1977.

Gerald of Wales. *On the Instruction of Princes.* Translated by J. Stevenson. Burnham-on-Sea, UK: Llanerch Press, 1991.

Gildas. *De Excidio Britanniae.* Vol. 7 *of History of the Sources.* Edited and translated by Michael Winterbottom. Chichester, UK: Phillimore, 1978.

Gilley, Sheridan. *A History of Religion in Britain.* Hoboken, N.J.: John Wiley & Sons, 1994.

Graves, Robert. *The White Goddess: A Historical Grammar of Poetic Myth.* London: Faber and Faber, 2011; first published 1948.

Hamerow, Helena, David Hinton, and Sally Crawford, eds. *The Oxford Handbook of Anglo-Saxon Archaeology.* Oxford, UK: Oxford University Press, 2011.

Harding, John. *Chronicle of England.* Charleston, S.C.: Nabu Press, 2011.

Harleian MS 3859. British Library, London.

Heledd. *Canu Heledd* (Song of Heledd). In *Llyfr Coch Hergest* (The Red Book of Hergest). Jesus College MS 111, Bodleian Library, Oxford, UK.

Henig, Martin. *Religion in Roman Britain*. London: Routledge, 1995.

Higham, Nick. *The Kingdom of Northumbria, A.D. 350–1100*. Stroud, UK: Sutton, 1993.

Hilary of Poitiers, John of Damascus. *Nicene and Post-Nicene Fathers*. Vol. 9, *Hilary of Poitiers, John of Damascus*. Second series. Edited and translated by Philip Schaff and Henry Wace. New York: Christian Literature Company, 1899.

Hughes, G. "Old Oswestry Hillfort: Excavations by WJ Varley 1939–40." *Archaeologia Cambrensis* 143 (1996): 46–91.

Jacobsen, Torsten. *A History of the Vandals*. Yardley, Penn.: Westholme, 2012.

James, Simon, and Valery Rigby. *Britain and the Celtic Iron Age*. London: British Museum Press, 1997.

Jarman, A. O. H., trans. *Aneirin-Y Gododdin*. Llandysul, UK: Gomer Press, 1998.

Joceline and Ailred. *Two Celtic Saints: The Lives of Ninian and Kentigern*. Burnham-on-Sea, UK: Llanerch Press, 1989.

Jolliffe, John Edwards Austin. *Pre-Feudal England: The Jutes*. Oxford, UK: Oxford University Press, 1962.

Jones, Arnold, John Martindale, and John Morris. *The Prosopography of the Later Roman Empire*. Cambridge, UK: Cambridge University Press, 1971.

Jordanes. *De Origine Actibusque Getarum: The Origin and Deeds of the Goths*. Translated by Charles Mierow. Princeton, N.J.: Princeton University Press, 1915.

Kennett, David. *Anglo-Saxon Pottery*. Oxford, UK: Shire Publications, 1978.

Kightly, Charles. *Castell Dinas Brân: Llangollen*. Ruthin, UK: Denbighshire County Council, 2003.

King James Bible. London: Collins, 2011.

Knott, E., ed. *Togail Bruidne dá Derga*. Dublin: Dublin Institute for Advanced Studies, 1936.

Lacy, Norris, ed. *Lancelot-Grail: The Old French Arthurian Vulgate and Post-Vulgate in Translation*. New York: Garland, 1996.

———. *The New Arthurian Encyclopedia*. Princeton, N.J.: Garland, 1991.

Laing, Lloyd. *The Archaeology of Celtic Britain and Ireland: c. AD 400–1200*. Cambridge, UK: Cambridge University Press, 2006.

Laycock, Stuart. *Warlords: The Struggle for Power in Post-Roman Britain*. Stroud, UK: The History Press, 2009.

Leland, John. *John Leland's Itinerary: Travels in Tudor England*. Stroud, UK: Sutton, 1993.

Lhuyd, Edward. *Archaeologia Britannica: Texts and Translations*. Edited by Dewi W. Evansand Brynley F. Roberts. Aberystwyth, UK: Celtic Studies Publications, 2007.

Llyfr Coch Hergest (The Red Book of Hergest). Jesus College MS 111. Bodleian Library, Oxford, UK.

Loomis, Roger Sherman, ed. *Arthurian Literature in the Middle Ages: A Collaborative History*. Oxford, UK: Clarendon Press, 1959.

Lucy, Sam. *The Anglo-Saxon Way of Death: Burial Rites in Early England*. Stroud, UK: Sutton Publishing, 2000.

Lynn, Chris. *Navan Fort: Archaeology and Myth.* Dublin: Wordwell Books, 2003.

Macalister, Robert, trans. *Lebor Gabála Érenn: Book of the Taking of Ireland.* Dublin: Irish Texts Society, 1941.

Malory, Thomas. *Le Morte D'Arthur.* Translated by Stephen Shepherd. London: W. W. Norton, 2003.

Marsden, Peter. "The Excavation of a Roman Palace Site in London, 1961–1972." *Transactions of London and Middlesex Archaeological Society* 26 (1975).

Martin, Paddy. *The Historical Ecology of Old Oswestry.* Church Stretton, UK: Shropshire Botanical Society, 1999.

Mathew, H. Colin, and Brian Harrison, eds. *Oxford Dictionary of National Biography.* Oxford, UK: Oxford University Press, 2004.

Maxfield, Valerie, ed. *The Saxon Shore: A Handbook.* Exeter, UK: Exeter University Press, 1989.

Mayr-Harting, Henry. *The Coming of Christianity to Anglo-Saxon England.* Philadelphia: Pennsylvania State University Press, 1991.

McNeill, John, T. *The Celtic Churches: A History A.D. 200 to 1200.* Chicago: University of Chicago Press, 1974.

Meaney, Audrey. *Gazetteer of Early Anglo-Saxon Burial Sites.* London: Allen & Unwin, 1964.

Mela, Pomponius. *De Situ Orbis.*

Mills, A. David. *Oxford Dictionary of British Place Names.* Oxford, UK: Oxford University Press, 2003.

Morris, John. *The Age of Arthur.* London: Weidenfeld & Nicolson, 1973.

———. *The Age of Arthur: A History of the British Isles from 350 to 650.* London: Phoenix, 2004.

Munby, Julian, Richard Barber, and Richard Brown. *Edward III's Round Table at Windsor.* Woodbridge, UK: Boydell Press, 2006.

Murray, Margaret. *The Witch-Cult in Western Europe.* Oxford, UK: Oxford University Press, 1967.

MS f. fr. 794. Paris: Bibliothèque National.

Nennius. *British History and the Welsh Annals.* Vol. 8 of *History from the Sources.* Edited and translated by John Morris. Chichester, UK: Phillimore, 1980.

Nitze, William, ed. *Le Roman de l'Estoire dou Graal.* Paris: Champion, 1927.

Nutt, Alfred, trans. *The Voyage of Bran.* London: David Nutt, 1895.

Osborne, Robin. "Hoards, Votives, Offerings: The Archaeology of the Dedicated Object." *World Archaeology* 36, no. 1 (2004): 1–10.

Owen-Crocker, Gale. *Rites and Religions of the Anglo-Saxons.* Lanham, Md.: Rowman & Littlefield, 1981.

Pennar, Meirion, trans. *The Black Book of Carmarthen: Introduction and Translation.* Burnham-on-Sea, UK: Llanerch Press, 1989.

Petts, David. *Burial in Western Britain AD 400–800.* British Archaeological Reports 365. Oxford, UK: Archaeopress, 2004.

Phillips, Graham, and Martin Keatman. *King Arthur: The True Story.* London: Century Random House, 1992.

Phillips, Graham. *The Chalice of Magdalene.* Rochester, Vt.: Bear and Company, 2004.

Piggott, Stuart. *The Druids*. London: Thames and Hudson, 1985.

Radford, Ralegh. *Arthurian Sites in the West*. Exeter, UK: University of Exeter Press, 2002.

The Red Book of Hergest. See *Llyfr Coch Hergest*.

Redknap, Mark, and Alan Lane. "The Early Medieval crannog at Llangorse, Powys: An interim statement on the 1989–1993 seasons." *The International Journal of Nautical Archaeology* 23, no. 3 (August 1994): 189–205.

Remfry, Paul. *Castell Dinas Emrys*. Worcester, UK: SCS Publishing, 1995.

Robert de Boron. *Joseph of Arimathea: A Romance of the Grail*. Translated by Jean Rogers. London: Rudolf Steiner Press, 1990.

Russell, Jesse, and Ronald Cohn, eds. *Preiddeu Annwfn*. Key Biscayne, Fla.: Bookvika, 2012.

Schofield, John. *St. Paul's Cathedral Before Wren*. London: English Heritage, 2011.

Scott-Stokes, Henry Folliot, trans. *Glastonbury Abbey During the Crusades: Extracts from Adam of Domerham*. Burnham-on-Sea, UK: Llanerch Publishers, 1934.

Silvius, Polemius. *Notitia Dignitatum: Primary Source Edition*. Charleston, S.C.: Nabu Press, 2014.

Skeels, Dell. *Didot Perceval or The Romance of Perceval in Prose*. Seattle: University of Washington Press, 1966.

Steele, Philip. *Llyn Cerrig Bach: Treasure from the Iron Age*. Llangefni, UK: Isle of Anglesey County Council, 2012.

Stephenson, David. *Political Power in Medieval Gwynedd: Governance and the Welsh Princes*. Cardiff, UK: University of Wales Press, 2014.

Stewart, R. J., Robin Williamson, and Chris Down. *Celtic Bards, Celtic Druids*. London: Cassell, 1999.

Strabo. *Geography: Books 3–5*. Vol. 2. Translated by Horace L. Jones. Cambridge, Mass.: Harvard University Press, 1923.

———. *Geography: Books 10–12*. Vol. 5. Translated by Horace L. Jones. Cambridge, Mass.: Harvard University Press, 1989; first published 1928.

Tacitus, Cornelius. *The Annals: The Reigns of Tiberius, Claudius, and Nero*. Translated by J. C. Yardley. Oxford, UK: Oxford University Press, 2008.

Taylor, Timothy. "The Gundestrup Cauldron." *Scientific American* 266 (March 1992): 84–89.

Thompson, Edward A. *Saint Germanus of Auxerre and the End of Roman Britain*. Woodbridge, UK: Boydell, 1984.

Toghill, Peter. *Geology of Shropshire*. Marlborough, UK: The Crowood Press, 2006.

Topsfield, Leslie T. *Chrétien de Troyes: A Study of the Arthurian Romances*. Cambridge, UK: Cambridge University Press, 1981.

Upward, Christopher, and George Davidson. *The History of English Spelling*. Hoboken, N.J.: Wiley-Blackwell, 2011.

Wace. *Wace's Roman de Brut: A History of the British*. Translated by Judith Weiss. Liverpool, UK: Liverpool University Press, 2005.

Wardle, David, ed. *Cicero on Divination: Book 1*. Oxford, UK: Oxford University Press, 2007.

Ward-Perkins, Bryan. *The Fall of Rome: And the End of Civilization*. Oxford, UK: Oxford University Press, 2005.

Warnicke, Retha. *Mary Queen of Scots*. Abingdon, UK: Routledge, 2006.

Watts, Niki, ed. *The Oxford Greek Dictionary*. New York: Berkley Publishing, 2000.

Webster, Graham. *Viroconium, Wroxeter Roman City, Shropshire*. London: HMSO. 1973.

Weiss, Judith. *Wace's Roman de Brut: A History of the British*. Liverpool, UK: Liverpool University Press, 2005.

Wilhelm, James, ed. *The Romance of Arthur: An Anthology of Medieval Texts in Translation*. New York: Garland, 1994.

William of Malmesbury. *Antiquities of Glastonbury*. Translated by Frank Lomax. Newcastle, UK: JMF Books, 1992.

———. *The History of the English Kings*. Translated by R. M. Thomson. Oxford, UK: Oxford University Press, 1998.

Williams, Ifor, ed. and trans. *Canu Llywarch Hen*. Cardiff, UK: University of Wales Press, 1935.

Wright, Thomas, ed. and trans. *The History of Fulk Fitz Warine*. London: The Warton Club, 1855.

Yorke, Barbara. *Kings and Kingdoms of Early Anglo-Saxon England*. Abingdon, UK: Routledge, 1990.

Zaluckyj, Sarah. *Mercia: The Anglo-Saxon Kingdom of Central England*. Hereford, UK: Logaston Press, 2011.

Index